Ancient Arts
of
Central Asia

Ancient Arts
of
CENTRAL ASIA

Tamara Talbot Rice

London
Thames and Hudson

Contents

Page 7 Introduction

11 CHAPTER ONE
The World of the Transcaucasian and Central Asian
Nomads

54 CHAPTER TWO
The smaller kingdoms of Transcaucasia and the Persian
highlands during the first millennium BC

75 CHAPTER THREE
Soghdia, Ferghana and Chorasmia from Achaemenid
to Islamic times

123 CHAPTER FOUR
Bactria and North-Western India from
Achaemenid to Islamic times

173 CHAPTER FIVE
Eastern Turkestan in the Roman and
Buddhist Periods

221 CHAPTER SIX
Armenia, Georgia and Caucasian Albania
in Early Christian times

Page 263 Bibliography

265 Maps

268 Chronology

270 List of Illustrations

282 Index

Introduction

Our interest in the past tends to centre upon the great civilizations which embody mankind's finest achievements. In consequence, we are inclined to disregard the peripheral cultures which flourished as offshoots of the main creative streams and to render ourselves the poorer thereby, for many marginal societies succeeded in ancient times in evolving artistic cultures of considerable merit. Though the number of major masterpieces which they were able to add to our store of outstanding treasures may be comparatively small, the majority of their works are nevertheless both surprisingly fascinating and extremely interesting. If they at times present a less inspired and clear-cut conception of beauty than do the works belonging to the major schools of art, they often display instead a remarkable liveliness of mind, sensitivity of eye and manual dexterity. These accomplishments enabled artists from the peripheral cultures to create works of lasting quality and to evolve distinctive, essentially national styles even when adopting motifs, mannerisms and idioms from their more gifted neighbours. Today it is stimulating to attempt to distinguish the foreign elements which they selected and to establish the use that they made of them. The task is an absorbing one, both because it provides a measure by which to assess their achievements and also because it directs our attention to those trends in the major schools which appealed most strongly to contemporary artists. These dual results serve to increase our pleasure in the marginal schools and to further our understanding of the great civilizations which helped to inspire them.

The rise of hybrid schools of art is possible only in those peripheral communities where a variety of cultures and traditions meet, and where men exist who are capable of fusing them into something wholly new and original. Conditions such as these prevailed in Central Asia, Transcaucasia and north-western Persia from deep antiquity till late in the Middle Ages. Throughout these centuries the eastern, northern and western borders of the countries which constituted the great powers of those times, that is to say of Mesopotamia, Persia, India, China and, in later years, to some extent also Tibet, abbuted on to the immense expanse of Central Asia's grazing lands and deserts. From very early times onwards nomadic cattle breeders pastured their flocks in the vast Central Asian plain, but certainly by the third millennium BC groups of settlers had started cultivating its productive southern fringes. In due course some of these agriculturists assumed the tricky yet profitable task of trading with the nomads. Soon they were acting as middlemen between the latter and the settled inhabitants of the neighbouring kingdoms, though friction between the nomads and settlers continued to persist, even though the respective advantages inherent in each way of life frequently won for the one group adherents from the ranks of the other.

As early as the third millennium BC some of the nomads living on the eastern borders of the Caspian Sea had established themselves in the neighbourhood of Astarabad. From 1932 to 1933 Arne excavated the site on which these people had settled and found that they formed a fairly large community with a surprisingly complex and well developed way of life. Their possessions were numerous and varied, and included a highly burnished form of black and grey coloured pottery which displays marked affinities with wares that are now associated not only with Iran, Mesopotamia and Asia Minor, but also with Crete and Greece. The link with the latter seems less surprising today than it did thirty years or so ago, for recent archaeological discoveries in Anatolia, on sites such as Çatal Hüyük, Beyce Sultan and Can Hasan have shown that contacts with neolithic Asia Minor must, almost as a matter of course, bring Crete and Mycenae under consideration. Unfortunately, by the second millennium BC, all traces of life had ended on the site, to reappear, according to Arne, with the rise of the Samanids in the ninth century AD.

From about 1500 BC the south-western corner of the Caspian served as the centre of a remarkably vital culture known as the Amlash, yet south-eastern Transcaucasia was one of the first areas on the western periphery of Persia in which a small kingdom is known

8

to have become established in the ninth century or so. As Urartu it rapidly became a satellite of Assyria. Five to seven centuries more were to elapse before a number of other virtually autonomous, small yet affluent principalities or fiefs were to come into being in several rather more easternly districts of Central Asia. Even then, however, the plain itself remained the nomadic preserve it had become in the hands of the Scytho-Sakian tribesmen at the start of the first millennium BC, when Scythian and kindred Asiatic nomads roamed its vast expanses. This large confederation of tribes shared a characteristic culture and way of life of their own, though the various clans remained distinct and autonomous. In the Asiatic section of the plain the rule of the Scytho-Sakians was in due course replaced by that of the Huns; then people of Turkish stock took control, to form in the sixth century AD a strong kingdom in what is now Mongolia and, after a temporary setback, to establish in Central Asia the dynasties of the Islamic Samanids, Ghaznavids and Seljuks. Finally the dreaded Mongols became masters of western Central Asia. Throughout the two thousand years covered by these events each of these powerful tribes and many smaller ones of kindred origins, roamed the plain and, as they did so, slowly moved westward, seldom missing an opportunity either to raid the settlers or trade with them.

Our knowledge of the political and economic events of those far-off times was until recently largely dependent upon Chinese documents and the complementary information contained first in the works of Greek, and then of Arab historians. However, in recent years many newly deciphered Assyrian and Urartian texts have become available to historians. The information that has come to light has stimulated interest in Central Asia, more especially among explorers and archaeologists. Indeed, it was largely due to the journeys undertaken during the opening years of the present century by such men as Sir Aurel Stein and A. von Le Coq that archaeologists set out to search for and uncover the ancient cities of what is now Afghanistan. At much the same time when Western scholars were becoming interested in Central Asia, Russians started to explore its western section. Since the Revolution many of them have followed the example set by their learned countryman, the late V. V. Barthold, and have devoted themselves to examining ancient texts whilst others have turned to field work, carrying out scientific explorations and excavations on numerous sites. As a result of these diverse researches, on either side of the Oxus, so much information has now been made available that it is possible to trace many of the political and economic changes and artistic developments which occurred in Transcaucasia, northern Persia and Central Asia from about the second millennium BC to soon after the close of the first millennium AD, when the Mongols put an end to a long-established way of life over most of this region. During this time the polital conditions which developed in various sections of the vast area dealt with in this volume were often so fluid and complex that, for reasons both of brevity and clarity, it has seemed best to deal with the artistic schools peculiar to each region on a geographical rather than a chronological basis, starting and ending with the more westerly regions. Even so, the various racial groups living in Central Asia during the period under review were so numerous and their cultures, even when basically similar, so distinct that it has been impossible to consider every group or each period in any detail. Instead, the first chapter sets out to provide the reader with an outline of the history only of those nomads who controlled large sections of the Central Asian plain and at the same time created significant works of art; the second will deal with several of the more important communities established on the western and southern fringes of the plain; Chapter Three will concern itself with the three kingdoms of importance in western Central Asia in classical and early Buddhist times and Chapter Four with similar developments in what is now Afghanistan and north-western Pakistan. The influence of both Rome and Buddhism in Eastern Turkestan will be discussed in Chapter Five, and Chapter Six will attempt to show how the Caucasian and Transcaucasian people, disregarding all geographical and political considerations, chose to become Christian rather than Buddhist or Muhammadan and thus became part of Europe's cultural world.

CHAPTER ONE

The World of the Transcaucasian and Central Asian Nomads

From time immemorial the vast plain which stretches from the low-lands of central Europe eastward to the borders of China constituted the undisputed homeland of a considerable number of nomadic tribes. In the Asiatic sector, which is the one with which we are chiefly concerned here, the nomads had taken possession of the grazing lands long before the presence of settled communities in the fertile areas bordering the plain's southern edge came to be recorded in history. The various tribes which succeeded one another as occupants of the region followed, even into the present century, very much the same pattern of life as that which their predecessors evolved many centuries ago. From roughly the first millennium B C to the end of the first millennium A D these nomads were able to affect events occurring in the ancient world to a quite surprising degree, for the political and economic stability of the petty states which grew up along the western, southern and eastern borders of the Central Asian plain during the latter half of the first millennium B C depended to a large extent upon their goodwill. Indeed, even the well-being of the great kingdoms whose frontiers and trade lay within easy striking distance of the tribesmen was adversely affected when the peace of the nomadic world became disrupted. However, the skirmishes which frequently broke out between various groups of nomads, as well as between nomads and settlers, do not seem to have interrupted the cultural give-and-take which, once established, was sustained.

To appreciate the various artistic developments which occurred either simultaneously in different areas of Central Asia or which succeeded each other in a particular region, it is necessary to distinguish the precise characteristics of each local culture. Over most of the area an animal style was in vogue, practised by the various groups of nomads who were often related, yet always distinct. The style flourished over so wide an area and so long a period of time that it is often called the art of the steppe peoples. According both to the region and the period in which they lived, each group of crafts-men was influenced, if in varying degrees, by the artistic trends pre-vailing in the great centres of civilization situated in their immediate neighbourhood, but they were in their turn sometimes able to leave a mark on the major schools of art which were evolving in those empires. This is especially true of the Scytho-Sakian-Altaian com-munities of nomads, and even of their successors, the Sarmatians. Each of these groups produced individual variations on similar themes, but the creative genius and technical skill of the Scythians were generally of a far higher order than those of kindred tribal communities.

Generations of nomads traversed the Central Asian plain without, in so far as we yet know, leaving upon its surface any traces of their passage. Fortunately, by the time that their chieftains had started to take delight in precious objects and had amassed sufficient wealth to enable them to satisfy their possessive instincts, many nomadic com-munities had come to believe in the existence of a life beyond the grave similar in every respect to that lived upon earth. As a result they began to provide elaborate tombs for their chieftains, equipping them with every necessity of earthly life, but choosing for the purpose the finest, most sumptuous and intrinsically valuable of the dead man's possessions.

The earliest princely burials as yet known to us in the area with which this chapter is concerned are to be found in Transcaucasia, in the vicinity of the great international routes which, in ancient times linked Europe and the ancient Orient with hithermost Asia. The district was richer in foodstuffs than in minerals, but by the end of the second millennium B C mining was being carried out in the Urals and the copper deposits which lie between what is now Tiflis (Tblisi) and Lake Sevan had been discovered and were being exploited. Tribesmen were readily drawn to the wild, beautiful and fertile region, and two of the earliest princely burial grounds, those of Maikop and Tsarskij (now renamed Novosvobodnyj) lie to the

1 Gold figurine of a bull, originally intended to hold one of the poles which supported the canopy placed over the body of a dead nomadic chieftain buried at Maikop. The animal's features – its head, horns, heavy hindquarters and massive legs – are emphasized to produce a realistic model of the beast. *c.* 2300 BC

south-west of the copper-mines. The Maikop burials have been assigned to various dates, but the earliest and most important are now generally regarded as belonging to the end of the third or the start of the second millennium BC. The objects which have been recovered from them are not only intrinsically valuable, but are also to be prized for their remarkable artistic and historic importance. They consist of articles of personal adornment, of bronze figurines of bulls (*Ill. 1*) and of vessels of bronze, silver and gold, the shapes and decorations of which are in a highly evolved and sophisticated style. Especially interesting are a series of silver bowls, a gold sceptre and diadem (*Ill. 2*), the figurines of bulls and the stamped gold plaques. The latter were intended as dress trimmings, and thus resemble and foreshadow similar gold decorations made by the Scythians for the same purpose in the course of the first millennium BC.

One of the silver bowls from Maikop is of outstanding importance for it is embossed and chased with decorations forming a precise, clearly thought-out composition (*Ills. 3, 4*). The neck of the vessel is adorned with a chain of mountains from which two rivers flow into

13

2 Gold rosettes from a princely burial at Maikop which were mounted on felt and worn as diadems. The rosette remained a favourite motif in Central Asian art for some two thousand years. *c.* 2300 BC

a lake or sea placed at the bottom of the bowl. Farmakovskij believed that the mountains were intended to depict the Caucasian range when seen from the north-west and the rivers to represent the Terek and the Kuban. If this is indeed the case then the decoration must rank as man's earliest known, if not his very first attempt at rendering an actual landscape in art. A bird is shown at the mouth of one of the rivers and a plant at that of the other. The remainder of the space is filled with animals disposed in two rows. A bull, a Przhevalski horse and a lion with a bird perched on its back and another bull facing the other way. Below them a wild boar, a panther and two antelopes stand in a circle. The work, for all its Mesopotamian affinities, is strongly Caucasian in style and the suggestion that it was made by a local craftsman is supported by the inclusion in its design of a boar, for no renderings of that animal appear in the arts of Egypt or the ancient Near East. The bronze figurines of the bulls do, however, suggest links with Anatolia. Recent excavations point to the existence of a bull cult not only in Crete, but at an earlier date in much of Asia Minor; it may thus have reached Transcaucasia with some Western art forms. The figurines also bear a marked resemblance to Georgian ones of a somewhat later date for they already display the marked preference for realism which characterizes both Georgian and west-Siberian art of the Bronze and Iron Age periods. The presence in the Maikop burials of lapis lazuli, cornelian and turquoise beads proves that even at that early date the Maikop tribesmen had established contacts with the inhabitants of Central Asia. The former are especially important since the lapis must have been obtained from the neighbourhood of Kabul. The naturalistic treatment of the bull statuettes may thus have been derived from western Central Asia and transmitted to Georgia at that very early date.

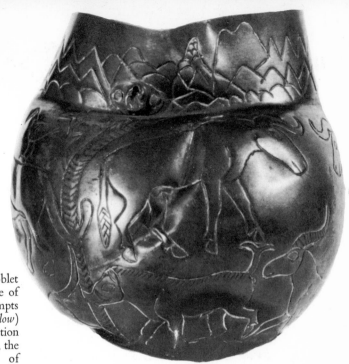

3, 4 (*right*) This silver goblet
from Maikop presents one of
man's earliest known attempts
to depict a landscape. (*Below*)
A projection of the decoration
shows the mountain range, the
rivers and processions of
animals

15

5 Gold cup from a royal tomb at Trialeti. Decorated in filigree, a form of metal work at which the Georgians excelled, and inlaid with turquoises and other precious stones. Second millennium B C

The style of the Maikop animal figurines reappears in a modified, somewhat lighter form, in some dating from the Bronze Age discovered in Georgia in the Trialeti burial field. The tombs in that vast cemetery range in date from the Obsidian period through the Neolithic to the Bronze Age. The Soviet archaeologist Kuftin examined forty-two of the Bronze Age burials and found that they dated from about the middle of the second millennium B C. The tombs were all in the form of single burials and many contained objects of marked intrinsic worth and artistic importance. In addition to a considerable quantity of fine pottery decorated with black designs painted on a red or natural ground, vessels of gold adorned with jewels and delicate filigree work were also found (*Ill. 5*). The shapes of some recall that of certain vessels discovered in Sumer and one of the oldest of the burials contained a cup resembling one found at Ur. Other vessels are adorned with embossed decorations displaying in their designs a blend of Mesopotamian and Transcaucasian elements. The most interesting of the motifs appear on a silver goblet (*Ill. 6*) which are disposed in two parallel bands each, as on a cylinder seal, recording a consecutive scene. The upper strip depicts a sacrifice with a procession of people advancing towards a seated god. Animal and plant motifs are also included. The lower section of the cup is decorated with a frieze of stylized leaves which serve as a setting for a file of stags and does. The people in the sacrificial scene wear hats of Hittite shape, but their clothes are of a different cut, and are thus presumably local.

6 Two views of a silver cup from Kurukh Tash, near Trialeti. It too dates from the middle of the second millennium B C. In so far as the animals are concerned, the art remains essentially naturalistic

17

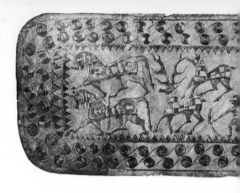

7 Bronze belt from Trialeti decorated with a lively hunting scene with an edging of dog-tooth, which may well have been derived from a textile. *c.* 1200 B C

The discovery at Trialeti of a bronze belt (*Ill. 7*) decorated with an embossed hunting scene is of particular interest because belts of this type are often regarded as Urartian in origin. The Trialeti belt is, however, earlier in date than known Urartian ones and thus suggests that the type may have been popularized first in Georgia even though its decorations must have been derived from Assyrian cylinder seals. The decorations of the Trialeti belt include lunar symbols which may well have been introduced into the design for a magical purpose, though the chequer-board patterning covering the bodies of the horses, even if originally imbued with religious meaning, seems to have been retained in this instance for purely decorative reasons.

Nothing is as yet known about the people of Trialeti, but they must have been of a peaceful disposition for practically no weapons were found in their tombs. The tombs also contained nothing to suggest that the Trialeti people had learnt to make use of the horse. They seem to have relied on bullocks as draught animals and the people depicted on the bronze belt are shown pursuing their game on foot.

In the Bronze and Iron Age periods the Caucasian and Transcaucasian areas developed into a thriving centre of metallurgy. During the second and first millennia metal workers in Colchis, that is to say in western Georgia, and the southern and northern slopes of the Caucasian mountain range, concentrated on the production of animal figurines and animal designs. They did not work in the realistic yet static style associated with Maikop, but evolved stylized, essentially mobile forms. Imaginery and fantastic beasts became as popular as the real animals indigenous to the area. The fabulous creatures were doubtless endowed with magical attributes. Some

18

resemble animals from the Scythian repertory though they antedate the latter, and thus tempt one to ascribe their presence to the influence of the Cimmerians, forerunners of the Scythians, whose art is still unknown to us. These animal designs continued to be produced in Colchis in Hellenistic times. To begin with, wild animals, and more especially wolves, figured most often; in later times domestic ones frequently took their place.

Whilst the metal workers of Colchis were creating a distinctive animal style those living in the northern foothills of the Caucasus created a culture known as the Koban, after the village where the first objects to be associated with it were found. This culture flourished from c. 1200 B C to as late as A D 500, but the axes which were peculiar to the region ceased to be made after c. 200 B C. Those which were intended for everyday use are rather coarse, but elegant, delicately shaped ones were made to serve a symbolic purpose. The latter were decorated with geometric designs, astral symbols and highly stylized animal forms; the majority date from between the twelfth and the tenth century B C. Somewhat later, that is to say from the tenth to about the fifth century B C, numerous articles in the form of personal adornments and votive figurines were produced in both bronze and iron in the same region. Bird and bull ornaments were especially popular also.

The bulk of the Koban metal work came from the Kumbulta, Phaskau and Kamunta burials. Dog-like creatures often figure among the motifs which decorate them. Typical of these is a belt buckle which must date from early in the school's history for it is made of bronze instead of iron, even though the bulk of the Koban objects are of iron. Another characteristic buckle displays a stag-like creature

(*Ill. 8*). It too is an early example, but it already includes, set in the space between the stag's antlers and tail, the dog-like beast which was popular in Georgia throughout the Iron Age period. Though the inclusion of the dog is typical of the locality its position on this buckle, no less than the choice of a stag for the main motif must surely be ascribed to Scythian influence. The stag figured prominently in Georgian art only in those centuries during which Scythian influence was strongly felt there. When the Scythians converged on southern Russia the horse replaced the stag in Georgia's applied arts. Two iron buckles dating from about the mid fifth century display a spirited horse rendered in high relief (*Ills. 9, 10*). Though the realism with which they are portrayed may be ascribed to Greek influence, Greek colonists having by then established themselves on the eastern shores of the Black Sea, it is more likely to be due in the first place to that of Persia.

That the art of Achaemenid Persia was known in Georgia is

(*left*) In this iron belt buckle from Georgia, Scythian influences are more strongly seen than in either 9 or 10, but the inclusion of a dog in the space between the stag's antlers, suspended by its tail, is typically Georgian and, more specifically, a Koban feature

9, 10 Bronze belt buckles from the Koban region of Georgia reflect Greek influence as well as Scythian. All are decorated with bosses, which may have held cabochon jewels, and spiral designs of which the Georgians were particularly fond. *c.* 500 BC

evident from the presence in the Akhalgorisk hoard of a pair of superb gold head-dress terminals (*Ill. 12*). The masterly modelling and fine proportions of the magnificently caparisoned horses forming their central motif must surely have been inspired by an Achaemenian sculpture of outstanding quality, but in the terminals the rendering of the horses shows a greater, essentially Georgian, vitality, being neither static nor in motion, as is usual in Achaemenid art. Instead they seem on the point of breaking into a gallop, the impression of movement which they create perhaps implying a link with Scythian art. Other objects found with the terminals suggest bonds with the ancient Orient. Thus a horse's gold breastplate or disc reflects, as is the case with certain of the Scythian objects found at Zakis, Assyrio-Babylonian rather than Persian influence (*Ill. 11*).

11 Gold disc from the Akhalgorisk hoard probably used as a horse's breastplate. Ducks, very similar to these in style, continued to appear in Central Asian art for many centuries to come. Fifth century BC

12 Gold head-dress terminals from the Akhalgorisk hoard dating from the fifth century BC. Achaemenid Persia was the prime source of their inspiration, but either the Greek colonials or the Scythian nomads contributed the considerable feeling of movement

13 Silver dish fro
Stepantsminda sho
how under Achaem
nid influence the
shaped spirals ha
been transformed in
confronted swans ga
ing at a stylized lot
flower. Sixth centu
B C

14 Detail of a silver dish
from Armazi showing a
portrait of Papak, the
Sassanian king, Ardashir's,
deputy and governor of
Georgia. Although Geor-
gian artists responded to
the influence of both
Rome and Persia, Sassa-
nian influence dictated
these decorations. Early
third century B C

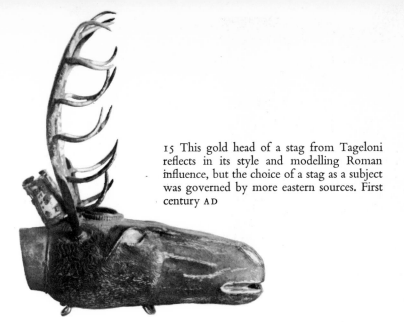

15 This gold head of a stag from Tageloni reflects in its style and modelling Roman influence, but the choice of a stag as a subject was governed by more eastern sources. First century AD

On the other hand the silver dish from Stepantsminda (*Ill. 13*), which is usually referred to as the Kazbek dish, must undoubtedly have been inspired by the art of Achaemenid Persia, though here again the S-shaped contours of the double-headed swan motif links it with the Scytho-Altaian nomads. The Achaemenids coveted the Caucasus, but it was the Sassanians who conquered it in the first half of the third century AD. Papak, the deputy of Ardashir (AD 220–241), marked the annexation of Georgia by having his portrait embossed on a silver dish which he presented to the governor of the new province (*Ill. 14*). Professor Amiranachvili was the first to notice the almost obliterated inscription which had been engraved upon it and which, he found, contained the earliest known text in which the word 'Georgia' appears. By the time that the Sassanians had made themselves the masters of Georgia, both the Romans and the Sarmatians had reached and departed from the country's borders. Their arrival there is reflected for us in the superb gold head of a stag from Tageloni (*Ill. 15*), for it was probably Sarmatian influence which dictated the choice of a stag as the animal to be portrayed, whilst it was Rome that set the standard alike of the quality and style of its execution.

Until the arrival of the Scythians in the Caucasus in the seventh century BC the Caucasians portrayed animals with considerable realism – a tendency which was likewise observed by Siberia's early metal workers. However, in the course of the first millennium BC Scythian stylization was often blended with Greek elegance, even though the synthesis was sometimes clumsily achieved. In the process the Scythian understanding of grace, balance and movement was at times replaced by unintelligent contortions and meaningless ornamentation, whilst Greek clarity of vision was superseded by stiff precision. Then, as the millennium sped itself, the nomadic elements began to recede from the Caucasian area and as they did so human forms started to replace those of animals. Figures such as these are generally of an anthropomorphic character. Some metal objects show them precariously poised on several tiers of animal horns for, in contrast to Scythian art, in Caucasian culture antlers are of secondary importance to horns. A. Tallgren ascribes the presence of horns in Caucasian art to the influence of Asia Minor, and the recent discovery at Çatal Hüyük, in the Konya plain, of an astonishingly complex and sophisticated neolithic culture associated with a form of bull worship seems to confirm this view. Typical of these votive figurines is an iron terminal from the Stepantsminda treasure (*Ill. 16*). It is obvious that it was made for a religious purpose. It shows a bearded male figure, naked but for his boots, poised on the horns of a bull, the animal's head being the topmost one of three; three similarly superimposed horned bulls' heads appear on either side of the central composition.

The arrival of the Scythians in Europe had been preceded by that of the racially allied Cimmerians. Nothing is as yet known of the art of the Cimmerians or even of that of the Scythians proper prior to their entry into Europe. J. A. H. Poïraiz's theory that Scythian art is in no way related to that of Siberia is difficult to accept, but there is not as yet enough evidence available to substantiate either view and the problem is shrouded in obscurity. So too is that concerning the origin of the Lurs. Some scholars contend that the people designated by that name were in fact Cimmerians; other authorities, however, assert that the Cimmerians were not a nomadic people and

16 An iron terminal from Stepantsminda takes the form of a cult figurine, and the multiplicity of horns seems to point to the existence of some form of bull worship. Late first millennium B C

they therefore dispose of the former theory to assert instead that the Lurs were Hittite craftsmen who, sometime between 1200 and 1000 B C, when their kingdom was being overrun by the Persians, fled to the Zagros. Settling there the Lurs are then thought to have transmitted their artistic traditions to the native Mannaeans. Supporters of this view sometimes go so far as to maintain that it was the Mannaeans who, during the second half of the seventh century B C, taught the Scythians, who had by then become the masters of Media, the rudiments of their animal art. Another school of thought is, however, of an entirely different opinion, believing that the Lurs were taught to work metals first by the Cimmerians and later by the Scythians. This is hardly the place in which to discuss these contradictory theories, but it is difficult to agree with the view that the Mannaeans inspired Scythian art, if only because the latter contains many indications that the Scythians had worked in wood and other non-precious materials for many centuries before producing the metal objects by which they are now known. Furthermore, although the metal objects associated with the Lurs often bear a superficial resemblance to the Scythian yet, basically, they are completely different in style. They embrace a wide range of articles but it is in the vessels, weapons and horse trappings that their artists are seen at their most characteristic.

27

17 The people of Luristan were skilled metal workers who made daggers, knives and axes of superb quality. This beautifully proportioned dagger carries a cuneiform inscription of the King of Babylon. Twelfth century

The dates which different scholars assign to the objects which they ascribe to the Lurs vary as much as do the theories they hold regarding the origin of these people, for their estimates range from about the year 2600 B C to A D 800. Some objects bear cuneiform inscriptions; many of these have been deciphered within recent years and found in fact to date from between the nineteenth and the twelfth centuries B C (*Ill. 17*). Often the names of kings or high dignitaries are mentioned in them. These persons were connected with Babylonia and Elam. The inscriptions also show that the objects on which they appear were intended for religious purposes and, though used by the Lurs, may not have been made by them. Indeed they form a quite different group from that comprising the horse trappings. The latter are of obvious nomadic origin. They probably date from between the seventh and fourth centuries B C and must have belonged to Lurs living, in the manner of some Scythians of southern Russia, in semi-settled communities, situated in their case in the central Zagros. Their dwellings appear to have taken the form of houses rather than of felt huts or *yurts*, and to have been grouped round a sanctuary similar to the one which E. Schmidt excavated at Surk Dum in 1937–8. There the dead had been buried outside the settlement and every tomb which the excavators examined was found to contain, lying beneath the dead man's skull, a bit with a rigid centre-piece and elaborate terminals fashioned into either human or animal forms (*Ill. 18*). The human figures are thought to have represented deities and it is assumed that the bits were placed in the tombs to speed the passage of the dead from the world of the living to that beyond the tomb. Ghirshman is of the opinion that these bits were made especially for funerary purposes and that they were not intended for daily use for none of those which he examined showed any signs of wear.

28

The animals decorating the Luristan bits are less complex and basically less tempestuous than the Scythian works which they call to mind. This fact, taken in conjunction with the appearance in some examples of Caucasian metal work of pre-Scythian date of animal forms and decorations of a Scythian type, may well be an indication that the Cimmerians did in fact practise a form of animal art. If so they may have introduced it both into the Transcaucasian and the Zagros areas before the Scythians appeared there with their own more accomplished and vital renderings of similarly conceived animal designs. In that case Cimmerian influence may be responsible for the somewhat coarse and more primitive elements seen in both the Luristan bits and the Georgian belt buckles.

18 The Lurs, too, delighted in making horse trappings. The designs chosen range from animal to human figurines. This cheek-piece takes the form of a spirited winged creature with human head and horns. The interest which the artist took in marking the creature's muscles is in keeping with early Persian and Scythian conventions

The Scythians proper, or Royal Scyths of southern Russia, created an animal art of superb quality. The earliest of their known works date from the seventh century B C and come from the Kuban district and from southern Russia – areas which lie outside the geographical limits set for this book. Yet Scythian art is so important a branch of the nomadic arts of Central Asia that it cannot be entirely excluded from this survey. Though essentially decorative in character and primarily animalistic in content it includes astral, geometric, floral and, on occasions, figural motifs. It is complex in its imagery and composition, and achieves great technical subtlety and polish. The finest examples include gold plaques representing stags or other wild animals such as leopards (*Ills. 19, 20*). Certain scholars now think that some of the best of these, including the plaques of the recumbent gold stags, are of Thracian and not Scythian origin. Should this view prove correct the basic conception of these works nevertheless remains essentially Scythian in character. The excellence of these plaques, as of other outstanding works of unquestioned Scythian origin owes something of its quality to the skilful use of the play of light on the surface by inclining sections of the metal, often gold, in slightly different directions in order to re-create the ripple of the animal's muscles and body when in motion.

In the Altai nomads sharing the way of life and outlook of the Scythians practised an art very similar to theirs from, at any rate, the fifth to the second centuries B C. Whereas in southern Russia climatic conditions were such that articles made of perishable materials failed to survive in the tombs of the Royal Scyths and only the indestructible ones remained, in the Altaian burials all the objects which had been placed in the graves were recovered in good condition. This was because the tombs had been insulated from the outer air by a layer of ice which had fortuitously formed above them, transforming each burial into a kind of deep-freeze. The Altaian burial grounds of Pazyryk, Tuekt, Shibe and Katanda, to name but a few, were excavated after the outbreak of the Revolution by Griaznov, Rudenko and other Soviet scholars, and found to contain, in addition to some metal objects, a great many in wood, felt, wool and silk. The Pazyryk tombs had been particularly lavishly

19, 20 (*above*) The gold stag from Kostromskaya, and (*below*) the gold leopard from Kelermes, show the art of the Royal Scyths at its best. The leopard's ears were originally inlaid with amber and its eyes with enamel, and both were probably intended as centre-pieces for shields. Seventh–sixth century B C

equipped and the objects, with their virtually all-over decorations – even the soles of the people's footwear were elaborately worked – are so similar in style and shape to their counterparts from the tombs of the Royal Scyths of southern Russia that it is evident that, even if the tribesmen who produced them were not Scythians, they undoubtedly shared the same culture, though they at times expressed themselves with less sophistication. Thus the Pazyryk burials, like the Scythian, are all horse burials. Stags frequently appear in the art of the Pazyryk people, yet they do not hold quite so important a place in it as in that of the Scythians (*Ill. 24*). Furthermore, the Altaians portrayed them in a more realistic manner, conforming in this to Siberian conventions, even though they introduced a touch of Scythian stylization into their more naturalistic creations.

As with the Scythians so with the Altaians, the art they produced was essentially decorative and rendered largely in the flat, either in the form of carvings, embossed metal or felt appliqué work, but some objects were rendered in the round. A rather barbaric and primitive head-dress (*Ill. 23*) decorated with savage-looking beasts is nevertheless close in style to the elegant Scythian gold aigrette (*Ill. 22*) of the fourth century BC discovered in the Oxus Treasure. Other examples of this local style are provided by the imaginary beasts tattooed on the embalmed body of the man recovered from

◀ 21 (*far left*) Detail of a combat scene from a saddle-bag from Pazyryk, made in appliqué felt work, shows the Altaian convention of dot and comma markings to indicate muscles. Fifth century BC

22, 23 It is interesting to compare the gold lion-gryphon aigrette of Scythian workmanship to the more barbarous and primitive necklet of carved wood from Pazyryk made by Altaian craftsmen working in the Scythian tradition. Fifth century BC

24 Carved wooden stag with leather antlers intended as a pole terminal. The style is more realistic than the Scythian and accordingly closer to that of western Siberia. Fifth century BC

Mound 5 at Pazyryk as well as on the appliqué worked felt-hangings from the same burial ground (*Ill. 26*). These creations, and others like them, should perhaps be accepted as offshoots of the style in which the Oxus Treasure ornament is made. The Altaian convention of using dot and comma markings both in their metal and felt appliqué work (*Ill. 21*) as a means of indicating the muscles of the animals portrayed, may on the other hand be a mannerism which they adopted from the ancient Orient, which they used far more often than did the Scythians.

33

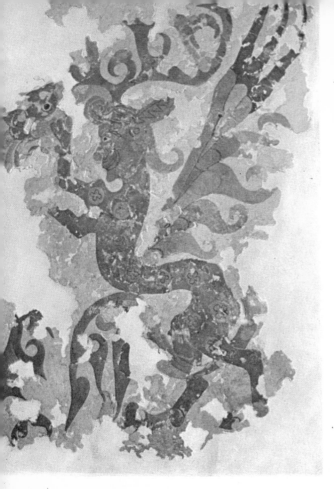

25 This fantastic creature, part human, part animal, fighting a lion-gryphon (not shown) is a detail from a felt appliqué hanging from Pazyryk. Fifth century BC

26 Detail showing a corner ▶ of the oldest woollen pile knotted carpet known to the world. The borders show horsemen of Achaemenian style and elks. It was found at Pazyryk, though probably made in Persia. Fourth–third century BC

The Pazyryk people must have been in regular contact with both China and Persia, for fine textiles produced in both these countries were found among their tomb furnishings. The Persian fabrics included two woven stuffs and the oldest knotted woollen pile carpets known to us. One of these is in almost perfect condition and now hangs in the Hermitage Museum in Leningrad (*Ill. 26*). It dates from the fifth century BC. In his recent book on Oriental carpets K. Erdmann, though he has not had an opportunity of examining these rugs, questions Rudenko's statement that they are made with the Turkish knot. Erdmann suggests that they are in the cut-loop technique, yet it is difficult to accept his view in place of Rudenko's.

27 One half of a gold, **B**-shaped, Siberian belt buckle showing a rider who has leapt from his horse to seek safety in a tree from a wild boar, whilst a second rider pursues the beast. First century BC–first century AD

28 One half of a gold, **B**-shaped, Siberian belt buckle. It shows a warrior sleeping under a tree with his head resting on a woman's lap; his gorytus hangs from the tree and an attendant holds the couple's horses. Compare the woman's dress to that worn by the Great Goddess (*Ill. 30*). First century BC–first century AD

Especially closely related to the metal objects belonging to the Scytho-Altaian schools are the Siberian gold and bronze belt buckles, plaques and articles of personal adornment acquired by Peter the Great. These objects first appeared on the market in about 1669, when Russian settlers in the Ob and Irtysh districts of Siberia started to burrow into the local burial mounds in the hope of finding valuable articles, which they could either sell or melt down. By the end of the century they had broken into so many tombs that the local markets were flooded with ancient metal objects. When Peter the Great was informed of this he instantly took stern measures to put an end to the looting, at the same time giving orders that as many of the stolen objects as possible were to be acquired on his behalf. The collection which he formed is now a treasured exhibition in the Hermitage Museum.

The belt buckles are among the most interesting objects in the collection. The majority are **B**-shaped and cast in bronze, but quite a number are in gold. In both cases the clasps were made separately and soldered to the plaques, the moulded designs of the former being then finished off by hand. In some cases additional decorations were carried out in gold wire or else by means of granulations or repoussé work. Occasionally buckles were adorned with cloisonné enamel, paste inlays or cabochon jewels, turquoises being used more often than other stones. Though contemporary pieces of jewellery were

29 Gold belt buckle from Siberia showing a wolf, which closely resembles the tusked beast of Central Asian and Sassanian art (*Ills. 96 and 97*), fighting a serpent. First–second century A D

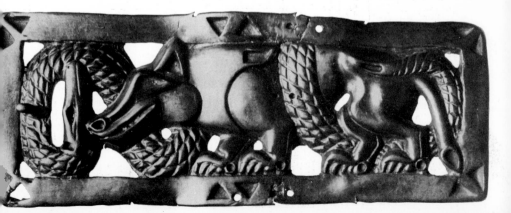

generally decorated with geometric motifs the buckles usually display animal designs, which are often Scythian in character. Occasionally, however, human beings appear on them instead. The animals shown are invariably those which were at the time native to Siberia, but although various species of the stag family were to be found there in large numbers and although stags frequently figure in Scythian art, almost as often in that of the Altaians, yet they seldom appear in Siberian art. Their place is often taken by the wolf (*Ill. 29*), generally shown as a large-eyed, snarling beast, a form which Rudenko traces back to Achaemenid art and which is found closely paralleled in such Altaian burials as Shibe and Katanda.

The people who appear on the Siberian plaques seem to belong to different racial groups for some have Mongoloid, others Aryan, features. However, all wear clothes of similar style and since these correspond to actual garments recovered in excellent condition from the frozen burials of Pazyryk and Katanda they must be accepted as the local form of dress. A belt buckle of outstanding importance was found in the eighteenth century somewhere between the Ob and Irtysh rivers. Made of gold enhanced with polychrome incrustations, it depicts a hunt in a wood (*Ill. 27*). Each section of the buckle is decorated with a different scene. One shows a rider abandoning his horse in order to escape from a wild boar by climbing a tree, whilst in the distance a goat wanders in a hilly landscape; the second portion of the buckle shows him shooting the boar. This buckle is dated to somewhere between the third and first centuries BC. Another gold buckle of even greater interest was found in the same district at much the same time (*Ill. 28*). In this case both sides of the buckle show the same scene, though they present it in reverse. The composition is an elaborate one. It centres on a man lying asleep in the shade of a tree with his head resting on a woman's lap whilst a groom stands at his feet holding his horse. The man's gorytus hangs from a branch, of Scythian shape, but unornamented. The woman's robe is very like a fur one which was found in 1953 in a mound at Katanda whilst her curious head-dress is, according to Rudenko, similar to the peculiar wooden crowns or hats which he found at Pazyryk. It also resembles the head-dress of the Great Goddess on the remarkable felt-hanging

38

30 Detail of a motif from a felt appliqué hanging probably showing an investiture scene. The Great Goddess is shown holding a tree of life in her hand and granting audience to a rider. Pazyryk, fifth century BC

found at Pazyryk (*Ill. 30*). Griaznov noticed that the horse's saddle and bridle, though devoid of decorations, are similar in shape to the real articles discovered at Pazyryk. This buckle dates from between the fifth and the third centuries BC. Its style recalls many aspects of the Pazyryk school, but the horse is rendered with greater naturalism and thus conforms more closely to the Siberian convention than the Altaian. Rudenko is of the opinion that none of the buckles in Peter the Great's collection is to be dated earlier than the sixth century or later than the second century BC. Thus they fall within the Scytho-Sakian period, yet some display an obvious relationship with certain objects in the Oxus Treasure. The similarity is, however, perhaps to be ascribed to the presence in both of Achaemenid elements which were probably transmitted in each case by nomads rather than obtained through direct contacts with Persia.

Certain Soviet scholars, notably Griaznov, have come to feel that the plaques showing human beings probably illustrate incidents from

31 Silver dish from Kulagysh showing two warriors deeply engaged in single combat. Their broken weapons lie scattered on the ground. Griaznov believes that the scene illustrates an incident from an ancient epic. Seventh century AD or later

local myths. He has aptly described the Scytho-Sarmatian period in Siberia as the heroic age of Kazakstan, for he thinks that the sudden ability to ride invested the nomad's life with a glamour and excitement new to it and never again quite equalled. Horsemanship not only made war economically profitable but also rendered it psychologically exhilarating, for his mount transformed every tribesman into a warrior capable of becoming a hero. This possibility led to the glorification of individual valour and eventually resulted in the most intrepid and successful warriors being acclaimed as heroes in epics, which may well have been as stirring and magnificent as Homer's, or as gallant and spirited as those written by Firdausi or Malory. Griaznov believes that these epics lived on until the Arab invasion of Central Asia in the seventh century AD, gaining fresh vigour from the exploits of Turkish warriors. He suggests that illustrations of incidents recounted in them figure on two silver vessels dating from the middle of the first millennium AD. The first of these appears on a

32 Bronze plaque from the Ordos region representing, as Griaznov suggests, an earlier scene from the same epic. The men, having abandoned their mounts, settle their disagreement by wrestling hand to hand, while the horses look on. *c.* third century BC

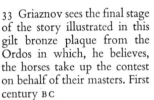

33 Griaznov sees the final stage of the story illustrated in this gilt bronze plaque from the Ordos in which, he believes, the horses take up the contest on behalf of their masters. First century BC

silver dish from Kulagysh in the Ural foothills (*Ill. 31*). According to the best traditions of medieval romance the two combatants shown on it have already used and discarded a number of weapons which lie broken and abandoned at their feet. The second vessel is a *kovsh*, which was found in the Tumen district of Russia. Its rim is decorated with figures of a rider, several animals shown in single file and four tree-like designs. The handle shows two combatants who have dismounted from their horses to continue their fight on foot. Griaznov found the same scene paralleled on two Ordos bronzes dating from the third to the first century BC (*Ill. 32*) and the discovery led him to think that the bronze plaques showing two horses locked in fight (*Ill. 33*), versions of which have been found not only in the Ordos but also in the Transbaikal and Minussinsk areas, present an elaboration of this theme, the chargers continuing the contest started by their riders. In Islamic times heroic incidents of this type were often described by writers of distinction the stories which inspired

41

them having probably been kept alive during the intervening period in the Persian world by the Persians.

In Achaemenid times the central section of the Asiatic plain was largely controlled by Saka tribesmen. They are believed to have come there from the easternmost parts of Turkestan, Tibet and the Tien-shan, and some scholars think of them as forerunners of the Turks. On abandoning their homelands these tribesmen proceeded to move steadily westward, advancing towards what are now Afghanistan and Persia till by the eighth century B C they had reached the foothills of the Arals. Then, spreading out from Lake Balkash, they appeared in the Altai and soon after set up their headquarters in what is now Kirghizia. They remained there till some time between the third and second century B C using weapons, cauldrons and lamps of the same types as those associated with the Scythians, but in addition they also possessed silks, jade and lacquer objects of Chinese origin as well as vessels of gold and bronze decorated in the Graeco-Bactrian style with figures of satyrs and Medusas. Today many of the objects which once belonged to them continue to be found scattered beneath the soil of the Semirechie, Tien-shan and the Pamirs.

The Sakas took part in all the wars which were fought in Central Asia throughout the centuries during which they roamed across its grazing lands. They were conquered by Cyrus, who then persuaded them to join him in fighting his arch enemies, the Greeks. Alexander the invincible subjugated them and in his turn used them in his wars against India. However, in about 159 B C they established a kingdom of their own in Ferghana and were on the point of defeating the Parthians when they were themselves conquered by the Usuns. Before they had had time to recover from this setback the Turks appeared to harass them and drove some into India where, in the course of the first century A D, they gradually became assimilated with the local population and in the process introduced Scythian characteristics into the Indian art of the region. Those Sakas who remained in Central Asia were in their turn gradually absorbed by their Turkish conquerors.

In the second half of the fourth century B C the Huns attempted to gain control of the Central Asian plain. They had by then established themselves on China's western borders where they had adopted the habit of raiding the Chinese settlers living in the empire's frontier areas. The Chou emperors determined to put a stop to their depredations and sent an army against them. To begin with the Chinese force met with a fair measure of success, then the Huns reasserted themselves and recaptured part of the territory they had lost. By the second century B C they had penetrated into the Ordos – a district situated to the east of Tun-huang, west of Peking and south of Mongolia – where they gradually founded a semi-independent kingdom of their own. A series of bronze objects, more especially of cast plaques displaying animal motifs carried out in a Scytho-Siberian style tempered generally by Chinese elements, are to be associated with the Ordos Huns, more particularly of the Han period. The plaques often display animals in the recumbent (*Ills. 34, 35*) or circular positions characteristic of Scythian art, though rendered in the more naturalistic manner which prevailed in western Siberia. This nomadic style even penetrated to China, reaching it both from the Ordos and from Central Asia, to advance as far as the point at which the Yellow River makes its bend. Between the fourth and second century B C Chinese artists became so attracted by the art of their nomadic neighbours that they not only adopted the maeander and interlaced spirals (*Ill. 36*) of which the latter made such frequent use, but occasionally also designed hunting scenes and animals bent into a circle in a style somewhat similar to theirs. Near Ulanfoo in the province of Chensu bronzes of fighting animals rendered in a Scytho-Siberian manner were very popular for a time.

The Huns were not prepared to stay in the Ordos but pushed on into northern Mongolia. In the third century B C they gained control of the grasslands to the north-east of the Gobi desert and then headed for the Transbaikal and moved into Mongolia proper. There, from the seventh to the fourth century B C, it had been the custom for the local inhabitants to be buried in slab graves. In early times pictures of galloping stags had figured prominently in their art but in the course of centuries, that is to say during the Iron Age, they had greatly widened their repertory. The Huns soon gained control

34 Bronze horse trapping from the Ordos region which shows, in its curled design, obvious Scytho-Siberian ancestry. Han period

35 Silver plaque of a tiger, also from the Ordos region, but lacking the splendid rhythm which distinguishes the work of the Scythian and related schools. Han period

of these people and became so powerful that, in about 50 BC, the Chinese resorted to another war designed to contain the Huns. After some fierce fighting they succeeded in forcing the latter to recognize their emperor as their suzerain. The humiliation and loss of their independence re-created such bitter dissensions among the Huns that, although the southerners decided to abide by their allegiance to China, the northern group proceeded to migrate to the Orkhon valley. In about AD 45 a prolonged drought led many of them to revolt against their Orkhon rulers whilst others decided to submit to the Chinese. The latter were resettled in the Ordos and their menfolk drafted to guard the Great Wall and Yellow River. In about AD 150 those who had remained in the Orkhon were evicted from it by the Sienpei, ancestors of the Mongols, who had appeared there from Khingau. They moved westward to found a kingdom of their own in what is now Kazakstan. The numerous mounds which stretch across Mongolia and the district of Baikal are a lasting

36 Chinese artists were frequently influenced by the animal art of the Eurasian nomads, as in the case of this bronze ritual vessel of high quality. Li Yü, Shansi, China; sixth century BC

testimony to their slow but steady advance westward. Many of their burials are situated at very much the same level as that occupied by the Pazyryk and other Altaian tombs. As a result some of the Hunnic graves have been subjected to partial freezing, and those in the Zidzha valley are the richest of these frozen tombs. The earth above them was topped with stones of such cyclopean dimensions that they attracted attention as far back as 1890 when the first of them were excavated. They were found to contain square burial chambers varying in length from 18 to 20 metres. Their walls were built of granite and their roofs of logs. Each chamber contained a coffin made of boards. Though all the tombs that were excavated then had been looted in antiquity, the archaeologists nevertheless recovered from them such important objects as bronze mirrors, silks and lacquer vessels of Chinese worksmanhip as well as some objects made of white nephrite and some trefoil-shaped arrow-heads.

The most important Hunnic cemetery known to us is situated

45

near Noin Ula, on the Sehenga, to the north of Ulan Bator. It was noticed as long ago as 1912 by some gold prospectors who came across it by chance, but whose stories of their discovery failed to arouse the curiosity of archaeologists. In 1922 P.K.Kozlov led a Mongolo-Tibetan geographical expedition into the area and happened to meet one of the gold prospectors who casually described the burial ground to him. Kozlov was quick to appreciate the importance of his remarks and set out to examine the burials. The first tomb which he opened was of the frozen variety. Like the remainder of those which he was later able to excavate it too had been looted in antiquity, but some of its contents still lay in their original positions. In contrast to the Pazyryk burials, where the walls of both the human and horse tombs had been hung with textiles, at Noin Ula it was the floors and ceilings of the human burial chambers which were covered with fabrics. All the tombs which Kozlov examined were so alike that he assigned them to a single period and group of people. Moreover, all proved to be princely burials and, in accordance with the invariable custom of the Scythian and Pazyryk people, all took the form of horse burials. In each case the wooden coffins in which the chieftains were laid had been so carefully and expertly made that Rudenko feels convinced that the work was done by Chinese craftsmen and as they were all embellished with lacquer this suggestion seems likely. The sixth tomb which Kozlov uncovered proved to be the richest as well as the most important from an archaeological point of view, for it not only contained the famous rug, but also the inscribed and dated lacquer cup which enabled the burials to be exactly dated. The inscription on the cup records the names of the three craftsmen who made it for use in the Shahlin Palace on the fifth day of September in the year AD 13.

In addition to some precious objects the Noin Ula burials contained such useful items as three-legged tables, wooden utensils of various sorts, bronze cauldrons with cylindrical bases and handles of Chinese appearance, chopsticks, pottery vessels of Chinese shapes, malachite and coloured glass beads and bronze mirrors of Chinese workmanship. The horse trappings were exceedingly elaborate and

37 Detail from a large woven woollen rug mounted on fine leather and decorated in purple, brown and white felt, first stitched onto the textile over a cord binding and then embroidered. Its central motif shows a gryphon attacking an elk. Noin Ula, first century A D onwards

included saddles, the pommels and front frames of which were covered with leather threaded with black and red wool closely clipped to resemble velvet. However, it was the textiles that proved of most interest. One of the finest was the superb rug found in Tomb 6 (*Ill. 37*). Its central design is executed in chain-stitch and is typically Scytho-Altaian in character for it shows a wild beast attacking an elk. Its border is worked in appliqué felts in the manner of the Pazyryk hangings. The most spirited of these designs display animals of the Perso-Scytho-Altaian type locked in combat. The rug is mounted on a fine leather lining. The ceiling in the same burial chamber was covered with another textile of almost equal interest. This was made of a woollen woven stuff on which black and white stripes had been embroidered to give the impression of a splayed out tiger-skin, the animal's head and paws being embroidered at each end (*Ill. 38*). Other important hangings display humans embroidered with great skill (*Ills. 39, 40*). This group of textiles is assuredly of nomadic origin, but the silk stuffs which were found with them are undoubtedly Chinese. In addition Rudenko assigns two of the woven textiles to Usun weavers, certain others to Graeco-Bactrian workshops and some others to Parthian or Graeco-Parthian craftsmen.

47

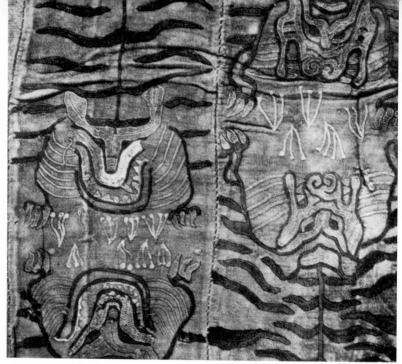

38 Textile embroidered with tigers, probably to give the impression of real skins, used to cover the west wall of Tomb 16 at Noin Ula. First century A D onwards

The diverse origins of the imported objects serve both to testify to the widespread nature of the contacts which the Huns had by then established, and also to illustrate the varied influences which were making themselves felt in Central Asia at the dawn of our era.

Some scholars think that the Turks were Hunnu tribesmen who had been evicted from the Ordos by the Huns. According to legend they came from the mythical land of Turan where their chieftains lived in great splendour, wearing golden crowns and sitting in tents of a vast size. They owned immense herds of horses and cattle, branding their animals with their personal crests. They gradually advanced into Kashgaria and then entered Turkestan. According to the story their ruler Feridun, 'one of the world's greatest kings', then divided his land between his two sons, giving Iran to Ir and Turan to Tur. In medieval works of art the Turks are shown wearing the

39 Embroidered fragment showing two riders. It is interesting to compare it with *Ill. 90*. Noin Ula, first century A D onwards

40 Embroidered fragment showing a head which has something of the quality of a portrait. Noin Ula, first century A D onwards

close-fitting tunics, broad trousers gathered in at the ankles, embroidered high boots and either felt bonnets or fur hats associated with nomadic horsemen, whilst their warriors appear in pointed helmets topped with a pin and ball (*Ill. 172*). As the Turks moved westward replacing the Huns some settled in Mongolia as vassals of the Avar rulers of Upper Mongolia and the Gobi; others pushed on towards the Sea of Aral and reached Bactria, where many of them settled. They are known to have reached the middle Syr Darya by the first century BC. They were splendid horsemen and skilful cattle breeders, but like most nomads they were predatory and restless. In about AD 78 they did not hesitate to plunder the Hunnic burials in the Orkhon district, a sacrilege which the Huns lost little time in avenging. They were also quarrelsome and their fights and skirmishes disrupted the economic stability of the Asiatic plain at the very time when the Han emperor, Wu-ti, wished to ensure its stability and safety so as to establish commercial relations with the Western world in order to obtain such luxuries as glass, vines and lucerne in return for silk. Realizing that the success of these plans depended upon China's ability to ensure the safety of the caravans carrying these precious goods, Wu-ti determined to control the Turks both by force of arms and by propitiatory gifts. The Turks were content to be kept quiet in this way until about the middle of the sixth century AD. By then they had grown so rich and powerful that they rebelled against the Avars, overthrew their rule and evicted them from their territory. The Avars moved westward as a result, overrunning Europe. The Turks, on the other hand, established a kingdom of their own in the Orkhon valley, with its capital near Karakorum. By 565 they had conquered the Mongolian Hephthalites and extended their rule to the borders of Persia. However, they soon quarrelled among themselves and eventually split into two groups, the eastern retaining the Orkhon and Mongolia, the western ruling on the Issyk Kul.

Chinese and Byzantine writers of the sixth century describe the wealth and strength of the Orkhon Turks. They mention the gilt thrones shaped in the form of rams which their chieftains used in Ferghana. The Khan of Bokhara and the Khan of the Orkhon each

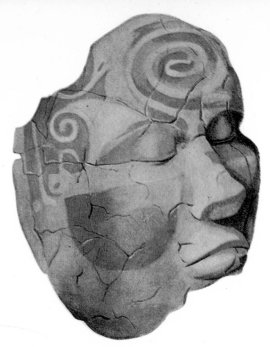

41 Death mask from a Tadjik burial, painted perhaps to represent tattooings. Second century B C–first century A D

had thrones supported by four golden peacocks and other animals made of silver which the Byzantine envoy thought as impressive as anything to be seen in Constantinople. These thrones must surely have been made by Central Asian goldsmiths rather than by Turks.

Both groups of Turks spent much of their time fighting their respective neighbours, the eastern the Chinese, the western the Sassanians. Then, in about A D 630 the *kagan* of the western group was murdered and his kingdom rapidly disintegrated as a result. The western survived it for little more than twenty years, to succumb with the rest of eastern Turkestan to China. But even though the Turks were not destined to remain in Central Asia these setbacks were little more than a momentary eclipse. After the Arab invasion had spent itself the Turkish tribes rallied again and eventually established the great, if comparatively short-lived, dynasties known to us as the Samanid, Ghaznavid and Seljukid, not to mention the Ottoman. In the tenth century those who were still concentrated in

51

the Samarkand region are said to have made life-size statues in wood of horses, oxen, camels and other animals and to have placed them in the public squares of Samarkand. Unfortunately none of these has survived to our time, but a building of that period was discovered in Kashgaria, in what is now Uzbekistan, and found to contain a room, the north wall of which was decorated with a painting representing the Emperor of China, the east wall with that of a group of Indian Brahmins and Turkish khans and the west wall with pictures of Persian kings and Roman emperors.

At the time when the Huns and Turks were abandoning their homelands in the east to move westward small groups of settlers were establishing themselves in the Minussinsk basin, the region lying close to the Altai which had in early times shared the animal art common to western Siberia. Many bronze objects have been recovered from the upper reaches of the Yenissei. They include tools and vessels decorated with animal designs which seem sometimes to point to tenuous links with China. The early inhabitants of the region had earned their living by agriculture. Until the fourth century or so BC these people were of Iranian stock, members of the Europoid race, but they wore the type of clothes associated with nomadic horsemen and, like the nomads, they knew how to work metals. Indeed metallurgy had been developed in the Minussinsk basin at a very early date. During the first millennium BC its inhabitants decorated their objects with motifs drawn both from the Scythian animal repertory and from that of the ancient Orient. By the third century BC people of Mongoloid race had come to live beside the Iranians. The features of the newcomers have been preserved for us in a series of some sixty masks (*Ill. 41*) which Soviet archaeologists have found in Tadjik burials dating from about the third century BC to the first century AD. Some of these masks are casts made from the faces of the dead, but others were modelled by hand; the vast majority of both types were painted with blue, red and green colours to indicate the pearl necklaces the women had been in the habit of wearing, as well as the eyelashes of the dead and lines on their foreheads, temples and cheeks. These may well represent tattoo marks. Tattooing cannot have been uncommon at that date in

Siberia for in the fifth century B C at least two of the Pazyryk dead had had their bodies entirely covered with markings. Certain of the Tadjik burials also contained scale armour made not of metal but of stone sections held together by straps; larger sections of similar stone particles were used to make their helmets. These were decorated with figures of real and imaginary animals of Scytho-Siberian appearance, which were doubtless invested by their wearers with magical attributes.

The Kirghiz were offshoots of the Orkhon Turks but it was not until the seventh and eighth century A D that they became renowned for the fine pottery and superb gold and silver vessels which they made. These were of local shape but they often embodied Sassanian and Chinese features in their decorations, and were much admired in T'ang times. Until the end of the first millennium A D the Kirghiz also made bronze belt buckles, decorated with designs in which Scytho-Siberian traits prevailed. They were also in the habit of embellishing their saddles with hunting scenes, the origins of which can be traced far back into the past, combining them with landscapes of Chinese character. The Kirghiz were practically wiped out by the Mongols in 1209 and their flourishing school of applied art never recovered from the blow which was inflicted on it then.

The smaller kingdoms of Transcaucasia and the Persian highlands during the first millennium BC

The Persian tribes, and more especially the Medes, were latecomers in the west for they did not appear in the Zagros area until about the tenth century BC. Shortly after that the majority of the Medes abandoned nomadism to live in walled towns where their houses were built round the fortified citadels belonging to their chieftains. The Medes bred horses of such excellence that their stallions were coveted by the Assyrians who frequently resorted to war as a means of procuring fresh stock from which to raise their own horses. It is therefore scarcely surprising that the first known written reference to the Medes occurs in an account of a campaign conducted against them by Shalmaneser III in 836–5. Fighting between Assyrians and Medes continued for many years with only short interruptions but the Medes took advantage of the peaceful interludes to wage war against other neighbours, more particularly the Urartians and Mannaeans.

At much the same time that the Median kingdom was growing up in the Zagros, the Urartian kingdom was developing in Armenia and the Caucasus. Originally a confederation of Hurrian tribes, the Urartians became a nation by the ninth century BC and just as the turbulence of the Medes aroused the suspicions of the Assyrians, so did the wealth of the Urartians excite their cupidity. Torn between anxiety and envy, the Assyrians failed to concentrate on the destruction of one of their enemies before turning on the other, but dissipated their strength in raiding Median cattle farms and repelling Median incursions into their own territory whilst at the same time harassing the Urartians. This policy gave the Median princes the opportunity to unite with the result that, by the second quarter of the first millennium BC, they were in a position to defy the mighty Assyrian emperor in a full-scale war. Its outcome was on the point of being decided when the victorious Scythian nomads swept into what is

42 Detail from a gold sword sheath depicting scenes from a hunt reveals that the Medes shared with the Assyrians their love of movement and their ability to render it in metal. Oxus Treasure, seventh–sixth century BC

now north-western Persia and eastern Turkey, to become the masters of the whole of that area for the best part of three decades. In the face of the common danger the Medes set aside their differences and joined forces with the Assyrians to fight their nomadic conquerors. In about 625 BC they succeeded in defeating the nomads and in chasing them northward across Urartu. There the retreating Scythians paused just long enough to pillage and set fire to the Urartian stronghold of Karmir Blur before continuing a flight which carried most of them to southern Russia. The Medes followed them as far as the Caucasian mountain range, taking advantage of their passage across Urartu to destroy that kingdom. Then, leaving part of their force to mop up behind them, the Medes attacked Assyria. Here too their troops achieved signal success with the result that within another fifty years Median territory extended to the Halys river in Anatolia. However, the victors were not to enjoy the benefits of their conquests for long, for within twenty-five years one of their Persian vassals had rebelled against them. He was to go down in history as Cyrus the Great and his revolt brought the Achaemenids to the thrones of both Assyria and Media. It was, however, his successor, Cyrus II, who was finally to destroy the Medes by defeating their ruler Astyages in c. 492 BC. This victory enabled him to establish his court in the former Median capital of Ecbatana (Hamadan).

43 A detail from the bronze gates at Balawat showing the conquest of Urartu by Shalmaneser III in 859 BC. Ninth century

Though the Medes came to the Zagros from the north, like most of Assyria's neighbours, they too were to be profoundly influenced by Assyrian culture (*Ill. 42*). To begin with, they even went to the length of adopting the Assyrian script, but they later abandoned it in favour of the old Persian cuneiform, which was itself derived from Akkadian and which Darius continued occasionally to use. Median art was likewise deeply influenced by that of Assyria, but at the same time it also adopted certain features of Urartian origin.

Urartu, the Khaldi of the ancient texts and the Ararat people of the Bible, occupied much the same area as does present-day Armenia with, in addition, the district of Van which now belongs to Turkey. Its king likewise used the Assyrian script for official purposes and encouraged the growth of a culture which, though basically Baby-lonian, had acquired an Assyrian veneer before it reached Urartu. The Urartians were Aryans, but they modelled their appearance on that of the Assyrians. The admiration they felt for the latter was, however, devoid of servility. Thus, from the start of the ninth century BC they tried to expand eastward and southward, then, in

44 Assyrian limestone relief from the palace at Nineveh showing the Assyrians melting down the bronze statues which they captured from the Urartians. From a drawing by Flandin. Seventh century BC

c. 834 BC, when Sardur was king, they advanced towards Lake Urmia. Thereafter, both under Sardur and his successor Argysht, they proceeded to encroach on Assyrian territory till the latter were goaded into retaliating. The war which ensued was fierce and protracted; one battle was recorded for all time on a bronze panel adorning the door of Shalmaneser III's palace at Balawat (*Ill. 43*). The defeated Urartians appear on it wearing clothes which resemble those worn by both the Hittites and the Assyrians. Fighting between both countries continued with only short pauses for the best part of a century. Major campaigns occurred in 743 and 714 BC, but eventually the Assyrians, who far outnumbered the Urartians, were able to impose ties of vassalship upon their enemy and to levy immense taxes on their unfortunate victims. Indeed, its intrinsic value proved so immense that the Assyrians were themselves astonished by it. Their records refer with wonder to the vast quantities of gold, silver, bronze, copper and iron objects which were handed in, special mention being made of the bronze sculptures (*Ill. 44*) and the textiles embellished with gold thread. As most of the enumerated metals could be obtained from the mountains situated on Urartu's northern borders, and were thus close at hand, the lavish use of them by the Urartians is hardly surprising.

On becoming vassals of the Assyrians the Urartians wisely applied themselves to improving their relationship with them. As a result, under Argysht II, the Urartians were able to rebuild the towns which had been destroyed in the fighting. They had scarcely finished doing so when the Medes broke into their territory in pursuit of the Scythians and, at the sight of Urartu's wealth and splendour decided to content themselves with evicting the Scythians from Trans-caucasia in order to apply themselves to overthrowing the Urartian rulers and putting an end to that country's existence. They fully succeeded in carrying out these aims, destroying the Urartian kingdom with all traces of the elaborate culture which had been evolved there.

In their day the Urartians were greatly admired by their neighbours for their remarkable skill in working metals. Their bronzes were frequently exported to Luristan, Asia Minor and even further afield, for some have been found in Thracian burials. The Urartians well deserved the esteem in which they were held, for their metal workers could cast life-sized statues and make so wide a range of objects as to include thrones and candelabra.

Our knowledge of Urartian art and culture is still largely based on excavations carried out on only three sites, those of Toprak Kale, in present-day Turkey, and Karmir Blur and Arin-Berd or Ereburi, in Soviet Armenia. Toprak Kale was the first of the three to be examined. It is situated in eastern Turkey, on the outskirts of Van, and was of such importance in its heyday that legends grew up ascribing its foundation to Semiramis. They averred that she employed 12,000 Assyrian labourers and 600 Assyrian master masons to build the town. A bronze plaque depicting a building (*Ill. 45*) and a fragment showing a tower (*Ill. 46*) were found at Toprak Kale and serve to give us some idea of the city's appearance.

Toprak Kale was excavated on behalf of the British Museum towards the end of the last century. The man chosen to direct the work was inadequately qualified and as a result the digging developed into a treasure hunt. No detailed records were kept and even the task of supervising the labourers was so inefficiently discharged that the men were able to steal many objects and, most disastrous of all, to smash the royal throne – a unique find – and later to sell the fragments to a number of museums. The pieces are thus widely dispersed; nevertheless they suffice to show that the throne was made of cast bronze sections which were welded together, their moulded decorations being finished off by hand. The fragments that survive are deeply influenced by Assyrian art. For the most part they take the form of creatures combining human, animal and bird attributes, but in addition many are also decorated with engraved or embossed designs of a similar kind. Typical of these creatures is a bronze human-headed winged bull, the face of which was once inlaid with stone, whilst its head is surmounted by an elaborate crown (*Ill. 48*). Another fragment (*Ill. 47*) is thought to be the arm-rest. Like all the other objects thought to have come from the Toprak Kale excavations these objects are dated to the eighth century BC.

45, 46 Two bronzes from Toprak Kale. (*Left*) A relief of a citadel or palace and (*right*) a model of a tower. The latter already displays a brick or stonework decoration of the type which is associated with medieval Persia. Eighth–seventh century BC

47 Bronze statuette, probably the god Teishab, from a bronze throne, now destroyed. Toprak Kale. Eighth–seventh century BC. The only other piece of monumental bronze work from Urartu is the statue now in Erivan, of which this may have been a replica

With the destruction of the throne only two major examples of Urartian workmanship are known to us. One is the life-size statue, in Erivan Museum, of Teishab, the Urartian god of war and storms, shown standing on a bull from Adilgzhevaza (*Ill. 47*). Similar to the other is a wall-painting from Arin-Berd, carried out in reds, blues and whites, with the scenes disposed, in accordance with Assyrian custom, in two parallel bands. The decorations on the lower band include a tree flanked by deities; only parts of the upper section of the work survive; these consist of stylized garlands which recall similar ones found at Nimrud, but whereas the latter are dated to the sixth century BC, B. B. Piotrovsky, the discoverer of the Arin-Berd paintings, assigns the latter to the eighth century.

48 Human-headed, winged bull creature, again probably part of the bronze throne from Toprak Kale. The face was originally inlaid with stone. Eighth–seventh century B C

49 Another fragment, probably the arm-rest, of the bronze throne from Toprak Kale. All three fragments reveal the static, essentially Assyrian style of Urartian court art. Eighth–seventh century B C

The minor works of art which Piotrovsky and his colleagues found in large numbers whilst excavating the sites of Karmir Blur and Arin-Berd also add to our knowledge of Urartian art. Both sites are situated in the outskirts of Armenia's capital, Erivan, Karmir Blur is the name by which the settlement was first known, but in the seventh century B C the Urartian king, Russa I, chose it as an administrative and military centre, and renamed it Teishabani in honour of the god Teishab. Thereafter the town quickly grew in size. Many of its houses clustered round the large, extremely impressive palace-citadel. It was unfortunate that its buildings were roofed with thatch, for the Scythians, whilst being evicted from Persia by the Medes, set fire to them. Though they pillaged and destroyed them they nevertheless overlooked many objects in the town's ruins for Soviet archaeologists to discover some 2,500 years later. The finds include a great deal of pottery and some articles of both intrinsic and artistic value. The pottery is of a reddish colour; the finer wares are decorated with painted designs which are generally geometric in character, though some represent bulls. According to Piotrovsky one of these closely resembles the bronze statuettes of bulls found on the Hittite site of Boğazköy in Turkey. Figurines of deities and animals were also found at Karmir Blur; so many of them represent bulls that it seems probable that some sort of bull cult was practised in the city at the time of its conquest. Ninety-seven bronze jugs were found in the citadel's cellars and are identical in shape to the numerous pottery ones which were also found there. Nevertheless, the most important finds consist of weapons, fragments of wide bronze belts and a cauldron in the form of a bird decorated with bull-headed creatures with human bodies.

Piotrovsky thinks that some two hundred of the objects recovered from the ruins of Karmir Blur were specially made for the king and his courtiers, and suggests that they were made in Arin-Berd, where many admirably equipped workshops were found when the town was excavated. Many of these articles are inscribed in Assyrian and can as a result be dated with exactitude. The weapons include fourteen shields and twenty helmets of Assyrian shape. The finest are adorned with elaborate decorations; and are inscribed with the

50, 51, 52 (*above left*) Bronze quiver case of Sardur II and (*above right and detail*) bronze helmet of Argysht I. Both objects follow Assyrian tradition in the method of decoration and similar types of shields and helmets can be seen engraved on the objects themselves. Karmir Blur, seventh century BC

names of their royal owners, Kings Argysht I, Sardur II and Russa I
(*Ills. 50, 51, 52*) The decorations on the shields were first embossed
and then finished off by chasing. The same method was used for
adorning the belts. Although these are rather wider than the belt
found at Trialeti in Georgia they are of the same type. Four of the
finest shields are dated by their inscriptions to the eighth century B C.
Their decorations are arranged on them in bands, in what must be
regarded as the Assyrian manner; the motifs include figures of gods,
sacred trees, lions, chariots and horsemen. The designs on the belts
follow the same system of arrangement, rows of animals alternating
with a line of trees.

Some boxes, amulets and statuettes of stone were also found at
Karmir Blur. Living as they were in a region rich in stone of
excellent quality it is hardly surprising that the Urartians were able
to work it as skilfully as they did metals, cutting inscriptions with
equal proficiency on both. In addition, they also knew how to inlay
paste and stone, and the more difficult art of engraving gems. They
were as ready to adorn their gems with the images of gods as with
scenes of either a religious or genre character.

53 Bronze statuette of one of Urartu's
well-trained and disciplined soldiers.
The figurine has a personal element
about it unusual for the period, though
it can scarcely be called a portrait.
Eighth–seventh century B C

Yet for all their technical proficiency and their ability to create impressive works the art of the Urartians is of a more pedestrian character than that of the Assyrians. The proportions they evolved for their renderings of the human figures (*Ill. 53*) produced stocky rather heavily foreshortened outlines so that they create a more prosaic impression than do the Assyrian works which inspired them. Furthermore, an almost Prussian-like regard for details, formality and conformity robs many Urartian works of the poetic element which is beauty's invariable companion. Urartian renderings of animals are, on the other hand, even when carried out in the Assyrian manner, far more spirited than those which the Assyrians produced – an advantage which they may well owe to the impact of the animal art of Central Asia. But whereas the nomads were fond of including fierce beasts, whether real or imaginary, in their repertory, the Urartians preferred to present even their lions as benign. They never showed animals contorted by the speed of their movements as did the nomadic artists, but presented them instead in poses of such static dignity that they seem even more immobile than their Assyrian prototypes. Urartian art is staid and tranquil, un-changing, and it must be admitted, somewhat repetitive both in theme and character. It lacks the touch of spontaneity which enlivens Assyria's narrative and essentially ceremonial art. Yet it remains immensely impressive. It is essentially religious, the majority of the decorative motives which appear in it being either of a propitiatory character or closely related to the people's faith. Nevertheless the scenes are rendered in a way which clearly shows that the artists who produced them were fond of decoration for its own sake, and as a result Urartian objects are often as heavily decorated as the nomadic ones of a similar date. The floral designs in particular often seem to exist in order to fill a vacant space rather than to provide an essential section of the design.

A series of magnificent objects of a different sort have been dis-covered within recent years in Iran, at the sites of Hasanlu, Marlyk and Ziwiye. They possess so many affinities with the artistic schools which grew up in Transcaucasia and the Central Asian plain that they must be mentioned here even though their sites lie just to the

54, 55 Gold repoussé bowl from Hasanlu which cost two Urartian soldiers their lives. It is decorated with ritual scenes. (*Below*) Details showing a goddess riding a lion and holding a mirror, attributes of the Great Goddess which appear on several Scythian objects found in south Russia. Tenth–ninth century BC

56 Silver spouted vessel from Marlyk with applied decorations in gold. Spouted vessels of this type made their appearance at Amlash at the end of the second millennium and continued to be made in north-west Iran until early in the first millennium B C

south of the geographical limits set for this book. They are situated in the Caspian–Lake Urmia districts. Hasanlu is perhaps the most important of the three for it probably served as the capital of the Mannaeans. It stands at the southern tip of Lake Urmia, at a point where the roads connecting Anatolia to the Caucasus, Kurdistan and Luristan met those linking Assyria to Kurdistan, Azarbeidjan and central Persia. The town was already important by 1000 B C and had probably been so for some considerable time before that. It was sacked by the Urartians in the ninth century B C and two centuries after the Medes put an end to the Mannaean kingdom. When at the height of its prosperity Mannaean metal workers ranked as second to none, yet our knowledge of their artistry is still largely derived from the objects found at Hasanlu first by Sir Aurel Stein then, in 1956, by R. H. Dyson, excavating on behalf of Philadelphia University. Dyson assigns the objects which he found to about 1000 B C when delicately shaped pottery vessels were first given elegant fluted bases and long, thin spouts.

Dyson's most important finds include a splendid gold bowl (*Ill.*

67

54), the workmanship of which recalls that of Trialeti. It has been suggested that the vessel was made in Urartu, but since it dates from a time when the kingdom scarcely existed this hardly seems likely. In 900 B C the citadel of Hasanlu was set on fire by the Urartians, and in the confusion and looting three Urartian soldiers saw the bowl and lost their lives trying to secure it, for the excavators found it lying beneath their crushed bodies. Also beside them was a sword mounted to a handle of red sandstone adorned with ivory and bronze, an iron sword handle, a star-shaped mace of Caucasian origin and an Urartian cup. The vessel reflects Caucasian influences, as well as Assyrian traditions, namely in the disposition of the decorations in two bands. Georgian influence is reflected with particular clarity in the figure of a fish-tailed monster with three dogs' heads which is seen emerging from a cave to fight a man wearing, what Dyson has aptly described as, boxing gloves. Other scenes include a goddess seated on a lion's back (*Ill. 55*). The animal displays a swastika on its flank whilst the goddess holds a mirror. In Scythian times mirrors served as attributes of women deities and they may well have had the same meaning among the Mannaeans. Another motif shows a god seated in a chariot which is harnessed to a mule. As mules rarely figure in the art of this period the animal's presence may be due to Anatolian influence, but another chariot included in the decoration of this bowl, once again occupied by a god, is harnessed to a bull of Caucaso-Urartian appearance. Other metal vessels from Hasanlu display motifs which were popular in Urartu though they are executed in a manner which is closer to the Assyrian, for they occasionally bear witness to the Hittite and Egyptian influences which at times made themselves so clearly felt in Assyria.

To the north of Hasanlu, at the southern tip of the Caspian, near Rudbar, in the foothills of the Gonar Rud, Iranian archaeologists recently excavated a mound called Marlyk. One of a group of five mounds of uniform size and character, it concealed beneath its earth topping a building, partly carved out of the underlying rock and partly built of stone, and thought to be a temple. An altar-like structure stood at its centre with a superb, long-spouted silver vessel like a teapot lying beside it (*Ill. 56*). The vessel was adorned with gold representations of a winged figure with a human body and two animal heads holding a sphinx in each of its extended arms while above a lion is seen in the act of attacking a stag. The composition is impregnated with deep religious feeling. Though the combat scene between the lion and stag is so old a motif that its origin cannot be established, the form in which it is presented here clearly stems from the nomadic world, yet the workmanship of the vessel as a whole recalls the style of the gold Hasanlu bowl and cannot have been made by a nomadic craftsman. Outside the building some twenty graves were situated, only two of which contained any bones. They varied in size and the excavators suggest that, somewhat in the manner of Goldilocks and the three bears, kings had been buried in the largest graves, queens and their children in the medium-sized ones, some of which contained dolls and dice, whilst the smallest of all were used for the burial of courtiers.

In addition to the beautifully shaped pottery vessels found at Marlyk, all of which were fine and delicately made wares, the tombs also contained many objects of intrinsic value. Some had clearly been made for a ceremonial purpose, others for religious needs and many more for daily use, whether in the home, out hunting or in warfare (*Ill. 58*). A series of gold and silver mugs (*Ills. 57, 59, 60*) assigned, by the archaeologists who discovered them, to about the year 1000 BC are perhaps the finest and most valuable of the finds. Their shapes are truly superb but, in addition, each is enhanced by animal designs of Scytho-Persian character often executed in such high relief that the creatures seem on the point of breaking free from the background. Both the animal and the floral motifs which are shown on the cups are native to the region, but the rosettes which stud the backgrounds are of much earlier local origin. Nevertheless, the basic characteristics of these cups, notwithstanding their links with Assyria and Urartu, foreshadow the Achaemenid style. It is unfortunate that nothing is as yet known about the people who either made or commissioned these splendid objects, but it is abundantly clear that those who did so were in close and regular touch with their immediate neighbours, and more especially with the Urartians and Mannaeans, as well as the Assyrians.

57 One of several gold mugs from Marlyk. This one, showing a winged bull in high relief, between trees, is amongst the finest. Ninth century BC

58 (*below left*) Pottery bear. Many animal-shaped vessels were found at Marlyk; the bulls are very stylized, but this bear is far more naturalistic. Ninth century BC

59 (*below right*) Like the bear, this silver mug may well have served some ritual purpose. It is engraved with warriors in close-fitting tunics holding a leopard in each hand. Ninth century BC

60 Gold mug from Marlyk is decorated, in the manner of so much Perso-Scythian art, with two rows of tusked beasts walking in opposite directions. Though Assyrian in inspiration, they are imbued with a vitality which may well stem from western Central Asia. Ninth century B C

The third group of objects to be mentioned here belongs to a treasure which was discovered shortly after the Second World War at Ziwiye, near Sakiz, some 120 kilometres to the south of Lake Urmia. It contained numerous articles made of either gold, bronze or ivory. Dr R. D. Barnett has shown that they must have been placed in a copper coffin and buried in it some time during the last quarter of the seventh century B C, perhaps at the very time when the Scythians had overrun the district. The coffin was, Barnett thinks, almost certainly made in Assyria though its central decoration contains animals rendered in the style of the steppe people and another motif shows a Median prince in the act of paying homage to his Assyrian suzerain. Ghirshman assigns the objects found in the coffin to four schools which he defines as the Assyrian, the Scytho-Assyrian (*Ill. 61*), the Scythian (*Ill. 64*) and the local, that is to say, the Mannaean. However, a gold pectoral (*Ill. 62*) is considered by many scholars to be of Scytho-Median workmanship and Barnett adds a fifth, Urartian group, so as to cover the superb gold plaque decorated with lion's masks alternating with Scythian-looking goats and stags which (*Ill. 63*) resembles a late Urartian metal belt from Zakin.

The objects which the Urartians, Mannaeans and their immediate neighbours created in the course of the first millennium B C are often

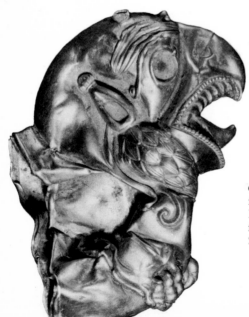

61 Gold handle of a cauldron in the form of a gryphon eagle from Ziwiye. Its majestic and authoritative air stems from Assyria, its vitality from the Scythian world. Seventh century B C

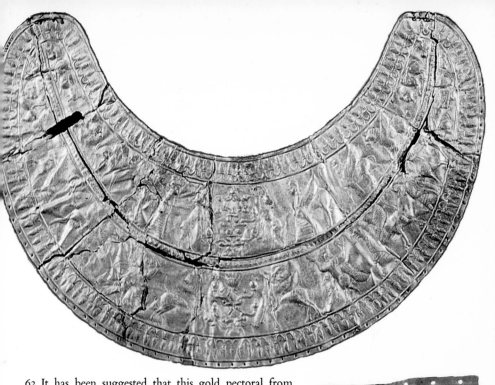

62 It has been suggested that this gold pectoral from Ziwiye may have belonged to the Scythian king Bartatue who married an Assyrian princess. The style of its decoration is either Assyrio- or Urarto-Scythian and is arranged in two bands. A tree of life occupies a central position and is flanked by ibexes, winged human-headed bulls of Assyrian origin, with a Scythian-looking hare and feline creatures in the corners. Seventh century BC

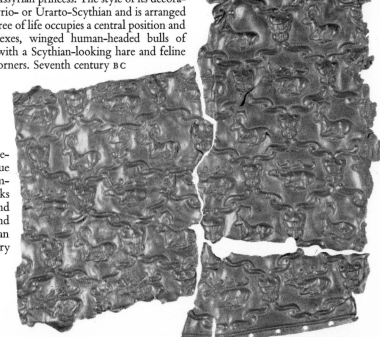

63 Fragments of repoussé gold plaque with lozenges terminating in lion's masks of Urartian type, and enclosing stages and ibexes of Scythian style. Seventh century BC

extraordinarily lovely and splendid. Nevertheless, their great fascination lies in the light which they throw on the taste of their times and on the way of life followed in quite small countries and communities living within the orbit of the great Assyrian empire. These objects also serve to show that craftsmanship was no less highly developed in many of the minor principalities than in the great centres of civilization, and that even if artists in the peripheral regions lacked some of the inventiveness and genius displayed in the masterpieces belonging to the Graeco-Persian schools, yet they possessed the technical proficiency and sense of style which are essential if a supremely well-made object is also to rank as a work of art.

64 Gold pommel decorated with an embossed and chased animal curled into a circle in the Scythian manner. The workmanship may be Median or Scythian. *c.* 600 BC

CHAPTER THREE

Soghdia, Ferghana and Chorasmia
from Achaemenid to Islamic times

Whilst the Central Asian plain remained a nomadic preserve, settlers with a highly evolved system of irrigation established flourishing townlets along the eastern and southern fringes of the plain. Both from an economic and a geographical point of view, conditions there favoured an urban way of life based to a large extent upon trade. Sociologically, no less than economically, the area comprising the regions now known as western and eastern Turkestan formed a single unit. Nevertheless, the geographical position occupied by the various countries into which the region was split resulted in their basically similar cultures developing along slightly different lines as a result of the impact made upon each of them by their respective neighbours. Thus, in the western areas the local styles were overlaid by Graeco-Roman and Persian elements, whereas, in the east, where Hellenistic traditions having once penetrated, persisted longer than elsewhere in Central Asia, it was India which provided the vital elements in the creation of a style which, with the years, acquired a Chinese overlay.

Owing to these differences it is more convenient to divide the arts of the urban dwellers of Turkestan into three sections, devoting one to what is known today as western or Soviet Turkestan – that is to say, the area which contains the republics of Turkmenistan, Tadjikistan and Uzbekistan – another to what is now southern Tadjikistan, Afghanistan, north-western India and a small portion of north-western Pakistan, and a third to eastern Turkestan and the modern Chinese province of Sinkiang.

In ancient times western or Soviet Turkestan was split into the three comparatively small though important states of Soghdia, Ferghana and Chorasmia (the Latin version of Kwarasm). They often enjoyed complete political independence, but at times they were reduced to positions of vassalship. Throughout their history all three were closely linked to Bactria, a state which covered most of present-day Afghanistan and the southern part of Tadjikistan. Soghdia in the west, Bactria to the south-east, were both centres of particularly vital cultures. Throughout the Achaemenid period, from about the sixth to the fourth century B C, both developed along parallel lines, adopting numerous motifs, themes and conventions from their Persian neighbours and fusing these with their own basically nomadic, largely Scytho-Sakian style of animal art.

When the Achaemenids succeeded in conquering Soghdia and Bactria they found that possession of these territories imposed certain troublesome obligations upon them. The most important of these was the task which the Medes had faithfully performed of protecting the settlers from raiding nomads. Indeed, Cyrus met his death in c. 530 whilst campaigning against the Massagetae to the east of the Caspian. It was, therefore, as much in order to establish a belt of buffer states along their northern borders, as for reasons of territorial gain that the Achaemenids set out to populate and develop the border territories which the Arabs were later to describe as 'the other side of the world'.

Soghdia comprised the Zaravshan and Kashka Darya river beds in what are now southern Uzbekistan and Tadjikistan, marching on the north-west with Chorasmia which extended over the lower reaches of the Amu Darya, in which is now the district of Tashkent. Both shared a frontier with Ferghana, and all three developed virtually simultaneously along much the same lines, evolving in the process an analogous way of life and producing artistic and architectural works which followed the same styles, though with certain regional differences. Soghdia was, however, politically the more important of the three; it figures with Chorasmia and Bactria in the inscription cut at the order of Darius on the great rock of Bisitun.

Soghdia and Ferghana were both very fertile countries, for although the central part of Ferghana was a sandy, uninhabitable desert, its edges were dotted with townlets which had grown up in ancient times at the points where the smaller rivers joined the Syr Darya. There the surrounding foothills were covered with trees and

65 This superb head of a thoroughbred horse, perhaps a Ferghana, was made in green jade by a Chinese sculptor of the Han period

lush grass which provided farmers with admirable pasture on which to rear the thoroughbred horses for which they were famous as far afield as China.

In early times Chorasmia was the least prosperous of the three states for although it is mentioned both in the Avesta and in Darius's Bisitun inscription, in the first millennium B C it was little more than a large oasis state in the Syr Darya's delta. However, in the time of Herodotus Chorasmia was already noted for the excellence of its agriculture. In the sixth century B C, when annexed by the Achae-menids, all three states were thus regarded as valuable additions to the Persian empire, yet Cyrus appears to have set greater store by Soghdia for he founded more new towns there than anywhere else in Central Asia, with the exception of Bactria. He also provided

77

66 Clay model of a horse. Here a Chinese potter immortalized a recalcitrant horse of a heavier breed. Docked tails are seldom seen on the thoroughbreds depicted by either Persian or Chinese artists. AD 220–589

Soghdia with a new capital, choosing for the purpose a town which he founded in the neighbourhood of present-day Samarkand and which he called Cyreskatu or Kyropolis after himself. It became the headquarters of a garrison and a major defensive outpost, yet in the fourth century BC Ferghana was to be in greater need of military aid than Soghdia for in *c.* 307 the Emperor of China decided to replace his regiments of charioteers by cavalry units capable of curbing the predatory raids of the Hunnic horsemen. The reform made it necessary for China's soldiers to lay aside their traditional dress in order to adopt the high boots, baggy trousers and close-fitting tunic evolved by the nomads as best suited to a rider's way of life; it also rendered it essential for them to possess swift horses on which to pursue their enemies. Furthermore, it brought Ferghana, where the best horses were to be found, within reach of the Chinese. When they required fresh supplies of horses of quality the Chinese therefore took to raiding Ferghana. In the first century BC they sent an army estimated 60,000 strong to conquer it; the size of this force enabled the Chinese to impose an annual tribute of a thousand stallions on their victims. They were convinced that horses of the Ferghana breed sweated blood; in fact they resembled the Anglo-Arab hunter and, as Grousset suggests, may well have served as models for Chinese potters and sculptors of the Han and T'ang periods (*Ill. 65*), though the native Chinese pony was still being shown in the low relief funerary sculptors of Chantung and Honan (*Ills. 66, 67*). However, two major campaigns mounted by the Chinese against Ferghana during the second century AD were not undertaken so much in order to obtain fresh supplies of thoroughbred horses as to establish communications between China and the Western world, and to increase the volume of goods entrusted to the caravans maintaining a lucrative trade between both continents.

Ferghana does not appear ever to have been incorporated in the

67 Chinese tombstone decorated with a scene showing a battle on a bridge. This time the swift Central Asian ponies are shown instead of the imported thoroughbreds. Han period

Achaemenid empire, but it was often obliged to recognize the Achaemenids as suzerains. Soghdia was less fortunate, but although it was joined to the empire, it was Soghdia which provided her conquerors with their first script; it is still known to us as the Soghdian. In return, however, the Soghdians adopted many ideas and customs from the Achaemenids. Some of these were of ancient origin having been learnt by the Achaemenids from the Medes; they included the retention of the Median stole as part of their ceremonial dress, the Median fondness for splendid jewellery, their delight in archery and horsemanship, which is a passion that persists into modern times among the Central Asian nomads, and also the reverence with which the Medes regarded their kings. The Achaemenids did not scorn the people they conquered. Even when they showed such scant consideration for individuals that, according to Herodotus, they did not hesitate to shift populations, moving Egyptians to Bactria, Thracians to Asia, Ionians to Susa and Greeks to Kuzistan, yet they showed themselves eager to make use of alien skills and resources. It was in this spirit that Darius levied a tribute of Yaka wood from Gandhara and, when building his palace at Susa, sent to Babylon for labourers, to the Lebanon, Kirman and Gandhara for cedar and other rare woods, to Sardis and Bactria for gold which he employed Egyptians and Medes to work, to Soghdia and Bactria for lapis, and possibly also for craftsmen, since some Soghdians are represented on his funerary monument. Darius also sent to Chorasmia for turquoises, to Ethiopia for ivory and to Ionia and Lydia for stonemasons. The intellectual ferment aroused by these movements of people and material, and the artistic cross-currents to which they gave rise helped to quicken an appreciation of beauty and quality not only among people living close to the empire's heart, but also among those whose lives were spent in its furthermost borders. As a result the urban inhabitants of Central Asia were able, without loss of time, to understand the aims which Western artists and thinkers, arriving in the eastern districts in the wake of Alexander the Great's advancing army, had set themselves. This in turn enabled them to react so warmly to the impact of Hellenism that they quickly came to delight in it. When, under the Seleucids, ever closer contacts with

Western artists were established the native inhabitants of Turkestan adopted many Greek customs. Seals which, in Achaemenid times, had been reserved for official documents were used for business purposes by the Seleucids who added monograms and inscriptions to the existing designs. The Sassanians employed seals engraved with portraits, crests or animal motifs both for semi-official documents and for private communications.

Following upon Alexander's death in 323 BC his Seleucid successors found their authority challenged by the Parthians who were rapidly extending their Central Asian territories and whose military successes in that area may well have been due in part to their Aryan origin, which led the Iranians to regard the Parthians as kinsmen. The bond had assuredly eased their entry into Chorasmia and helped them to conquer Media. Even so, their rise was both unexpected and spectacular. It was largely brought about by Arsaces, who founded the new dynasty by revolting in c. 250 BC against the Seleucids, though he was probably employed by them at the time as governor of Bactria. He captured much of northern Persia, proclaimed himself king and advanced towards Transcaucasia, but failed to reach the Caspian. Nevertheless, the kingdom which he founded continued to grow after his death until it came to stretch from the borders of north-western India to the borders of western Persia. The various stages of its growth were marked by changes in its capital. Thus from about the second century BC until, according to Masson, the year AD 10, its capital was at Nisa, a town founded in c. 171 BC by Mithridates I. Nisa is now situated in Tadjikistan, on the edge of the Karakorum, some 18 kilometres south of Ashkabad, and Soviet archaeologists have been engaged during recent years in excavating the site. It lies slightly to the north of the later, equally ruined walled town of New Nisa. The earlier city contained a royal palace, necropolis and several temples. The latter were built round a large hall containing either four square piers or round pillars to support the flat wooden roofs. Over life-size statues of men and women made of unbaked brick were placed between the pillars. Domestic architecture probably resembled the religious, for one of the largest houses to be excavated was built round an internal courtyard

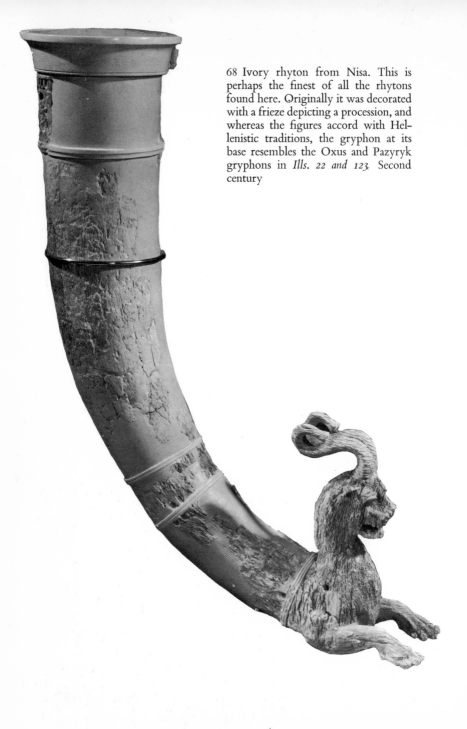

68 Ivory rhyton from Nisa. This is perhaps the finest of all the rhytons found here. Originally it was decorated with a frieze depicting a procession, and whereas the figures accord with Hellenistic traditions, the gryphon at its base resembles the Oxus and Pazyryk gryphons in *Ills. 22 and 123.* Second century

surrounded by a portico made of wooden columns set on stone bases as in the temples. Its large rooms opened onto the courtyard; during the last phase of occupation one of them had been used as a royal strong-room, and even though the building had been robbed in antiquity, a great many valuable objects were recovered from it. They included some silver-gilt statuettes representing both local and Hellenistic deities such as Athena, as well as sphinxes and mythological and imaginary beasts. Bronze and iron weapons, burnished and painted pottery, fluted glass vessels and ivory objects were also found there. The most interesting group of finds included the bronze legs of a throne in the form of a gryphon's claw holding a spray of acanthus leaves, and also several magnificent rhytons. The finest of these were embellished with jewels and polychrome glass incrustations as well as with friezes showing human and animal heads (*Ills. 68, 69*). Their bases were made of silver or gold which were often given the shape of an animal's head. The loveliest rhyton of all is assigned to the second century B C. With it were found some twenty sherds bearing inscriptions written in the Parthian language with Aramaic letters. The majority of those which have been deciphered consist of wine receipts dating from the first century B C.

Arsaces dressed in the nomadic style and his adherents did likewise. A number of large statues were found at Nisa. Stylistically

69 Detail of the ivory rhyton from Nisa showing a procession probably including Zeus, two satyrs and a youth who could possibly be Apollo. Originally the eyes were painted blue. Second century

70 Colossal stone statue of the Sassanian king, Shapur II, which lies fallen from its base in the cave where it was originally set up. The importance which the Sassanians attached to details of costume and insignia of office is clearly apparent, but the face shows far more regard for psychological likeness than was usual in royal portraits of this type. Late third century

71 Life-size bronze statue of a Parthian prince from the temple at Shami. It may have been statues such as these that led the Sassanians to produce the vast figure of Shapur. Second century

many resemble Parthian sculptures coming from such widely scattered areas (*Ill. 71*) as Chorasmia, the Kushan sanctuary of Surk Khotal in Afghanistan, or Nimrud. Statues of comparable size were nevertheless rare at that time, and those at Nisa are therefore thought to be portraits of Parthia's early kings. They may well have served to inspire such Sassanian works as the immense statue of King Shapur which lies fallen and broken in a high cave above Bishapur in Persia, in the district of Shiraz (*Ill. 70*).

The Parthians chose Dara to be their second capital. Its site is still being sought in the region of Damghan. Later they moved their

72 Silver dish from the Oxus Treasure showing the triumph of Dionysius, with, beside him, Ariadne and Heracles. Parthian artists were profoundly influenced by Hellenism which often provided both the subject and the style of a composition. However, Central Asian customs dictated the inclusion of a solar disc or rosette and that the animal be flanked with flowers. Second century

headquarters to Hekatompylos, then they transferred them to Ecbatana and finally they settled on Ctesiphon. In AD 226, when the Parthians succumbed to the Sassanian emperor Ardashir, Ctesiphon remained the capital of the new Sassanian empire.

During the second phase of Parthia's history, that dated by E. Masson from the year AD 10 to 226, the territory over which the Parthians ruled was so vast that three major artistic styles flourished simultaneously in different parts of it. Thus Babylonian and Assyrian traditions prevailed in the western areas, blending there with those of Rome, whilst in the north, where Parthia marched with Transcaucasia, Hellenism, in the form which it assumed when taken over by Rome, continued to serve as a source of inspiration longer than it did anywhere else in Asia (*Ill. 72*). Parthians in the Central Asian area, on the other hand, assimilated certain local, that is to say Central Asian traditions such, for example, as the desire and ability to convey an impression of movement in art (*Ill. 73*). They had perhaps learnt to appreciate the beauty of motion from the Scytho-Sakian nomads as well as from the Greeks who entered Asia with

Alexander. The use which the Parthians made of unbaked bricks and the adoption of the *iwan* or barrel vaulted chamber with only three walls as the central feature of their houses should perhaps be ascribed to Asian influences. Soviet archaeologists have found the ruins of vast fortified palaces in the desiccated areas of south-western Turkestan. The building techniques employed in their construction cannot be entirely traced to the Greeks. Furthermore, though Alexander enclosed the towns which he founded in Central Asia within walls, with the result that he is often credited with having introduced walled fortifications into the area, *vallae* dating from far earlier times have been found in Siberia. The ruins of the fortified palaces discovered in western Turkestan, though they date from the early centuries of our era, include architectural features which may

73 This Parthian terracotta relief of a rider, like the works of both Scythian and Sassanian artists, succeeds in conveying a sense of rapid movement, yet it is less stylized than works of the former schools and thus more realistic

well prove to have originated with the Parthians. Their discovery tends to confirm the idea tentatively put forward prior to it by M. Rostovtzev that what he described as the Neo-Perso-Parthian style acted as a formative influence in Persian Asia in late Hellenistic times. It is tempting to develop this idea by suggesting that the royal residences of very much the same type which the princes of the early Islamic period built in what is now the Iraqi desert, as for example the Khaja-i-Khodja palace with its arcaded façade and Hellenistic murals or Kusair Amra or Ukhaidir, were inspired by Parthian prototypes, just as their stucco decorations were in many respects derived from Central Asian sources. Rostovtzev went so far as to ascribe the Persian renaissance with its pleasure in the chase, armed contests and great banquets to Parthian influence (*Ill. 74*). Delight in these motifs crystallized under the Sassanians, who also adopted the frontality of Parthian art as well as the zest, shared alike by Parthian and nomad, in movement and animal forms (*Ill. 75*).

88

74 Wall-painting of a hunt from Dura Europos shows the same delight in movement as *Ill. 73*. However, the animals show no trace of Central Asian influence. Second century

75 The difference between Parthian and Sassanian art becomes evident when this superb dish is compared to provincial products. This rhythmical, vital and spirited scene shows Shapur II out hunting. Fourth century

The Parthians owed much of the wealth which enabled them to live in the luxurious manner prevalent at Nisa to the decision of the Han emperor of China, Wu-ti, to sell silk to Europe. The silk industry had become established in China in the ninth century B C, but for many centuries the precious fabric was produced for the exclusive use of the imperial family and court circles. By the fifth century B C the emperors had begun presenting lengths of silk to the nomad chieftains whom they wished to propitiate. In the second century B C Wu-ti's desire to obtain certain Western products induced him to start exporting silk to Europe. Many difficulties had to be overcome in order to do so. The most important was the need to establish international routes which the silk caravans could travel along in complete safety. Several roads of a suitable character were already in existence. The western was the least difficult and it therefore quickly became the most popular. It led from China across Ferghana, Soghdia and Chorasmia to northern Iran where it could either turn eastward to Afghanistan and India, or proceed to Ecbatana where goods could either be directed to Syria and Asia Minor or sent northward to the Urals or the Black Sea. However, the north-eastern section of this road traversed areas which lay within easy raiding distance of the Hunnic and Sakian nomads. The Chinese were therefore obliged to mount costly punitive expeditions against them and even when they had restored peace they were often forced to placate the nomads with expensive gifts in order to maintain it. A vital section of this route was owned by the Parthians who levied heavy dues from the caravans traversing their territory.

India had already been making use of part of this route to provide the West with food, linen, cotton, jewels, ivory, dyes and hardwoods, directing these goods to Ecbatana. China, using the same road, obtained from the West lead, woven Egyptian and Syrian stuffs, Syrian cut glass and crystal as well as lucerne and vines from Ferghana in return for her silk exports. The glass factories which were founded in Central Asia at about this time were probably a direct result of these exchanges. The West was no less anxious than China to enter into trading relations for it had for long coveted China's lovely silks. From the start the revenue which China obtained from the silk trade was so considerable that the emperor decided to expand exports by ensuring the safety of the caravan routes. To do so it was necessary for him to put an end to the Hunnic raids. He therefore despatched an army into the Orkhon in about AD 91. Its presence there brought the Chinese into direct contact with the Parthians who, they firmly believed, wished to gain control of the Roman silk trade. On the face of it this theory was a sound one for the Parthians were all-powerful in Iran; their ruler Tiridates I had been crowned in Rome in AD 66, with the result that peace reigned between Parthia and Rome for fifty years, but in fact, in Mesopotamia the interests of Rome and Parthia conflicted so sharply that for some fifty years silk intended for Rome travelled through Media and Armenia to Colchis and the Black Sea coast. Thus, until they were supplanted by the Sassanians, the Parthians did in fact control that section of the silk trade. However when, with the rise of Byzantium, Constantinople supplanted Rome as the main centre of consumption, the silk caravans followed a different route. Even so politicians of all countries continued to manœuvre for control of the silk trade. In the sixth century AD the Byzantine emperor, Justinian, attempted to acquire it by persuading Ethiopia to export silk by sea from Ceylon only to find that the Persians were already in command of the Ceylon market. Justin II (565–8) tried to achieve the same results by arranging with the Central Asian Turks for supplies of silk to reach him via the route bordering the north of the Caspian and traversing the Caucasus, but these efforts were rendered unnecessary in 552 when some missionaries smuggled silk worms and the secret of silk production out of China and brought it to Constantinople. Though by the end of the sixth century, enough silk was being produced in Byzantium to meet the Court's need, yet the demand for Chinese silk was scarcely affected by this development and all those connected with the silk trade continued to prosper. Indeed, the Parthians grew so rich on it that they could afford to use figured silks for their banners, and even the Huns were able to wear silk underclothes.

The intellectual stimulus which was brought about in Central Asia by the arrival there of Alexander the Great and his Greek troops

76, 77 (*left*) A fragment and ▶ (*right*) a reconstruction of a terracotta ossuary with stamped relief decoration from Bia Naiman. Four figures, possibly religious personnages, for one holds an altar whilst his crowned neighbour may be a Zoroastrian priest or a king, stand within niches which, with the columns which support them, are closely of Western inspiration. Note their snake-headed walking sticks. The lid of the ossuary is decorated with plant designs. Fifth–sixth century, or even seventh century

encouraged the Soghdians to respond quickly and warmly to the beauty of Hellenistic art. Their delight in it was kept alive by the silk trade. When, under guidance of the Parthians, they embraced the teaching of Zoroaster, the Soghdians were able to apply the skill in sculpting which they had perfected under the Greeks to producing figurines as decorations for the ossuaries in which, according to the tenets of their new faith, they were obliged to lay the bones of their dead after these had been stripped bare of flesh by bird and beast. Clay ossuaries came into use in the Samarkand area with the dawn of the present era and remained so, more particularly in Uzbekistan, until Islamic times (*Ills. 76, 77*). Their shapes varied from the box to the room-like and their decorations from stamped relief ornament to cult-figures ranged along their sides, either in niches or arches of Western inspiration or seated or reclining on their lids. Hellenistic influences were also responsible for the introduction of caryatides first on the ossuaries, where they took the form of small human figures supporting the arcades, then in architecture, where they were used internally to uphold the wooden ceilings.

After the collapse of Alexander's Seleucid successors, in the second century BC, Soghdia became part of the Tokharian, or as it is now generally called, the Kushan empire. The Kushans were rapidly

to absorb the whole of Bactria and northern India, and gradually to extend their western boundaries to the Sea of Aral, annexing Chorasmia in the second century AD. Then, in the fifth century AD the Kushans were in their turn overthrown by the Hephthalites – an Altaic people who may have been racially allied to the Huns. The latter retained many aspects of Kushan culture, even to the adoption of the Greek alphabet. When the southern Hephthalites found it expedient to throw in their lot with Seistan, those living to the north of the Hindu Kush looked towards Soghdia and accepted many of the cultural forms which had become established there.

The Hephthalites chose Badakshan as their capital, but their political aims were based on the conquest of India rather than upon becoming the ruling power in Central Asia. They might well have succeeded in achieving this ambition had not the Turks, in the process of overthrowing the Sakas, attacked and defeated the Hephthalites, thereby superseding them as masters of Soghdia. However, the Hephthalites living in south-eastern Soghdia retained much of their political freedom till AD 538, when the Sassanian emperor Chosroe I conquered them. Those living south of the Oxus escaped Chosroe's grasp but in the seventh century they in their turn fell to the Arab invaders of Central Asia.

Bitter experience had taught the Soghdians to take advantage of every opportunity that presented itself, so that throughout this period they contrived to a large degree to govern themselves. They used their freedom to remain in close contact with the Chinese whilst continuing to be on good terms with their western neighbours, managing in the general confusion to gain control of the section of the silk road which passed through their territory. The Turks were too much occupied in quarrelling with the Persians and in trying to persuade the Byzantines to join them in attacking the common enemy to realize what had happened.

Recent excavations have shown that towns such as Afrasiab (ancient Samarkand) or Rindad (Tali Barzu) which grew up under the Kushans had, by Hephthalite times, become cities of considerable size and importance. Afrasiab had by then acquired a triangular shape; it was surrounded by massive walls and towers built of unbaked brick. Entrance to it was gained by gates situated at the main points of the compass. The majority of its inhabitants had become Zoroastrians, but they continued to produce statuettes of Greek inspiration, the most popular being of the goddess Anihita, generally shown holding a pomegranate. However, statuettes of other personages prominent in Greek mythology were also made in considerable numbers. Yet documents discovered in the ruins of Mug in Uzbekistan show that even though the inhabitants of Afrasiab had been quick to establish regular links with the western world they had formed equally close contacts with China. It is probable that the Chinese taught them to make the fine paper for which they were renowned in early times, though some scholars think that this did not happen before the eighth century AD.

Excavations were first carried out in Afrasiab in 1913. Some fragments of mural-paintings were found there at the time and although none of these has been preserved the tracings which were made then are still in existence. They have enabled the archaeologists who have within recent years excavated other important, well preserved mural-paintings in what was once Soghdia to date the Afrasiab fragments to some time between the sixth and eighth century AD. They also serve to show that the Afrasiab paintings were executed in the same style as those of a similar character which have recently been found in other parts of Soghdia. The period to which these works are assigned coincides with one when great advances in irrigation were bringing prosperity to many outlying regions of Central Asia. In Soghdia increased productivity enabled the wealthier agriculturists to live in the manner of feudal lordlings and Afrasiab developed into so rich and important a centre that its ruler ranked as a supreme prince and was entitled, together with only the ruler of neighbouring Piandjikent, to mint his own coins. The designs he chose bear testimony to the closeness of his ties with China for, in accordance with Chinese custom, made his coins square in shape with a hole punched in the centre.

The discovery of the castle of Mug and its remarkable hoard of documents was due to chance. A shepherd happened one day to notice a basket protruding from the desert's sand. He examined it and found that it was made of willow and was filled with manuscripts. He reported his find to the local authorities and an archaeological mission was quickly directed to the spot. The site lay in the Upper Zaravshan valley, in the Mug foothills, some 200 kilometres to the east of Samarkand. Excavators soon recovered a vast number of documents from the sand which rank as a sensational discovery. All are in excellent condition, even though some are written on paper, and others are on leather or wood. All date from early in the eighth century A D. The majority are written in Soghdian, but others are in Arabic, Turkish and Chinese. The Arabic texts are the only ones to have been as yet deciphered. They date from the years 717 to 719 when the ruler of Piandjikent sent them to the Arab governor of the area. In 722 the prince revolted against his conquerors but fell into their hands and was executed. His castle was then sacked and abandoned, and the desert sands gradually crept over it. Excavations show it to have been built in the form of a vast fortress having stout outer walls and massive defence towers. It was constructed in unbaked bricks on lines which may well have influenced the Seljuks when, several centuries later, they set out to create an architectural style of their own in Anatolia. Its rooms, like the Seljuks', were in the form of barrel-vaulted halls connecting one with the other by means of narrow corridors. Numerous coins, seals, articles in silver and bronze, weapons and fragments of silk and cotton stuffs were recovered from the site but, apart from the manuscripts, the importance of which can hardly be equalled, the most interesting find consisted of a wooden shield (*Ill. 78*) covered with fine leather decorated with a painting of a rider. Though only the central panel survives, with the result that the rider's head and feet are missing, the painting is in good condition. Enough remains to show that it was executed in the same style as the mural-paintings which have been discovered more recently in various parts of Soghdia. All clearly belong to the same flourishing, distinctive and accomplished school as the lost fragments from Afrasiab, and the group as a whole provides enough evidence to justify the suggestion that it was works such as these that played an all-important part in fashioning the style of Persia's school of Islamic painting.

The first Soghdian mural decorations to be discovered were found at Varaksha in a series of excavations carried out from 1947 to 1953 by V. A. Shyshkin. The town had been the capital of a long-forgotten fief in the Bokhara oasis, but it was abandoned to the desert sands in

78 Though only the central portion of this painted shield survives, it suffices to show that the broad-shouldered, wasp-waisted hero of Islamic Persia was already admired in the eighth century. It was found at Mug castle

79 Carved stucco panels with rosette decoration from Varaksha. Panels such as these were used in Persia and Mesopotamia as a form of architectural decoration from the first century AD onwards, but the initial idea may have come from Central Asia. Eighth century

the ninth century AD. Archaeologists started work at the southern end of the mound, where the citadel and palace had once stood, and soon came upon its walls of unbaked brick. The citadel had been defended by high towers and walls, and the palace within it was found to have contained an astonishingly large number of rooms. The earlier portions of the palace dated from the third century, the latest from the sixth, but the majority of the mural-paintings and

80 Drawing of a fragment of wall-painting from the Hall of Gryphons at Varaksha. Its antecedents can be traced back to Pazyryk (*Ill. 25*) and its successors can be found in Islamic painting and metal work of late medieval date. Fifth–seventh century

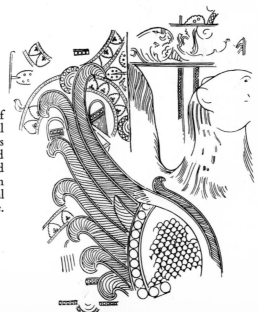

81, 82 Wall-painting from the west wall of the central hall of the palace at Varaksha. It con-
sists of two scenes: the first shows a man mounted on an elephant fighting an imaginary beast;
in the second another man, also mounted, in combat with a leopard who sinks his fangs into

carved stucco work decorations (*Ill. 79*) of the interior are assigned
to the eighth century. The rooms were roofed with flat ceilings
resting on columns, and opening onto a great central hall. One of
the rooms had built-in benches; its mural and stucco decorations
were particularly elaborate. They included a scene showing huntsmen pursuing birds with human faces through a wooded landscape.
Much of this painting was in poor condition, but some of those
found in other buildings were better preserved. One room contained
a painted frieze on which a procession of animals was set against a
red ground; below it was represented, in the form of a repeat motif,
a fight between elephants decked in rich trappings and fierce, winged,
imaginary beasts resembling leopards and gryphons (*Ills. 81, 82*). The
wings of the latter, and those of the gryphons in a room called after
them 'The Hall of Gryphons' (*Ill. 80*), are in a style which recalls that
of the semi-human semi-bird creature fighting a phoenix executed
in felt appliqué work on a wall-hanging found at Pazyryk, dating
from some twelve hundred years earlier (*Ill. 25*). Another frieze
shows a warrior riding an elephant on whose head an archer is

98

the elephant, while a small figure sitting on the elephant's head thrusts a spear into another leopard. Shyshkin discovered these paintings and stresses their resemblance to those found at Piandjikent, where even the elephant trappings are similar. Fifth–seventh century

shown shooting at an imaginary winged beast. Bands of an ornamental or geometric character usually decorated the walls at floor level. Paintings of water, fish and small trees were popular and are generally skilfully executed. Most impressive of all, however, is the mural-painting of a battle in which warriors appear seated on white elephants and huntsmen pursue goats. Both these scenes are dated to between the fourth and seventh century A D. The majority are executed in a style which retains clear traces of both Achaemenid and Pazyryk ancestry. In another tomb a scene of a hunt was carried out in carved stucco and paint. The warriors and huntsmen who appear in these paintings often have a markedly Sassanian look, differing in this respect from the expressive votive statuettes which show a closer resemblance to the sculptures which were produced in Bactria in early Buddhist times than to Persian works. The Persian elements made themselves particularly strongly felt in a room in the palace where the south wall was adorned with a painting of an enthroned king shown surrounded by his courtiers, whilst the west wall presented a group of warriors wearing pointed helmets and armour very similar to those shown on some silver dishes found in eastern Russia, more especially in the district of Perm as well as on paintings in eastern Turkestan, as for example at Sorçuk (*Ill. 172*).

The Varaksha paintings are closely linked both to that of the rider decorating the Mug shield and to the remarkable mural decorations discovered on two other Soghdian sites. The resemblance is not only a stylistic one, but also extends to details of clothing, furnishings and the like. The first of these sites, Balalyk Tepe, is situated on the northern bank of the Amu Darya, in the very south of Uzbekistan, close to the Afghan border. A fortified castle dating from the third or fourth century AD, though altered in the sixth century, and a sixth–seventh-century temple have been excavated there. The walls of both buildings survive to little more than a metre high, but even though many interesting objects were found by the excavators it is the paintings which once adorned the interior walls of these buildings that constitute their most important discovery. Some of the most interesting of these were found on the walls of a windowless room in the temple. Originally the room had had a wooden cornice with the decorations executed in a blend of terracotta and carved wood. The paintings were in poor condition, but men and women could be distinguished sitting cross-legged holding gold and silver vessels of Sassanian shapes by their bases, using only three fingers of their right hands (*Ill. 96*). The vessels belonging to the men were flatter and more elongated in shape than those held by the women. Servants stood behind the seated personages. In all some fifty people were included in the composition, the more important being larger in size than the rest. The men wear belted tunics with single revere – garments which appear in most Soghdian paintings as well as in some early Buddhist ones executed in eastern Turkestan (*Ill. 83*). The women's clothes consist of sleeveless tunics, some having wide reveres, worn over long-sleeved robes. Similar minor details of costume reappear in the Buddhist paintings of Bamyan and Kuça, where the same tendency of setting pale figures against dark backgrounds is also to be observed. L. I. Albaum has also observed them in some of the stone statues of Balbals or 'Stone Dames' (*Ill. 84*) which exist in quite considerable numbers in Kazakstan and Mon-

83, 84 It is interesting to compare the clothes worn by the figure (*right*) from Kizil in western Turkestan with the clothes of the life-size stone 'balbal' (*far right*) and also with the clothes shown in paintings discovered in Russian Central Asia (*Ill. 180*)

golia. He suggests that the Balbals may be statues of Soghdians who died fighting the Turks as soldiers in the Hephthalites army, and that they stood on the graves in which the ashes of the Turkish warriors who had killed them were buried.

The most important and best preserved Soghdian paintings have been discovered at Piandjikent. The city's ruins lie some 65 kilometres south-west of Samarkand, in the Zaravshan valley, straddling the road linking Zaravshan to Samarkand, and only some 35 kilometres from Bokhara. Founded in the fourth and fifth centuries AD to serve as the Hephthalite capital, Piandjikent was at the height of its prosperity in the seventh century. Soon after that date it was destroyed by the Arabs, but it recovered from the disaster, lingering on until the ninth century when, having been rendered useless by the growth in both size and importance of Samarkand and Bokhara,

85 Carved wooden statuette from Piandjikent. It is the product of an accomplished, assured and established school of art. Seventh century

86 Reconstruction of a wall-painting from the south wall of the main hall at Piandjikent. It shows the death of the god Syavush and his rebirth in the spring (not shown), a symbolic interpretation of the birth of the new year. Persia's Nu Ruz. In it the dead youth is seen through the rounded arches of the bier which is being carried by pall bearers and surrounded by weeping mourners. Other mourners appear in the foreground, and it is possible that some of the men are Turks and others Soghdians. Seventh–eighth century

it slowly died. By the seventh century it had developed into a city of impressive appearance. Its *Shahristan* or city centre had by then been surrounded by high walls strengthened by ten oval towers built of unbaked brick. The citadel, several temples and the richer houses were situated in that area. The earliest caryatides used in Central Asia were found there. Some measured as much as $3\frac{1}{2}$ feet in height. All were made of wood, as were a number of elegant statuettes. One, a woman, with carefully dressed hair, and wearing a rich necklace, wore such a low-cut robe that it savours of Indian influence (*Ill. 85*).

The main temple stood in the centre of the town. It too was built of unbaked bricks and contained a large central hall, the roof of which rested on four columns. The eastern end of the hall was left open to face onto a courtyard in the manner of an iwan, but the western end led to a windowless and doorless room but for this single entrance. This chamber had been used as an inner sanctuary.

103

Other rooms were disposed round the square central hall and many of them retained fragments of wall-paintings. However, the most important of all the known Soghdian paintings were found in another, similar temple. Many of these were in relatively good condition. Its columned hall displayed an elaborate composition which some scholars believe represents the Soghdian burial rite expressed in a scene illustrating the death of the god Syavush (*Ill. 86*). The god is represented by a youth who personifies the dying year, with its re-birth in the spring seen through an archway in the far distance. This method of presentation was devised in order to achieve the two-tiered effect popular in Soghdia, where it was generally attained by the division of the walls into two horizontal bands.

In his death scene Syavush is shown surrounded by mourners who are grouped below his bier in various attitudes of grief; six of them are placed below the others and differ so much in their appearance that Soviet archaeologists have attempted to recognize Soghdians in some of them and Turks in others. The decorations of the room's southern wall include a group of courtiers and three members of

87 Drawing of a mural at Piandjikent representing a ritual scene which is probably connected with the spring festival. The men in the right-hand section hold branches of almond blossom and gold vessels of Sassanian shape. The left-hand section shows a priest kneeling on a carpet beside an altar, his attendant close by. Seventh–eighth century

88 This wall-painting from Piandjikent of two men engaged in a game of chess has a symbolic meaning, for it is probably based on an incident in Buddha's earlier life. Seventh century

Syavush's bodyguard. In addition all four walls had had niches cut in them to hold clay statues, none of which survived in a recognizable form.

The mural decorations of Piandjikent include both religious and genre scenes (*Ills. 87, 88*). The former reveal the existence in Central Asia of a somewhat different form of Zoroastrianism from that practised in Persia for it retained certain local forms of pagan sun and moon worship. Soghdian religious paintings are therefore of particular interest to students of religion, but their importance is perhaps secondary to that of the genre scenes, the subject-matter of which is both fascinating and unusual. Soviet scholars regard them as illustrations of national epics of the type usually associated with the literature of Islamic Persia. Orientalists such as the late J. Orbeli, A. I. Jakubovski and Krachkovski have in fact succeeded in relating some of the paintings to specific passages in Firdausi's *Shah-nama* (*Ill. 89*). This great Persian poet was born at Tus in northern Persia at the end of the tenth century and wrote his masterpiece whilst living in Ghazni, in what is now Afghanistan, at the court of the Ghaznavid sultan Mahmud. Like Homer, he too was inspired by the legends which were current at the time. Some scholars believe that some very early ones were kept alive throughout the intervening centuries, fostering local patriotism and the survival of native traditions. Krachkovski found fifteen passages in the *Shah-nama* which he was able to relate to scenes appearing in the mural-paintings of Piandjikent and one which, in describing the discovery of Jamshid's treasure, refers to sculptures. Thus, when describing Syavush's palace at Syavushgird, Firdausi records that the walls of its iwan were decorated with painted scenes:

'Of kings and feasts, and battles
First shah Kavus is shown, wearing a necklace, a club in his hand;
Near the throne stands Rustem, the elephant bodied,
And Zal, with all the courtiers assembled there.
On his other hand are Afrasiab and the captain of his army.'

Another verse tells us that 'when the golden iwan was built Jamshid was depicted on its walls worshipping the Sun and Moon'. Scenes such as these occur more than once in Piandjikent's surviving paintings, but Krachkovski noted that the one of Bahram Gur out hunting, though a favourite theme in Islamic times, has not as yet been met with in Soghdian art. Instead a woman harpist (*Ill. 92*), battles between horsemen and contests between knights, all of which are often mentioned by Firdausi, frequently appear as does the picture of an enthroned king and dekhans sitting cross-legged (*Ill. 91*).

In contrast to Bactrian artists, whose works will be considered in the next chapter, the Soghdians do not appear to have been interested in portraiture. Rather was it the pomp and ceremony of court life which appealed to them. Painting with little regard for perspective but with a conscious endeavour to present light figures

89 Some of the wall-paintings at Piandjikent have been found to relate to specific passages in the *Shah-nama* by Firdausi, the well-known Persian poet. In this particular scene Rustam is shown slaying the dragon. Seventh century

against dark backgrounds, they set out to record royal audiences, contests between riders of a type still practised today by Central Asia's horsemen, battle scenes and beautiful women such as the poets of medieval Persia delighted in describing. The people they portrayed wear clothes of Central Asian cut which, however, include many Sassanian details. Thus the shape of the crowns worn by kings, together with their veils and bells are culled from the Sassanian repertory. So too are the cups and other vessels used in the libation scenes, the elaborately cut hair and carefully trimmed beards worn by men whose faces are, however, often rendered in a manner which is closer to the Indian or Hellenistic convention than the Persian. On the other hand the haloed figure discovered at Piandjikent beneath a slightly later overpainting displays such strong

90 There is something strangely evocative and appealing about this mural painting of two riders accompanied by attendants which decorated a room in Piandjikent in the seventh century

91 This scene of noblemen at a libation, from the north wall of a room at Piandjikent, is presented against a Pompeian red background. The head-dresses resemble in shape that worn by the Sorçuk warrior (*Ill. 171*). The painting shows great regard for composition and mastery of the sinuous line. Seventh century

92 Wall-painting of a harpist, in its elegance resembling the wooden statuette (*Ill. 85*), whilst its poetic quality is as marked as in the painting of the two riders opposite. Piandjikent, seventh century

93, 94 Details of silk textiles found in eastern Turkestan, but made in Soghdia. Both strongly resemble Sassanian textiles, especially in the way in which the confronted animals – ducks and elks – are placed in roundels. Eighth century

Byzantine influence that it must have been executed by one of the Nestorians who lived, preached and worked in Central Asia in early Christian times.

Zoroastrians fleeing to Central Asia to escape being persecuted by the Persians must have played a part in establishing Sassanian motifs in the area even if it was the Parthians who were responsible for introducing them to Central Asia. The commercial contacts formed between Soghdia and Persia doubtless also played an important part in keeping Sassanian culture alive there. Many of the people depicted in Soghdian painting wear clothes which are made of what were obviously real, contemporary stuffs. This is especially the case in the seventh and eighth century paintings of Varaksha (*Ill. 98*) and the fifth and sixth century ones of Balalyk Tepe (*Ill. 96*). The designs on these stuffs often resemble Sassanian ones, yet the material was obviously made locally. Textiles are known to have been manufactured in Soghdia from a relatively early date. At the time of the

Arab occupation Bokhara and Zendam were already renowned for their carpets and textiles, many of which were exported to Egypt. Contemporary Samarkand, Vedar and Darbucci were no less famous for their silver-threaded stuffs, brocades and silks. Prototypes for some of the designs seen in Soghdia's paintings can be found in the Pazyryk material. Similar designs, though made up of different motifs, also appear in the paintings of eastern Turkestan, where Sir Aurel Stein found fragments not only of Chinese silks but of actual textiles made in Central Asia (*Ills. 93, 94*). The finest Soghdian material was, however, discovered in southern Russia, at Moshchevaja Balka in the Kuban. As late as the eighteenth century it was customary to give the Ossetians, who transported bales of material across the Caucasian mountains to Russia, a length of stuff which they instantly cut up, dividing it between them. A shirt sleeve found at Moshchevaja Balka and now in the Hermitage Museum had been decorated with four fragments of this sort (*Ill. 95*). When assembled they formed a geometrical design of elaborate character. This textile is dated to the first century AD and is undoubtedly of Central Asian, more probably of Soghdian, manufacture. The materials shown on the Soghdian paintings display more traditional, and basically Sassanian designs. Many are worked in a repeat motif consisting of a pearl-studded circlet containing either a human face of Sassanian appearance, a typically Central Asian motif or an animal of either Sassanian (*Ill. 99*) or Siberian character. Typical of the latter is the

95 Soghdian textile from Moshchevaja Balka in the Kuban. Four fragments of silk sewn onto the sleeves of a tunic were reconstructed to produce a geometric design closely related to Sassanian motifs. First century AD

96, 97 (*above*) This damaged wall-painting of the fifth–sixth century from Balalyk Tepe shows how fabrics made in Soghdia were influenced by Sassanian motifs. The tusked beasts shown on the garments are very closely related to *Ill. 97* (*below*) which is a fragment of Sassanian material. The fact that it was found far away in Astana in eastern Turkestan also shows in what esteem Sassanian textiles were held all over Central Asia at this time

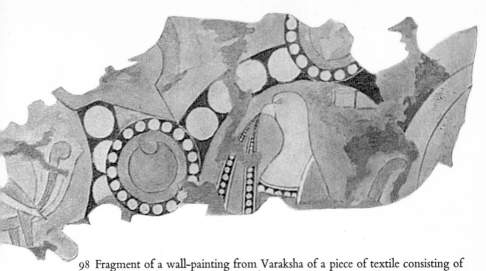

98 Fragment of a wall-painting from Varaksha of a piece of textile consisting of a design formed of pearl-studded roundels and a pigeon, which, according to Sassanian custom, holds a pearl necklace in its beak. It can be compared with a wall-painting from Bamyan (*Ills. 155, 156*)

99 This fine silk textile of Sassanian origin shows a *senmerv* or bird-dog. As in *Ill. 98* small pearl-studded roundels containing a crescent moon are used to link the larger roundels, as they are in the illustration above

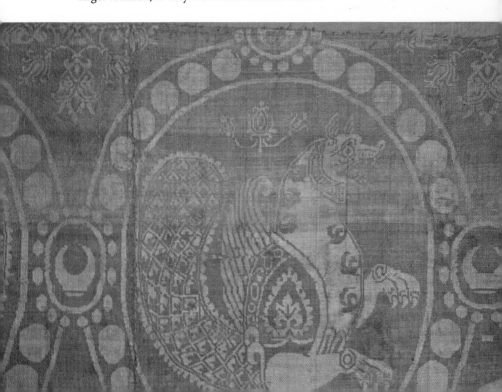

100 Ewers of this type have until recently been ascribed to Sassanian Persia, but it now seems probable that they were made in Soghdia. The seminude figure reflects Indian influence, but the niche, though made up of rosettes, and its banded columns point to Hellenistic influence and stems from the same series of designs as the Bia Naiman ossuary (*Ill. 77*). *c.* sixth–seventh century

snarling, tusked beast of prey (*Ill. 97*) which, though perhaps of Siberian origin, for it recalls the wolves of early metal work, was appropriated by the Sassanians who thereby ensured its continued popularity in Central Asia, and more especially in Soghdia.

It was Sassanian rather than Byzantine art which in early Christian times exercised most influence over the Soghdians. Until recent years it was customary to ascribe a series of silver vessels decorated with figural scenes either to Sassanian or to Bactrian workshops. Now, however, it has been suggested that many vessels resembling Sassanian ewers decorated with renderings of nude women presented in niches or beneath garlands in a manner somewhat reminiscent of the Bia Naiman ossuaries (*Ill. 100*) or dishes displaying hunting scenes (*Ill. 101*) may well have been made in Soghdia. They are dated by Diakonov to between the sixth and eighth century A D. All bear a marked stylistic resemblance to the work carried out in Piandjikent and the warriors are shown wearing armour of a similar type. In the eighth century the Arab invaders of Central Asia put an end to Soghdia's lively and fascinating school of figural art, but here and

101 Silver dish from Soghdia. Its decoration is derived from the large series of hunting scenes similar to that shown in *Ill. 73* produced by the Sassanians. Seventh century

there individual works either survived or continued to be produced to delight and inspire later generations of artists. Love of figural art is difficult to eradicate and the wasp-waisted, broad shouldered heroes of Soghdian art were to set the standards aimed at by Firdausi and Islamic artists of late medieval times. The Arabs never accepted the style and were, indeed, so shocked by the presence of human figures in the paintings which adorned the façade of the Great Mosque of Bokhara that they hurriedly destroyed them. It is because of their opposition to work of this type that no figural paintings of early Islamic date survive in Central Asia, but Soghdian art provides good evidence that the roots of Islamic figural art are nevertheless to be sought in that area.

Chorasmia had as long a history as Soghdia yet virtually nothing was known of it until 1930 when Tolstov discovered some neolithic remains dating from the fourth and third millennia BC at Djambas Kala and applied himself to the study of Chorasmia's past. He found that the fishermen and hunters who had lived in the deltas of its river beds during the Bronze Age had been in contact with inhabitants of the Volga's shores, the western Caucasus and the Urals, as well as with people living in northern Persia. By the eighth century BC an elaborate system of irrigation had enabled them to live in large settlements. Even though they were conquered by the Achaemenids in the sixth century BC the Chorasmians regained their independence in the fourth, but lost it again in the first or second century AD, this time to the Kushans. However, in the second and third century AD they were once again independent and able to mint their own coinage. They were to remain free until the twelfth century, when their kingdom included Rey, Hamadan and Isfahan, and when their political power and military prowess was such that they aimed at supplanting the Seljuks in what is now eastern Turkey.

Though the Kushans incorporated Chorasmia within their empire they did not prevent the rise there of a powerful class composed of feudal gentry and rich farmers. It may have been due to Parthian influence that some of them built fair-sized villages and large castles in remote country districts. Owing to the unsettled political situation the more isolated of these were fortified. Often they were enclosed by two sets of high defensive walls strengthened with towers and topped with archer's galleries, look-out posts and firing slits. As an additional precaution their entrance gates were laid out on a labyrin-thine plan. The villages within these fortifications frequently had at their centres two storeyed citadels topped by galleries. These strongholds were palatial in scale. They contained a great many rooms all of which opened onto a central court but which were lit, doubtless for defensive reasons, by only small windows set high in the walls. Many of the rooms had barrel-vaulted ceilings. These features appear again in Anatolia in the buildings constructed there between the eleventh and thirteenth centuries by the Seljuks. The store rooms in the Central Asian castles were generally well stocked, wine and oil being kept in enormous jars. One of third-century date is inscribed in Aramaic and provides us with the earliest known Chorasmian inscription. Clay rhytons and flasks were also widely used, many of them being decorated with designs which feature the horse and gryphon. In about the third century AD the bulk of the Chorasmians

102, 103 Apart from fragments of paintings found at Afrasiab, this tiger head and human head are the earliest examples of paintings from western Turkestan known to us. They once adorned a room at Toprak Kala and date from the third to fourth century

appear to have been Zoroastrians who, like their Soghdian neighbours, retained in their creed many religious customs dating from earlier times. A great many ossuaries have been found in Chorasmia. The majority are square in shape and their lids are adorned with human figures which are often shown seated. Many are half life-size and probably meant to represent the dead person, whereas the numerous clay statuettes and figures in high relief which have been found during excavations are thought to portray a male deity, a companion of the god Syavush, and a personification of the Mother Goddess and guardian of water and irrigation. The male figurines show the god wearing high boots and short, tight-fitting, belted tunic of nomadic cut with a hat surmounted by three horns. The goddess is more richly and elaborately dressed.

In 1938 excavations of the fortified town of Toprak Kala near Termez were put in hand and have continued at intervals ever since. The town was inhabited from the first century AD serving, in the

104 Head of alabaster – a stone readily available in Afghanistan from Toprak Kala. This link with the East is also reflected in the treatment of the face, which is closer in style to the Indo-Hellenic art of the Kushans than to Western schools. Third century

opinion of Tolstov, as the capital of Chorasmia until the sixth century. It remained rich and important until its destruction in the seventh century by the Arabs. Its existence depended upon the maintenance of its skilful and elaborate irrigation system. In Kushan times the town was extremely prosperous. The larger houses built at the time contained an average of ten to twelve spacious, square or rectangular rooms. Their inhabitants owned slaves and employed numerous retainers, running their households on patriarchal lines. The town was widely noted for its large and busy bazaar. In addition to a palace it contained at least three large fire-temples. The palace was excavated between 1945 and 1950. It was built of large blocks of unbaked brick on a high platform overlooking the town and was originally three storeys high and defended by three massive towers measuring at least 100 feet in height. It contained several hundred rooms, but the ground floor consisted of store rooms and offices, in which storage vessels and chests stamped with the ruler's crest were

105 On the other hand this statue, though it also comes from Top-rak Kala, is directly based on Hellenistic example. It is over life-size and was found in the Hall of Kings, which has led to the assumption that it may be a portrait of one of the king's wives. Like much Kushan work, it is made of clay and painted. Third–fourth century

106 Stucco frieze with rosette design which decorated a room in the ruined castle

found. The top-floor rooms have not survived, but those on the middle floor included both vaulted and flat-roofed halls which have successfully withstood their long years of burial. Even though their stucco and painted decorations have deteriorated beneath the desert's sands, enough of each remains to give us some idea of their original splendour.

Mural decorations survived in three sections of the building. The sculptures are so correct anatomically and so naturalistic in conception that they may well have been inspired by Hellenistic works (*Ills. 102, 103*). They are of stucco and, as at Piandjikent, form an integral part of the painted decorations. Both are dated to the third and fourth century AD. The paintings originally covered the whole surface of the walls, but it seems to have been customary either to divide the designs into panels adorned with decorative compositions, finishing them off with a frieze, or to have used frame-like borders set against a background of garlands. Both in style and detail the decorations closely resemble those of Piandjikent and they must therefore be assigned to the same artistic school. The finest murals appear in a room which the excavators called The Hall of Kings. Here the walls had pinkish borders with white lilies painted above them on a blue ground. Niches with grilles fixed across them as in regency book cases were ranged along the tops of the walls to hold clay statues of Chorasmia's kings, their wives and courtiers. Two ornaments recovered from the rubble recall the devices which appear on the crowns worn by the kings represented on the country's coins.

120

of Teshik Kala. Whereas the Varaksha panels were carved, these were moulded

Another room, named by the excavators the Alabaster Hall because its walls were decorated with floral motives cut and engraved on alabaster, led to a Hall of Victories. The latter had been decorated with sculptures of seated kings feasting in the company of the goddess of Victory. Their guests are shown carrying clubs and holding the bases of mugs and goblets of Sassanian shapes with three fingers, as at Varaksha. Beyond this chamber was the Warriors' Hall, so called because of its sculptures of warriors wearing chain-mail armour painted black and holding cane shields. Other decorations included a painted frieze of gryphons, dancing couples, vividly rendered musicians and a decorative composition of women gathering pears and grapes. Spirited paintings of tigers, horses and birds survive among the fragments recovered from the fillings.

Although the paintings and sculptures (*Ill. 104*) are executed in the style which is now associated with Soghdia they nevertheless reveal an interest in portraiture which is not apparent in the works found at Varaksha, Balalyk Tepe or Piandjikent. Furthermore, whereas in Soghdia interest in decoration was largely the result of the regard in which court furnishings, costumes and customs were held, in Chorasmia it was experienced for its own sake, and it therefore expressed itself there by the presence of ornamental backgrounds which generally turned to nature for their themes. The figural sculptures (*Ill. 105*) are realistic and anatomically correct in Chorasmia, and if the full face or frontal position in which the figures are shown may be traced to Parthian influence the inclined position of their

121

heads, bearing as it does an evident link with Bamyan, suggests a more easterly and Oriental source of inspiration. The stucco decorations (*Ill. 106*) in the fortified castle or manor-house of Teshik Kala are, however, largely of local inspiration and consist of rosettes, palmettes, diamond and ace of spades designs. It is motives such as these that reappear in the carved stone decorations of Anatolia's Seljukid buildings, and their origins may well lie in Chorasmia rather than in the Seljukid empires of the Near and Middle East.

Chorasmia's mural decorations suffice as testimony to the skill of the country's native artists. In addition they throw fresh light on the standards attained there both in daily life and culture during the first millennium of our era. By their existence they enabled local traditions to survive the upheavals resulting from the Arab invasion, with the result that the country was able from the tenth to the thirteenth century once again to play a vital part in Islamic politics. The Arabs were lenient masters for they were anxious to be on good terms with the native merchants on whom they depended for many of their luxuries. They were, nevertheless, resented in Central Asia, perhaps on account of their determination to put an end to the region's ancient figural art. A general restlessness gripped the people; its effect is apparent in the acceptance of a new religion, Islam, and the spread of heresies, such as Shamanism. The peculiarly Central Asian conception of chivalry, based as it was on the existence of numerous fiefs, each supporting a court and royal way of life, left a void which later Islamic rulers, such as the Ghaznavid and Samanid tried unsuccessfully to fill. Then, in the thirteenth century the all-conquering Mongols swept away all the remaining vestiges of Central Asia's ancient way of life. Her monumental arts perished with it, yet her craftsmen lived on. Her potters, above all those of Urgench, and her metal workers produced some of their finest wares for their Mongol masters and it remained for Tamerlane to destroy the last flowering of her talent. Amongst so much else he also destroyed Chorasmia's carefully built-up irrigation system, thereby leaving the insidious desert sands free to creep in and cover much of what man had so laboriously built up there in the course of some five thousand years.

CHAPTER FOUR

Bactria and North-Western India
from Achaemenid to Islamic times

Bactria occupied the northern slopes of the Hindu Kush and, though separated from Soghdia by the Amu Darya it nevertheless often included within its boundaries, from Achaemenid times to the end of the Kushan age, both Samarkand and Merv. Culturally, politically and economically Bactria had always formed part of the same complex as that which comprised Soghdia, Ferghana and Chorasmia, and it is for this reason that many of the sites which have been excavated on both sides of the Amu Darya have produced objects and results of a similar character. Like Soghdia Bactria possessed few mineral resources other than lapis lazuli and alabaster. Her people were therefore obliged to look to Badakshan for their rubies and to Chorasmia for their turquoises. For many centuries their gold came from Siberia by means of such devious and secret routes that it acquired increased appeal in the process.

Darius conquered Bactria at much the same time as he did Soghdia. In his Bisitun inscription he ranked it as a satrapy. It was indeed a valuable addition to his empire for its elaborate and admirably maintained irrigation works had transformed the country into what contemporaries described as a 'veritable paradise'. Bactrian agriculture was in fact the most advanced in Central Asia and, largely as a result, the general standard of living there was a high one. Houses built of unbaked brick generally contained numerous store rooms and more than one living room furnished in a manner both varied and elaborate. Many of the smaller towns could trace their foundation to the fourth and third centuries BC. In most of them craftsmanship was highly developed, potters having in some cases been in the habit of using the wheel from as early as the third millennium BC. At that early date the finest wares, whether moulded or turned, were frequently decorated with geometric designs or with very stylized renderings of local animals, such as panthers or mountain goats. Many of the later animal designs often showed an affinity with those produced by the Central Asian nomads.

However, nomadic traditions were never as important in Bactria as in western Turkestan or Siberia, and the country's acceptance of Zoroastrianism as its main religion altered the outlook and artistic conventions of the Bactrians as profoundly as it did their religious observances. According to tradition Zoroaster was born in Balk; he was certainly welcomed there by King Vishaz when he fled there seeking protection from the Persians. Many objects used by the fire worshippers have been found in Bactria where people attached much importance to votive figurines. These resemble in style the contemporary statuettes produced in Soghdia for a similar purpose, and this makes it seem probable that the majority were intended to represent the goddess Anihita and the god Syavush.

Bactria fell to Alexander the Great at much the same time as did Soghdia. The Macedonian conqueror and his Seleucid successors increased the number of existing townlets by founding military colonies, which were laid out on the rectangular lines followed in Greece and which, at any rate to begin with, were populated by Greeks. However, under the Seleucids, Thracians and Greeks born in Asia Minor were also made to settle in them. It was the duty of the settlers to protect the new provinces from marauding nomads. Many must have ended by marrying local girls. In doing so they would only have been following the example set by Alexander when he chose the famous Roxana as his second wife. She was a daughter of the Bactrian baron Oxyartes. The Seleucids also ended by having a good deal of Central Asian blood in their veins; thus, the mother of Seleucus I was a Persian, and although his wife Apamea was an Achaemenid on her mother's side, her father was a Soghdian baron called Spitamenes.

What is today known as Kabul had been captured from India by the Persians, but when Alexander conquered it, it was joined to Bactria proper. Realizing the importance of this area as a gateway to India, Alexander founded, at the meeting point of the rivers Pasishir and Ghorband, the town which was to serve as the region's capital. He chose a site some 60 kilometres north of Kabul, straddling the

107 Ivory statuette of a *yakshi* or river goddess from Begram. Although it shows close affinities with Indian art, it is also related to the wooden figurine from Piandjikent (*Ill. 85*). First–fourth century

108, 109 Two fragments
of ivory inlay from a piece
of furniture found during
excavations at Begram.
Indian influence is even
more strongly shown in
these water goddesses and
especially in the niches,
which feature on Indian
stupas. They may also be
linked with the Bia Nai-
nan ossuary (*Ill.* 77).
First- fourth century

caravan route leading to India. It is known today as Begram, but he
called it Alexandria-Kapisu or Kapisha in order, according to Tarn,
to express its future international character, for he wished it to be as
much Greek, because of the Greeks he had settled there, as it was
local and would, he hoped, become Indian. The multi-racialism
which Alexander wished to establish at Kapisu is reflected in the
region's art. This is partly due to the efforts of the Seleucid emperor
Demetrius I for, in his desire that Bactrians, Greeks and Indians
should regard themselves as equal and indivisible, he strove to
become as Indian in outlook as he was Greek by blood.

For a time Kapisu served as the capital both of the Seleucids and
the Kushans. Excavations were started on the site in 1936 and the
famous treasure (*Ills. 107–110*) which was discovered, hidden for

127

safety in a room in the citadel, suffices to show that the city had been quick to enter into commercial relations of a well-nigh international character. Thus, on the one hand, there is a group of finds consisting of Graeco-Roman objects, for the most part of Syrian origin, which Schlumberger assigns to the second half of the first century BC and, on the other, numerous fragments of Chinese textiles. Other finds included important carved and stucco decorations of local taste, statuettes and statues of various sizes and some Buddhist paintings reflecting at times strong Sassanian influences, but, as in the case of the paintings of Fundukistan, even more marked Indian elements.

For seventy-five years following upon Alexander's death the Seleucids ruled Bactria as a province, governing it by means of a Greek *eparch* chosen from among the younger scions of the Seleucid house. In about 250 BC the task was assigned to Diodotus but he soon started to break free from the central administration. With the help of numerous Greek sympathizers he eventually contrived to establish himself as an independent ruler of Bactria. His descendents proved still more ambitious. Thus his immediate successor murdered him in order to rule in his stead. It was the latter's son, Demetrius I, who set out with his own son, the future Demetrius II and his general, Menander, to conquer India, leaving another son Euthy-demus, to govern Kapisu. Demetrius I and Menander were remark-ably successful generals and as a result the king was able in *c.* 190 BC to install his third son, Pantaleon, as ruler of Gandhara whilst estab-lishing Menander as king of northern India. Another Seleucid, Eucratides, was to succeed Demetrius I as supreme ruler of the Bactrian kingdom in *c.* 167 BC, that is to say at very much the same time that Mithridates became ruler of Parthia. The interests of both dynasties were soon to conflict sharply but, to begin with, their strength was fairly equally matched. In the long run, however, the Parthians were to prove the more powerful. Indeed, at Menander's death in *c.* 165 BC the greatest of the Greek rulers of Central Asia passed from the political scene and with him Greek power in Turkestan came virtually to an end, even though some autonomous pockets of Greeks and several petty rulers survived in the remoter districts for the best part of another century.

110 Glass bottle, made in Syria, and found at Begram. It was no doubt transported there by a Roman merchant trading in luxury wares. First–fourth century

When at the height of its power, that is to say during some sixty years following the death of Diodotus, Seleucid Bactria's territory was so vast that, in the west, it included much of present-day Tadjikistan and southern Uzbekistan as well as parts of north-west Iran, and in the east the whole of present-day Afghanistan together with Kapisu, Taxila (Rawalpindi), Mathura in the Punjab, and Gandhara. In addition, from *c.* 187 to 155 BC it also comprised Seistan in western Afghanistan. And wherever a Seleucid ruled, even if he did so for a few years only, the art of the region acquired an Hellenistic or, rather, a Graeco-Roman stamp.

The Bactrians were a gifted, war-like and clever race. Under Greek tutelage they rapidly became politically mature and intellectually sophisticated. They were thus soon producing native astronomers, physicists, mathematicians and philosophers of distinction. Their culture quickly became eclectic, and one result of this is reflected in the facility with which they used the Aramaic, Soghdian or Greek alphabets when writing their native Persian tongue and the

111, 112 Stone sculptured frieze, a detail of which is shown below, once adorned a Buddhist monastery at Airtam, near Termez. The style is clearly Kushan, the workmanship local. Hellenic influence was responsible for the use of acanthus leaves to separate the youths and girls, some of whom hold musical instruments of local origin. First century

readiness with which they adopted the Seleucid calendar. Nevertheless, many continued to adhere to their pagan beliefs though some
became fervent Zoroastrians whilst others began to worship the
deities of Greece, and then proceeded to invest them with local
attributes till the resulting faith acquired a mixed character. Then,
when Bactria's military conquests had brought her into direct touch
with India, Buddhism penetrated into the country, swiftly gaining
so many converts that the new faith spread eastward into Central
Asia. Yet even among the Buddhist communities Greek influences
often prevailed and were frequently able to hold their own against
the rising tide of Sassanian Persia. The earlier Indo-Hellenistic blend
is seen at its best in the fragments of a superb sculptured limestone
frieze (*Ill. 111*) of the first century A D recently discovered at Airtam,
a fortified Buddhist settlement, situated some 18 kilometres north-
west of Termez, in what is now Soviet territory. It is thought
originally to have adorned a Buddhist monastery, but the work is
clearly Bactrian. The frieze displays a row of youths and girls shown
half-length bearing garlands and musical instruments, some of which
are of local origin (*Ill. 112*), set against a background of acanthus
leaves. Hellenistic and Indian elements are reflected both in the
modelling of the people and in the choice of such decorative motifs
as garlands, but the vitality with which they are rendered points to
the hand of a native artist.

Bactrian sculptors were fond of including architectural details such
as columns and capitals of Greek origin in their compositions. They
cannot have been altogether unacquainted with Greek buildings,

since the walled towns which the Greeks founded in quite large numbers in Central Asia must have been laid out and built by Greek architects according to their native styles. These towns must have contained temples and *agoras*, and the reason why none of these buildings are known is surely because no serious attempt has been made to find them, and not because they do not exist. In 1939 Evert Barger happened to notice either a Greek or a Roman column of Ionic order standing *in situ* at the bottom of a 10-foot deep clay pit at Kundar, near Khanabad, and it is surely only a matter of time before some classical sites of importance are discovered in Afghanistan. Though in Seleucid times the Greeks constituted only a small minority of Central Asia's population, they formed nevertheless its most important group, for it was they who provided the civil servants and commissioned ranks in the army, both of which were essential to the administration and protection of the country. Their hold over it was undoubtedly strengthened by their intermarriage with local girls. One result of this is that by the time that Taxila was captured by the Parthians, Greek culture was so firmly established there that its conquerors adopted the Greek language as their own.

Though the presence of Greek artists in Bactria cannot as yet be proved, it alone can account for the firmness with which the Hellenistic tradition took root there. Still today in the village of Istalaf, situated some 30 kilometres to the south-west of Kabul, the founding of which is ascribed by tradition to a group of Greek potters, clay figurines are being spontaneously made in the archaic Greek style. Furthermore, in early Seleucid times no one but Greeks would have thought of providing Bactria with the superb

113, 114, 115, 116 These four examples illustrate the quality of Bactria's coins. From left to right are shown the obverse and reverse of Eucratides' silver tetradrachma, *c.* 180–150 BC, with on one side the king's head and on the other the Dioscuri on horseback; Demetrius helmeted on his silver tetradrachma of the late third century BC; the usurper Euthydemus in old age, *c.* 230 BC, on his silver tetradrachma and, finally, Eucratedes' gold stater, *c.* 170–65 BC, the largest gold coin now in existence

coinage which now ranks as one of her chief glories, and only Greek artists would have been able at that time to satisfy the demand for one of so high a quality. Many Bactrian coins rank with the finest in existence (*Ills. 114, 115, 116*). They possess an elegance, forcefulness and perfection of line which, together with the excellence of their minting, characterize the loveliest coins of Greece. In addition certain of them show so great a gift for portraiture that they recall the best Roman sculptures. To be numbered with these is one showing Eucratides wearing a topee-like helmet which makes him resemble a young nineteenth-century English officer of the Indian army with, on the reverse, the Dioscuri riding horses that may well have been bred in Ferghana (*Ill. 113*). Could Bucephulus have been of that breed? Bactria's nickel and copper coins are as well minted and designed as her gold and silver ones. Foucher is surely right in thinking that they must have been produced by Greek master craftsmen, who may well have employed local men as assistants.

It is now evident that many of the fine metal objects which have been accepted as Sassanian are in fact Bactrian. They are as splendid in their own way as the coins and must have been widely admired in their own day for they appear to have been exported far afield. Bactria's metal workers are seen at their most characteristic in objects such as vessels (*Ill. 117, 118, 119*). These were so much admired by their contemporaries that even Chinese artists of the Han period, who were assuredly among the finest artists of their time, were enchanted by them and often let themselves be influenced by them

117 In their metal work the Bactrians looked both to India and the West for inspiration. This silver bowl from north-west India shows that Persia provided both the subject and the style. Vessels such as these may well have served as models for Daghestan artists working a thousand years later (*Ill. 248*). Fifth–sixth century

(*Ill. 122*). Many Bactrian vessels have been found in western Russia. A bronze phalera which comes from there is of particular interest. It displays the head of a youth executed in high relief work and finished off by chasing and gilding. C. H. Trevers considers it to be a copy of Praxiteles' famous statue of Dionysus, the head of which, she thinks, was chosen in the first half of the second century to appear on the Bactrian coin of Agathocles. This phalera was not unique. Others (*Ill. 120*) were also made in two sections held together by bronze studs, and also display Hellenistic heads often finished off in the same way. Many of the earlier Bactrian works were doubtless produced by Greeks for Greeks, but it cannot have taken long before local patrons, the first of whom may well have been drawn into the Greek orbit as a result of intermarriage, started to commission works in the Greek style for their own use. After that it can surely have been only a matter of years before the growing demand led native artists to work in the Hellenistic manner.

118 Silver bowl found in Russia, but of Bactrian workmanship. The scenes, which are executed in high relief, drawn from Euripides' tragedies of Alcestis, Alope, Bacchae and Ion, are a blend of Hellenistic and Persian elements. First–second century

119 Though dating from the seventh century, the designer of this silver Bactrian dish once again turned to Greece for his subject-matter, chosing to show Heracles as a slave of Syleus and slaying his master during a feast

120 This silver phalera is the work of an outstanding Bactrian master who has once again turned to the Hellenistic world for inspiration and produced this image of a female divinity holding a bow

121 This silver d stresses the country's li with India and is anot fine example of Bactr metal work

122 Bactrian metal workers were so much admired by their contemporaries that even China's artists did not hesitate to look to them for ideas. The Han metal worker who made this bronze mirror drew his motifs from the Graeco-Bactrian world

137

123 Armlet from the Oxus Treasure made of almost solid gold. The terminals – a mixture of gryphon and mountain goat – were originally inlaid with coloured stones and paste. It bears a strong resemblance to Altaian art (*Ills. 23, 24*), although it is of Persian or Bactrian workmanship. Fifth century BC

Some fine examples of the Bactrian jeweller's art are to be found in the Oxus Treasure. The treasure was discovered in 1877 buried near one of the busiest ferry-crossings on the road to Samarkand. It is thought to date from about the year 200 BC. Included in it are examples of Assyrian, Achaemenian (*Ill. 123*), Greek, Bactrian, Scythian (*Ill. 124*) and Indian workmanship (*Ill. 128*), and some objects which were probably made in western Turkestan. Contacts with Egypt are proved by the inclusion of a sphinx in the form of a dress trimming. Among the Bactrian objects are a superbly modelled bronze lion-gryphon of exquisite delicacy and great vitality (*Ill. 125*). The latter is reminiscent both of Achaemenid versions of the creature and the far more barbaric ones from Pazyryk.

124 Gold ring embossed with the figure of a contorted beast, possibly a lion, once adorned with colour inlay. Scythian, fifth–fourth century BC

The Bactrians had taken to trade in very early times but even under the Seleucids they failed to establish direct links with China. Goods from that country destined for Bactria, whether in the form of imports or as transit consignments, had to be transferred from hand to hand in order to reach her borders. The same conditions prevailed when Bactria first started to serve as a clearing house for India's trade with the Western world, even when the quantities of ivory being exported were so immense that Parthia derived the major part of her wealth from the dues she levied on their transit.

125 Cast bronze statuette of a lion-gryphon showing Bactrian art at its best. The foliated treatment of its mane is particularly accomplished. Fourth century BC

The Bactrians were endowed with an innate love of luxury. It was stimulated by the sight of the precious wares transported across her territory. Under the Seleucids their demands for gold rose steeply yet the supply remained unchanged for deliveries continued to depend upon imports which remained sporadic. It was as much in order to organize more regular deliveries of this coveted metal as to increase the amounts available that Eucratides attempted to discover the northern route along which gold was transported from China to Mongolia. On failing to find it he looked eastward, to the Tarim region. There he proved more successful for he was able to arrange for regular supplies of gold, silver and nickel of Chinese origin to be brought to Bactria. However, it was only in 106 B C that the first through caravans from China traversed Bactria carrying silk direct from China to Persia. By that time, however, the Greeks had been ejected from Bactria and it was the Kushans, who had replaced them there, who benefited by the change.

The Greeks had the misfortune to lose Bactria in 130 B C to a nomadic hoard composed largely of Asiani and Saka tribesmen, and some Yueh-Chi. The Greeks were forced to flee in the face of their onslaught, but they managed to close the Hindu Kush pass behind them and thus to deflect the Saka advance towards Parthia. Ten years of warfare followed between the Sakas and Parthians, and it was not until Mithridates II (123–88 B C) came to the throne and assumed command of his army that the Parthians were able to contain the Sakas. The latter then turned towards Seistan where, on joining forces with the Scytho-Sakian tribes of that region, they contrived to enter India and to establish themselves in its northern districts.

The Yueh-Chi were probably of Turkish origin. They are thought to have included in their numbers some Hephthalite Huns, Asiani tribesmen and some of the Tokharians who had been living in Bactria since the fourth century or so B C. Most of the Yueh-Chi were later to abandon Bactria and to form a short-lived kingdom in the Tarim valley. They were probably accompanied by some Sakas for it is known that they spoke a Persian language which, there is reason to think, was either Sakian or Soghdian. Tarn is of the opinion that the group which invaded Bactria and ejected the Greeks was led by Asiani Sakas and that it was they who remained in Bactria to rule there under the name of Kushans. Tarn therefore regards the name Kushan as a dynastic rather than a political or ethnic term. He suggests that the Tokharians, who are known to have spoken a European language before they adopted the Sakian tongue, may well have been the Indo-Celtic people who migrated from Europe and settled eventually on the borders of China. If so, he suggests that the blue-eyed people represented on some of the wall-paintings discovered in Turfan and Koço by Sir Aurel Stein and A. von Le Coq may represent Tokharians.

The Indo-Scyths or Kushans, as they are now called, remained the undisputed rulers of north-eastern Bactria, rivalling first the Parthians, then the Sassanians, growing rich on the commerce conducted along the silk road. They continued, however, to wear the nomadic dress of their ancestors, though they enhanced it by the addition of jewels, for the Bactrians had taught them to delight in luxuries and personal adornments (*Ills. 126, 127*). They also took over the alphabet used by the Greeks of Central Asia and adapted it to their own needs. Until the first century A D Transoxiana served as a buffer state between them and the Chinese, but in *c.* A D 94 the Chinese penetrated to the Orkhon and came into direct touch with the Kushans. The former then thought it wise to propitiate their new neighbours with costly gifts in order that they should not interfere with the caravans on which so much of China's prosperity depended.

126 This tiny circular pendant from Taxila is adorned with a delicately worked head of Hariti executed in repoussé and enhanced with pearls and garnets. Third–fourth century

These caravans carried goods from both India and China by means of a network of roads. Those coming from India generally crossed the Khyber Pass, for at Kabul that road converged with a number of others. The Kushans guaranteed the safety of these routes and established additional roads with a view to linking Balk eastward to Bamyan, Kabul and Kandahar and northwards across the Karakorum. The old road which connected the Ganges to the Aegean also continued to be used. Starting from Patna it passed through Mathura, Taxila and Kapisu, crossed the Hindu Kush and eventually reached Ecbatana where, like the newer routes, it linked up with roads leading either to Damascus and Phoenicia or to Antioch, and thence by way of the Taurus and Asia Minor, to Ionia. By these means the Kushan empire was brought into contact with the world's great cultural centres. And wherever caravans, and more especially silk caravans passed, intellectual and cultural exchanges took place, Graeco-Roman influences flowing eastward and Indian westward. Everywhere along these routes the creative spirit was stimulated by these exchanges, yet Kushan art saw its finest flowering in the second century B C, when Buddhism started to advance westward in the wake of India's growing export trade with the West.

127 The delight which the inhabitants of Taxila took in exquisite jewellery is illustrated by this pendant made of gold and encrusted with jewels. First century B C–first century A D

128 Silver bowl with a central design of a yaksha drinking. Like so much else in Kushan art it is a blend of Hellenistic and Indian elements. North-west India, third–fourth century.

The Kushans had won their territories in north-western India from the Parthian autocrat Gondolphus in *c.* 90 BC. They joined them to Bactria and, in their hands, the entire area entered upon a period of great prosperity. Central Afghanistan is rich in archaeological sites dating from those times. Surk Khotal is one which has yielded particularly interesting results. Excavations were started there in 1952 under the direction of the French Archaeological Mission to Afghanistan. Surk Khotal lies in the Kunduz-ab valley, on the banks of the main Afghan tributary the Oxus, close to the main road leading from Kabul to Mazar-i-Sharif. It was built on virgin soil to serve, in Schlumberger's opinion, as a dynastic shrine and fire-temple of the Kushan rulers, and was abandoned for ever in Sassanian times. The buildings climb up a hill and were surrounded by two lines of defences which followed its contours. Some houses stood at the highest point, but they proved of secondary importance. The most spectacular building was a sort of acropolis occupying the most impressive site within the enclosure. This temple was clearly

143

the reason for the entire complex. An immense, truly monumental staircase led to it. Both the staircase and the lower levels of the building's walls were constructed of vast blocks of dressed stone instead of the unbaked bricks generally used in the region for building purposes. The temple faced an impressively large courtyard surrounded by a peristyle. Its flat roof rested on columns of the Corinthian order and the sculptures which adorned the building likewise followed Hellenistic conventions, the floral and animal motifs assuming the forms which had been evolved in Gandhara from Western prototypes, whereas the human figures were rendered in a manner which recalled the Scytho-Parthian school of Mathura. The building's plan, on the other hand, vividly reminded Schlumberger of those followed in Achaemenid palaces built in Persia some six hundred years earlier. The decorative brickwork introduced at the top of Surk Khotal's outer walls and the shape given to the arrow slits with which they were provided likewise appeared to have been inspired by Persian prototypes. Schlumberger has commented on the absence at Surk Khotal of all Buddhist, indeed of all Indian influence. The discovery of an inscription which though in Bactrian was written in letters resembling the Greek used by the early Kushans has fortunately been read by A.D.H.Bivar and found to refer to the time of King Kanishka. Various dates have been suggested for his reign, but the French archaeologists working in Afghanistan now agree in assigning it to the first half of the second century A D. They believe that Surk Khotal was built just before Kanishka's conversion to Buddhism, and the sympathy he felt for the religion and the rapidity with which Buddhist missionaries were able to win converts among his subjects may help to account for the sudden abandonment of so important a Zoroastrian site. Thus Surk Khotal remains as a typically Kushan monument of early date, embodying the principles which were evolved west of the Hindu Kush, largely in Bactria, before the Buddhist elements in Gandharan art had started to express themselves there.

Taxila had had a culture of its own before Demetrius transformed it into a Greek halting place on the road to India. In 185 B C the entire region was annexed by the Scytho-Parthian king Azes I, only to

129 Reliquary in repoussé gold set with rubies which originally contained a relic of Buddha. It was found in a stone vessel in the ruined stupa of Bimaran in Jelalabad, together with some coins of the Sakian king, Azes, of the second century BC. The figures in the niches include those of Buddha, Indra and Brahma. The style is typically Gandharan; that is, a blend of Western and Indian elements. First century AD

fall in c. 60 BC to the Indian king of Mathura. Then the Scytho-Sakian king Mauryas invaded northern India and established a kingdom there bearing his name. It included Gandhara, where St Thomas is believed to have visited him. Throughout these unsettled years Taxila failed to benefit from the transit trade crossing her borders, even though it included consignments of silk, but in the first century AD her merchants decided to by-pass Bactria and, together with some traders from northern India to attempt to improve their affairs by dealing direct with China via Khotan. Some of them started to travel in Chinese Turkestan, and colonies of Indian and Indian speaking merchants soon came into being in Khotan. Some of the colonists used the Karoshti script for their business transactions and are thought by Tarn to have been Greeks. Tablets have been found enclosed in envelopes bearing the clay imprints of their seals. Many of these display Graeco-Roman designs; some are so accomplished that they may well have been engraved in the Western world, but others are so archaic in style that it seems probable that they were made in local workshops.

In the year AD 19 the Scytho-Parthian king Gondolphus became ruler of Taxila. His dynasty was overthrown in c. AD 64 by the Kushans, who then established close contacts with Augustan Rome. In 1913 Sir John Marshall directed the first excavations carried out on the site. He found remains belonging to all the various phases of its history. Relics from the local Mauryas dynasty lay on virgin soil;

above them Marshall came upon a Graeco-Roman layer dating from the first century BC to the first century AD and Kushan remains filled the upper levels. The Greek objects included coins and sculptures, one of them a head of Dionysius. At that time the town had been laid out on the rectangular lines characteristic of Hellenistic cities. Under Gondolphus it underwent radical alterations, winding streets replacing the earlier straight ones. The palace was found to date back to Sakian times and to have been built on an Assyrian plan. A temple in the Ionic style had a square tower resembling a Persian fire-temple, and was probably intended to serve the same purpose. The ruins of several Buddhist temples dating from the Kushan period were also found. Both in the Parthian and early Kushan periods the buildings were of rubble, though handled differently; from the third century AD rows of ashlar blocks alternated with layers of rubble. In each case, the walls were faced with polychrome stucco.

Hackin considered Kanishka to have been both the great legendary figure extolled in Bactria's epics and also the real ruler of a kingdom which extended from the Ganges to the Jaxartes. He is indeed the most intriguing of the Kushan rulers known to us. A low-relief sculpture discovered at Mathura bearing his name presents a figure which was probably intended as his portrait (*Ill. 130*). It is, therefore, particularly unfortunate that the top of the slab is missing and, with it, the king's head. It shows Kanishka holding a sword and mace, and with his feet planted on the ground in so masterful a manner that he seems to bestride his vast kingdom. He wears nomadic dress and even though he was to end his days as a fervent Buddhist, there is no trace of Indian influence in this sculpture. Both in style and conception the work is basically Parthian or, if it stems from the direction of the Ganges, Scytho-Parthian. Schlumberger has defined Kushan figural art as a blend of Greek, Achaemenian and nomadic elements; the term Greek must be interpreted as Graeco-Roman, and the nomadic must be taken to include Scytho-Parthian. In this instance, however, Greek elements are absent but other sculptures of this school and period reveal Sassanian influences in addition to those enumerated by Schlumberger. The latter expressed themselves with particular vigour in the rendering of horsemen, most of whom are shown

130 Carved figure in pink sandstone inscribed, 'The King, King of Kings, His Majesty ▶ Kanishka'. Although the head is missing, it was originally about life-size and probably represents a portrait of the king. Kushan, second century

wearing nomadic dress. Gandhara played a most important role in the development of Buddhist sculpture and thus of Kushan culture. It was not an offshoot of Bactrian art, but a local creation which may have evolved under the stimulus of Alexandria, the influence of which may have reached this eastern region in the wake of commerce. The climate of Gandhara is such that wall-paintings cannot survive there for long; as a result her artistic creations have come down to us in the form of sculptures. The Gandharan school of sculpture was important already in the second century BC, but it was only when the region became the centre for the production of Buddhist works that its influence made itself felt among its neighbours, more especially in what are known to us today as Afghanistan and Pakistan.

Gandhara proper occupied the area bounded on one side by the Kunduz river, on the other by the Indus, that is to say it lay at the lower end of the Kabul valley. Skylax was the first Greek to reach it, choosing it as his base when ordered by Darius to trace the course of the Indus. Alexander captured Gandhara in the spring of 327 BC and at his death it passed to the Seleucids. Whilst in their hands it became the fountain-head of Hellenism in northern India (*Ill. 133*). As a result Hellenistic culture took so firm a hold there that it continued to flourish in Gandhara after its capture by Chandragupta, the first Indian emperor to be recorded in history. It was Chandragupta's grandson, Asoka, who sent the first Buddhist missionaries to Gandhara, but who, at the same time, used the Aramaic instead of the Brahmin alphabet for his famous Gandharan rock inscription. It was

131, 132 (*left*) Gold coin stamped with Siva's bull and (*right*) coin with, on the obverse, Kanishka, and on the reverse, the goddess Ardoksha holding a Hellenistic cornucopia

133 Limestone relief of Hariti and Pancika showing strong Hellenistic influence. Gandhara, third-fourth century

Kanishka, the third of the Kushan rulers whose name is known to us, who was to adopt as his own the religion which had come into being on the Ganges sometime in the sixth century BC. Under his influence the Gandharans quickly became such fervent Buddhists that their sculptures of Buddha soon outnumbered those of the Graeco-Bactrian goddess Artemis-Anihita and of the Indian god Siva, even though the latter had been so popular there that he was known to the Greeks as the god of Gandhara and his emblem of a bull figured for a time on Gandhara's coins (*Ill. 131*).

When Buddhism reached Gandhara Hellenistic ideals were so firmly entrenched there that converts to the new faith must have turned to Western artists for the new votive statues they needed. These artists must in their turn have felt drawn to the new faith for

149

134 Head of Bodhissatva shows the softness and simplicity of line which characterizes the Kushan sculpture of Mathura. Second century

they showed no reluctance in working for it and, indeed, during the first century BC, many Greeks are known to have become converted to Buddhism. The impact made by the Buddhist sculptures produced by Hellenistic artists was soon to make itself powerfully felt not only in western and eastern Turkestan, but also in Kashmir, Mathura and Amurat. Tarn presents convincing reasons for thinking that it was the Indian sculptors who became Hellenized and not, as certain scholars maintain, the Greeks who became Indianized. He puts forward cogent arguments to support the view that it was Greeks who, in the first century BC, created the first known naturalistic representations of Buddha, pointing out that prior to that date, that is to say, from the third to the first century BC, Buddha was always depicted in Indian art by a symbol, such as his footprint, umbrella or throne. Then, sometime during the first century Mauryas, the Scytho-Sakian conqueror of northern India, had a coin struck showing, not as was assumed, a figure of a seated king, but according to Tarn, one of Buddha. This suggestion still awaits general acceptance, but Tarn was convinced that the coin was made by a Greek, if only because no Saka of that place or period would have been capable of such work. The coin antedates by the best part of a century the renderings of Buddha produced by the Indian sculptors of Mathura which many scholars regarded as the earliest of their kind. Yet these date from the very time when the last Greeks to emigrate from Bactria were reaching India. Tarn suggests that these refugees carried eastward with them the Greek conception of Apollo and, on reaching their new homes, proceeded to Indianize it by transforming it into the figure of the Greek-featured Buddha seated in the Yuga pose found on early seals from the Indus valley, which show Siva seated cross-legged. This creation was adopted by the Greek sculptors of Mathura later on and was retained by them with but little change until the Gupta period, when Indian artists transformed this Greek creation into something wholly different and entirely national.

135 Pink sandstone relief of a tree spirit from the Jain stupa at Mathura. Acanthus leaves are cleverly used to separate the figure from its neighbours. Second century

136 Head of Buddha from Mathura, the southern province of the Kushan empire, showing, therefore, strong Indian features. The eyebrows form a continuous delicately curved line, the lips turn upward in an enigmatic smile and the hair has lost its Greek waves. The elongated ear lobes were once adorned with earrings. First century

138 (*opposite*) This magnificent he of Buddha is in grey schist and sho Gandharan sculpture at its fine Second–third century

137 Head of Buddha from Gandhara. Although later in date than the preceding head, it is closer to the Romano-Buddhist sculptures of the early years. This hair is wavy, the eyebrows form a continuous line with the nose, the smile and expression are withdrawn, reflective and serene. Fourth–fifth century

The Buddhas produced by the earlier local sculptors wore no jewels, but the lobes of their ears were already extended as though drawn down by the weight of earrings to represent one of the thirty-two magical marks or *lakshanas* of Buddhahood (*Ill. 136*). Their profiles remained regular, their eyes elongated and their features delicate, their expression withdrawn, reflective and serene. To begin with, their draperies were rendered in a Hellenistic manner, but they were later transformed into linear compositions (*Ill. 140*). It is thought that most of these sculptures were originally painted or gilt. In Gandhara the style of the statues of both Buddhas and Bodhisattvas remained Romano-Buddhist (*Ills. 137, 138*), which amounts to the same as saying Romano-Indian. No trace of the Persian elements which appear so frequently in Bactrian art are to be seen in them, nor is the influence of China apparent, even though, under the Han emperors, it had made itself felt in Central Asia and was to predominate in the Buddhist art of eastern Turkestan and the Tarim basin. The absence of these elements is surely yet another indication that Buddhist art originated in Gandhara, spreading thence into Central Asia and eastward into China. That Hellenistic influence

139 Statue of Buddha seated in the Oriental or yoga pose. Tarn observed that Siva was depicted in the same position on early seals from the Indus valley. Gandhara, second–third century

140 Standing statue of a Bodhisattva. The draperies of Hellenistic origin are beginning to acquire the linear appearance which characterizes late Gandharan work. Second century

retained its hold over this art during some six centuries is also largely due to the silk trade, for it brought so much wealth with it that the Romans and the Kushans were equally anxious not only to maintain, but also to develop it to the utmost. To do so they made new roads in order to link China to the Oxus, and so on to Ecbatana. Western sculptors, many of whom probably came from Rome's Syrian provinces, must have taken advantage of the improved communications to seek a livelihood in the East. It was they who probably infused the passive renderings of Buddha which they found there with a Syrian or Alexandrian expressiveness which had in it a touch of Parthian vitality. In the process the Hellenistic element underwent a measure of Romanization, and it was in a Graeco-Roman form that Western influence survived in the figures of Buddhas and Bodhisattvas sitting cross-legged in the Indian fashion in what soon became a fixed iconographic form (*Ill. 139*).

Especially characteristic of the Gandharan school of sculpture are the scenes which were generally worked on slabs of Gandhara's grey coloured schist, though limestone was sometimes used instead. The vast majority are of a religious character for they were intended as adornment for the outer walls of the *stupas* and *vishanas* built to contain statues of Buddhas. Stupas (*Ill. 141*) had originally been intended to serve as funerary monuments for the ashes of people of distinction. However, they gradually acquired the character of shrines and an alcove-like opening was then cut into one side of them to hold a statue; eventually the larger stupas came to be used as chapels. The form was invented in India where the earliest examples were in the shape of low, rounded mounds topped by a balustrade. With the years they became elongated and their plinths were then divided into pagoda-like sections known as 'parasol' layers. According to legend the three original divisions were created by Buddha when he made the first stupa by tearing three of his garments into pieces which he folded into squares. He laid them one on the other

141 Model of a stupa from the Swat valley. Its base is decorated with scenes from the life of Buddha. Stupas rapidly acquired great height. According to Chinese pilgrims, Kanishka's stupa at Peshawar was seventy feet high.

142 Limestone relief depicting a scene from the early life of Buddha. As Prince Siddhartha he is shown driving to school in a chariot with his companions, holding inkpots and writing boards, walking beside him. Gandhara, second–fourth century

according to size and placed his pilgrim's bowl upside down on the top one, sticking his staff through its centre. If the early Chinese pilgrims are to be believed, the stupa in Peshawar was already 27 feet high. It was the parasol form which penetrated to Gandhara; there it was again elongated and the number of parasol layers increased, though never to the same extent as in Nepal, where they often numbered as many as thirteen.

The vishana was first intended to serve as a monk's hermitage or cell, but soon it too was being used to hold a statue or act as a shrine. Its shape was probably inspired by that of the stupa, for although vishanas took the form of triangles with their apexes flattened out, others were roofed with a sort of double dome, that is to say one having two sections which, when seen from the inside, created the impression of a threefold arch.

The sculptures which were produced to adorn the outer walls of the stupas and vishanas, picture incidents drawn from the three phases of Buddha's life, that is to say from his earlier existence

143 Sculptured relief from a stupa illustrating the death of Buddha. The style is basically Hellenistic, showing interest in drapery. Note the way in which vegetation is used to isolate the scene and also the contemporary-looking bed. Second century

(*Ill. '142*), his last phase (*Ill. 143*) and that of his Illumination. Each incident was carved on separate blocks of stone of uniform size, all of which were then arranged in the prescribed sequence, with the narrative unfolding horizontally from left to right, that being the direction in which worshippers circumambulated round the shrine. Each incident was presented in a border formed either of trees, corinthian columns, acanthus leaves or horseshoe shaped arches of Indian origin, which served to separate each scene, though this type of separation was probably due to Western influence. Acanthus leaves seem to have been as popular in Gandhara as they were in Palmyra. Rosettes similar to those found on early Indian works as well as on the considerably later ones created by the Seljuks in Anatolia are often scattered on the backgrounds. The slabs were held together by iron clamps and fixed to the walls of the shrines with large iron nails. Some of the sculptures bear mason's or sculptor's marks. The majority are in fairly low relief, but in others the under-cutting is so deep that the figures give the impression of being in the round. The modelling is always highly accomplished and the narrative vivid and graphic. The emotional content of each scene is conveyed by means of gestures, the sense of movement being expressed according to Indian rather than Greek conventions, but the draperies are treated in the classical manner. It has not as yet proved possible to date any of these slabs with exactitude, but in those which seem to be the earlier in date, the figure of Buddha is always larger than those of the other people appearing in the scene, whereas in what are probably the later works all the figures are of uniform size. Many wear head-dresses of Palmyrene style, but the frontal position in which so many of them are presented may well denote Parthian influence. In contrast, the inclusion of figures shown three-quarter face must be accepted as Hellenistic in inspiration.

The sculptures abound in details culled from everyday life (*Ill. 144*). The comfortable-looking beds well stacked with cushions and the chariots drawing the sun-god obviously reproduce contemporary forms. The women accord more closely with the Indian than the

144 Another scene from Buddha's early life shows the prince in his harem. Once again furnishings and objects used in daily life are included, together with architectural details of Romano-Hellenistic origin. Gandhara, second–third century

145 It is interesting to compare this limestone statue of a goddess with flowers from Hadda with the Bactrian silver phalera (*Ill. 120*). The Hellenistic element is so strong in both, that it has won for the statue the appellation of Antinoïs. Third-fifth century

146, 147, 148 Follow Rome's example the sculp of Hadda strove to ach physical as well as psyc logical likenesses in t works. (*Left*) Monk's h (*centre*) warrior's head (*right*) head of a demon. fourth–fifth century

Greek ideal of feminine beauty for their limbs are rounded and they wear a great deal of jewellery. They seem to belong to a single social class. The men are shown bare-headed as in the Western world yet many wear nomadic dress. Their racial characteristics range from the Indo-European to the Mongoloid and include men with moustaches trimmed in the Parthian manner. Bacchic scenes and farcical figures of Greek inspiration sometimes occur. Cherubs of Greek origin, bejewelled in the oriental manner but with their hair dressed in the Gandharan style whilst their draperies are moulded according to the classic convention appear holding garlands of Western origin and musical instruments of local types. Buddha's triton adorers are likewise of Greek origin and figure frequently. Broadly speaking, it can be said that the setting of these Buddhist themes is largely Indian but the treatment Greek.

Though a number of excavations have been conducted in Afghanistan very little concrete information has emerged concerning these sculptures. All that is known is that the school came into being in either the second or first century B C and that it survived until the end of the fifth or sixth century A D, when the invasion of the White Huns put an end to Buddhism in Gandara. Throughout the whole of that time it exercised a profound influence over Buddhist sculptors working in eastern Turkestan, but its most creative phase probably lasted from the first century B C to the second century A D, that is to say to the years when Buddhism was making such headway in north-western India that Kanishka became converted to it, celebrating the event by striking some splendid bronze coins bearing his representation and inscribed with Buddha's name. Though Shapur I destroyed the Kushan dynasty in *c.* A D 241, the school lingered on after the original impetus had spent itself and probably owed its long survival to Roman conservatism and influence, for the example of Rome was such that, as in Alexandria and Palmyra, the Hellenistic tradition continued to hold its own in the east for as long as Roman merchants retained control of the oriental trade. That Romans, or Rome's eastern citizen, remained in touch with what are now north-western India and central Afghanistan is proved not only by the presence at Begram of Syrian glass (*Ill. 110*) of the fourth century and by the discovery of hoards of Roman coins as far as Saripul, on the northern slopes of the Hindu Kush, but also by the predominance of Roman influence in the late sculptures discovered at Hadda (*Ills. 145–148*).

Though it was largely as a result of Greek influence that Gandhara became the centre of an important school of sculpture, it was due to Buddhism that religious architecture developed along Indian lines. From the start India provided the models for the Buddhist buildings erected throughout Turkestan, whether as far west as the Termez area, where monastic remains dating from the first to the third century AD have been found, or north of Balk, or in the east, in the towns of the Tarim and Taklamakan oases. The Termez ruins are the most westernly as yet known. Numerous inscribed sherds were found there; forty-two of these were written in Indian, three in Karoshti and the rest in Brahmin. Stupas and vishanas were built throughout the entire Buddhist area both as individual shrines and as essential parts of Buddhist monasteries. The latter were invariably laid out on a rectangular plan and had one gateway only. It gave onto a courtyard where the monastic buildings were separated from one another by narrow corridors. The main shrine always stood in a central position and the monastery's statues were assembled in the corridors where they were arranged in such a way as to face the shrine. Some of the statues were free standing, others were set in stupas built to face the temple but at the same time leaving room to enable the worshippers to walk round them. Early Chinese travellers noted the existence of a thousand Buddhist monasteries in Gandhara alone, but today some of the most impressive remains of these foundations survive to the west and east of Gandhara, at Bamyan and Begram, and in eastern Turkestan.

In Kushan times central Afghanistan became largely Indian in out-look and, notwithstanding the presence there of Graeco-Roman and Persian influences, it remained so until the Arab invasion. The reason for this lies in the fact that Buddhism not only provided the country with its religion but also with a specific culture. Bamyan is typical of this culture. The town grew up in the fourth century AD and the two immense statues of Buddha (*Ill. 149*) representing him as Locatarra, the Lord of the World, were cut in the rock at the eastern and western approaches of the town. The one dominating the road linking Bactria both with Taxila and the Oxus has more than a touch of Parthian assertiveness about it. These statues epitomize the Kushan

149 Immense statue of Buddha carved in the rock to the west of Bamyan. It represents Buddha as Locatarra, or Lord of the World. Fourth–fifth century

outlook on life no less than the serene aloofness inherent in Buddhism. Bamyan lies pretty well midway between Peshwar and Balk. Starting as the capital of a small kingdom it rapidly developed into a leading centre of *Hinayana* Buddhism, as such attracting numerous monks who transformed the caves abounding there into cells and sanctuaries. Often they decorated the inner walls of these shrines with paintings (*Ill. 145*) and, since none survive in Gandhara itself, it is to the Kabul area that we must turn to see what early Buddhist paintings were like.

Among the oldest as yet known to us are the paintings of Tepe Maredjan near Kabul. They date from the fourth century A D. Those at Bamyan are only very slightly later, but they have the advantage of providing us with valuable fixed dating points. Like all the murals executed in western Turkestan they are in tempera and intended to provide a setting for statues of Buddhas and Bodhisattvas. The latter were generally made of pisé, that is to say of a mixture of earth, straw, horsehair and clay, which was the only material easily procurable in many of the areas concerned. Most of the statues were then painted and some were gilded. Some were free standing so as to enable worshippers to walk round them, but their backs were often unworked, thus suggesting that they were conceived rather as reliefs than as sculptures in the round. All adhered to the traditional iconography and Buddha was generally presented seated cross-legged in the Indian fashion. Some of the wall-paintings were set off by relief sculpture work designed as an integral part of the painted scenes, in this respect recalling Soghdian mural decorations.

Hellenistic influence had been much to the fore during the second and third centuries A D. In painting it survived in the figures of a series of Buddhas and Bodhisattvas which, though never as Hellenized as the Apollo Buddha, nevertheless remained closer to the earlier renderings than to Indian or Chinese variants. However, in all the arts it was Gupta India that became the prime source of inspiration during the fourth century and which remained so during the fifth, for the rulers of the Gupta valley had by then absorbed the humanistic traditions which invest Indian sculpture of the second century A D with so much of its quality. Under the impact of these

150 Painting from the dome of one of the many cave shrines at Bamyan, showing Buddha in a mandorla preaching. He is surrounded by minor divinities, all smaller in size, sitting in the yoga pose. Fifth–sixth century

various influences, it became customary in the Bamyan area in the fifth and sixth centuries to adorn the domes of the Buddhist cave sanctuaries with paintings showing Buddha enclosed within a circle or hexagon (*Ill. 150*), these being linked to other concentric circles or hexagons to symbolize the heavens peopled with Buddhas. Other scenes included rosettes or eight-pointed Bactrian stars in their backgrounds. Both devices remained popular with the Seljuks of Anatolia some six hundred years later.

It is thought that Mani lived and studied at Bamyan. His love of painting must have helped to endear the art to the people of that area, more especially if, as has been suggested, the great teacher himself sometimes used the brush. So many paintings were produced in Buddhist times in the Bamyan and Begram regions, that even in their fragmentary and damaged state the shrines and temples which have been discovered there appear as veritable picture galleries. Sassanian Persia brought its own contribution to the predominant influence of Gupta India. Today the best Sassanian paintings are to be found outside Iran's borders, as at Duchtar-i-Nashirvan, a little to the

151 Painting of a hunter king from Kakrak, from the drum of a dome. The style is derived from Sassanian Persia. Fifth–sixth century

north-west of Bamyan. There the work recalls the magnificent Sassanian rock carvings of Naksh-i-Rustem in Iran. The most impressive composition shows a Sassanian king flanked by horsemen and attendants. These are assigned to the fourth century. Bamyan's scarcely less important paintings are dated to the fifth and sixth centuries as are those in the rock-cut temples of Kakrak, where there is a splendid rendering of a deified king shown wearing a diadem surmounted by three crescents (*Ill. 151*). Though, doubtless as a result of its proximity to Bamyan, the paintings must for stylistic reasons be classed as belonging to the Bamyan school both they and the fine, very stylized sculptures recall those of Balalyk Tepe, whilst, in addition, reflecting the influence of Gupta India. The Sassanian elements in the art of the Bamyan region were not brought about by chance, but rather as a result of regular contacts. Indeed, the links were so strong that several Sassanian princes fled to that area when trying to escape from the Hephthalites. After *c.* AD 670 some pushed

152 Wall-painting showing a Bodhisattva, probably representing Sakyamuni before he ▶ attained the rank of Buddha, surrounded by minor divinities. Sassanian elements can be seen in the pearl-studded roundel and streamers flowing from the head. Fifth–sixth century ·

on to Kuça and even to China. Furthermore, coins of Shapur (247–72), the Sassanian conqueror of Asia Minor and suzerain of Transoxiana, have been found as far afield as Zan Tepe where, regardless of the existence of local cults and the spread of Buddhism, Sassanian religious beliefs based on magic gained considerable support. Hackin discovered coins of Chosroe II (590–628) in Fundukistan, where the Buddhist paintings include Buddhas of the Hellenistic type, but where the women resemble Hindus in appearance and the men Sassanians.

In many paintings from central Afghanistan streamers similar to those flowing from the crowns worn by the Sassanian kings adorn Buddha's head (*Ill. 152*). Equally widespread there are motifs showing the winged Hellenistic horse and ducks set in pearl-studded medallions, but these are more likely to have reached the area from Soghdia than direct from Persia. Pigeons enclosed in similar medallions appear from an early date, recalling in their outlines the far earlier ones met with at Pazyryk. Yet it must have been from Sassanian Persia and not from the Altai that the motif passed into the

153, 154 Another example of the influence which the Sassanians exercised over their neighbours is seen in these two illustrations. (*Left*) This painting of Buddha from Balawaste shows him wearing a tunic very similar to that (*right*) seen on a rock relief at Tak-i-Bustan, Iran, in which the king wears a tunic lavishly adorned with emblems

155, 156 A Sassanian origin is again responsible for the motifs of these two wall-paintings from Bamyan, although they may have reached the area from Central Asia rather than direct from Iran. Compare them with *Ills. 97, 98*

Buddhist repertory. It may have been then that it attracted the attention of the Turks, with the result that their Seljukid descendents sometimes reproduced the form in Anatolia. At Bamyan, as in Sassanian Persia, the pigeons are shown in pairs and, like their Sassanian parents, they hold necklaces in their beaks (*Ill. 156*). Sassanian lunar deities and symbols also appear at Bamyan, together with, as Hackin remarked, weapons of Palmyrene type clothes. The latter are often carried by people wearing clothes of Sassanian cut. However, the discovery since Hackin's untimely death of such Soghdian paintings as those of Varaksha or Piandjikent prove that, for all their resemblance to Sassanian models, the clothes bear an even closer one to those which were worn at the time in Central Asia. They reappear again in some of the Buddhist frescoes of Kizil and other sites in eastern Turkestan such as Sorçuk (*Ill. 179*). Hackin believed that, on reaching Central Asia, Sassanian influence expressed itself first only in details of a decorative character but that with the years it came to dictate the manner in which the scenes were presented.

Sassanian influence continued to make itself felt in central Afghanistan till late in the seventh century; it was the invading Arabs who

157 Painted terracotta sarcophagus cover from the monastery at Fundukistan. It depicts a princely couple which, though in no way resembling Etruscan art, recalls it in sentiment. Sixth–seventh century

brought it to an end. When Arab rule was in its turn superseded the Guptas were reigning to the east and west of the Punjab and their influence naturally started to make itself felt in neighbouring lands. Within a short time Indian conventions were being widely accepted and nude female figures came to be included in Bactria in most sculptured and painted composition. Buddhism reached the height of its power in the eighth and ninth centuries. Then it fell into disfavour and many Buddhists fled to Kashgaria yet, even there, they were to remain free for only another century. With their decline Shamanism revived in Central Asia, but it always remained a secondary religion, for the Muslim communities which had become established there succeeded in quickly transforming the area into an Islamic stronghold. With the establishment of Muhammadanism Central Asia entered upon a new phase in her history. Though memories of olden times survived and a love of figural art persisted, both were so sternly frowned upon by the devout that they were relegated to inferior positions, although neither was wholly

158 Wooden painted
panel, which though
small in size, has all the
qualities of a monu-
mental work. It has the
elegance, delicacy and
grace that are generally
associated with precious
objects of small dimen-
sions. Seventh century

abandoned. It took several centuries for them to recover from this set-back, but had they not done so the literature and art of Iran's late medieval period would have become very different from what it is.

Fundukistan was both a less prosperous and somewhat less devout centre of Buddhism than either Bamyan or Begram and, as such, in Hackin's opinion, it was more typical of Central Asia than was the Kabul area. Its inhabitants were poorer and used pisé more often than stone, marble or bricks as a building material. Their sculptures were made of coarse plaster which was often painted, but they were generally very skilfully modelled and display great sensitivity (*Ill. 157*). Its Buddhist sanctuaries and monasteries were generally built of unbaked brick; the latter were laid out in a square plan with their inner walls lined with niches taking the form either of somewhat plain arcades or of more ornate ones making use of pseudo-corinthian capitals. There too the statues faced the central, generally stupa-shaped shrine. Many adopted the poses associated with the representations of Sassanian kings, the people in some cases appearing in Persian dress. Both the paintings and sculptures are sophisticated and elegant. Indian influence is often apparent, more particularly in such paintings as the enchanting Blue Lotus Maitreya (*Ill. 158*). These date for the most part from the start of the seventh century.

CHAPTER FIVE

Eastern Turkestan in the Roman and Buddhist Periods

Although the vitality of China's trade depended largely upon her exports to the Western world, in the second century A D she was more immediately concerned with establishing business contacts with the Indo-European merchants who had settled in the oases townlets of the Tarim basin than in her exports to the West. These towns were disposed along two curved lines bordering three sides of the Taklamakan desert, one skirting its north-western fringe, the other the south-eastern. The Chinese realized that, by making use of these towns and thereby avoiding the sandy wastes of the Takla-makan desert, caravanners would be in a position to provide them with new outlets for their luxury wares as well as with additional ways by which to communicate with the Roman empire, where her more lucrative markets were situated. However, the value of these towns depended, in so far as China's trade was concerned, on the efficiency and safety of the roads by which they were linked. Unfortunately, the majority, and more particularly those forming the north-western network, lay within easy reach of the nomads and were thus in constant danger of being raided. It was chiefly in order to confine the Huns and the Turks to Kashgaria, which was by then virtually in their hands, that the Chinese decided to transform the belt of defences they had constructed between 221 and 206 B C along their western borders into the continuous Great Wall. The officers chosen to command the special force raised to man it were given the title of 'Scourge of the Barbarians'. In *c.* 121 B C a twenty-nine-year-old commander, Ho Ch'üp'ing, was put in charge of a force of ten thousand men and sent across the Gobi to capture outer Mongolia. He took eight Hunnic chieftains prisoner and at his death in 117 B C a sculpture of a horse trampling on a barbarian was erected over his grave at Hsing-p'ing near Tch'ang-ugen.

Notwithstanding all the measures taken by the Chinese to protect

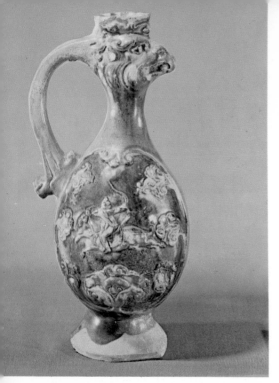

159, 160 Sassanian metal workers greatly influenced those of Central Asia, who in turn influenced China. This influence can be seen from this T'ang earthenware ewer (*left*) which is not only decorated with a typically Sassanian scene, but resembles this type of vessel (*right*)

the caravan routes the danger remained so acute that in *c.* 108 BC the Chinese set out to annex Lopnor and Turfan. The former proved particularly difficult to conquer, and even when they at last managed to occupy it the Chinese were able to hold it for only a few years. In *c.* 99 BC a large section of their army, led by the young general Li-Ling, was annihilated in the Gobi. It was only under Sinan-ti (73–49 BC) that the Chinese at last succeeded in conquering the Tarim area, occupying eastern Turkestan with, in the north, Turfan, Karuchaka and Yarkand. By capturing these regions the Chinese were able to split the northern Huns and, in 51 BC, to inflict so severe a defeat on the Mongolian group as to reduce them to the position of vassals. Many of the defeated men could not reconcile themselves to this affront and migrated to the west of Balk, to what is now Kazakstan. The Chinese pursued them and, in *c.* 35 BC, managed to capture and kill their commander. At his death such chaos ensued among the Huns that it probably delayed their invasion of Europe by some three centuries. The Chinese, however, continued to press westward and in due course came into contact with the Parthians and, later, with their Sassanian successors. The artists among them responded warmly to the beauty of Sassanian art, adopting not only certain decorative motifs as embellishments for their own pottery and metal wares (*Ills. 160, 161*), but also the amphora-shaped vessel (*Ill. 162*), which the Sassanians had themselves acquired from the Greeks. At the same time Chinese influence penetrated westward, reaching as far as Abakhan where a ruined building of the first century AD bearing a Chinese inscription has been found.

When the Chinese became the undisputed masters of the Tarim, the caravan route linking China to the West was brought into regular use, though the Chinese were obliged to maintain a large security

161 The T'ang amphora is also derived from the Greek amphora, but the dragon-shaped handles recall the animal designs of the Siberian nomads

162 Seal impressions in clay found on a document excavated at Niya, in Khotan. The one on the left is typically Eastern, whereas the right-hand one seems to depict a figure of a Roman god

force in the area to keep the old and the new roads open to traffic. The main north-western route round the Tarim led from Turfan through Karasahr, Sorçuk, Kuça, Kizil, skirting Kumtura to Aksu and Tumsuk, to converge with the existing western route either at Kashgar or at some other point in the Pamir area. Thence the great caravan road proceeded to lead them across Ferghana, Soghdia, Chorasmia and northern Persia to Ecbatana where the Indo-Afghan and Syro-Ionian routes met, and where the roads leading to the Urals and the Black Sea also converged. The eastern route round the Taklamakan started from Tun-huang and traversed the Lopnor, where it was joined by a branch road from Loulan; it continued thence to Miran and on to Cerčen, Niya and Keriya, avoiding the Altin Dag, to reach Khotan. Another route led north from Kashgar to Kuça, then down through Loulan to Tun-huang, whilst the Fundukistan route followed the Kabul valley, traversed Termez, which was an important staging point, and continued thence to Ecbatana. However, in the seventh century the T'angs were defeated by the Turks and forced to withdraw from the Tarim. They reoccupied it from AD 637 to 710, ruling over Transoxiana from 659 to 751, but they were defeated on the Talas by the Tivetans, who held the Tarim from 670 to 692. The Tarim was again cut off from China in 766, but by then the days of Buddhism were already numbered there.

The oases townlets had ample supplies of water and had the appearance so much admired at the time of garden cities. By the first century AD they had come to rank as important trading centres. The majority of their inhabitants were still of Indo-European speaking stock but, in the south, the number of Indian and Turkish residents was increasing rapidly. To begin with all used Khotanese as the international language, but when trade with the West became of prime importance Soghdian superseded it as the *lingua franca*. Then China's conquests in eastern Turkestan drew Chinese settlers to the area in such numbers that they soon ceased to be a minority and, even though Indian culture had by then taken firm root, that of China started in its turn to attract admirers. In so far as the arts were concerned it was obliged to blend with the existing styles, and in the process of doing so a new school of art, the Serindian, came into being.

Buddhism reached China in about the year 120 BC, mainly by way of the caravan route following the south-eastern oases route. It brought some native motifs with it, such as the lotus design. Sixty years later merchants from Taxila wishing to trade direct with China set out for the Tarim and China from north-western India and Afghanistan. They belonged to the Graeco-Roman cultural world and when they first came to the Tarim they used Roman seals engraved with the figures of Zeus or Pallas Athene, as well as of other classical deities. Many had been cut by Greek, Syrian or Bactrian jewellers and are similar to the seals used by the merchants at Niya (*Ill. 162*). Gradually the newcomers started to feel drawn to certain aspects of China's culture and to use Chinese seals, sometimes

163 Wooden chair from Niya. It is carved with designs which include the rosette which figures so often in contemporary arts of India and western Turkestan. Third century

164, 165 It has been suggested that the glazed pottery pilgrim flasks made for funeral purposes during the T'ang period (*left*) were inspired by pilgrim flasks made in Syria (*right*). Even the decoration of a flute player and dancer are of Western inspiration

stamping the same envelope with both a Chinese and a Western seal. At the same time, regardless of their nationality, Buddhist missionaries and pilgrims started to make converts among them and their Chinese neighbours. Indeed, numerous pilgrim flasks (*Ill. 164*) have been found in Chinese graves which, though unusable, and thus clearly intended for symbolic purposes, were modelled on Western prototypes which must have been introduced to eastern Turkestan by pilgrims from far afield. Basil Gray suggests that the flasks made in T'ang times in a glazed brown and green ware may have been copied from Syrian models dating from the time of the Arab conquest (*Ill. 165*). They were decorated with designs which he thinks probably inspired such figural works of the T'ang period as the pottery statuettes of dancers, musicians and riders in all of which he sees strong traces of Central Asian influences (*Ills. 166, 167, 168*). Though China lost control of the Tarim during the seventy-five years which followed the fall of the Han dynasty in AD 220, she

166, 167, 168 These three pieces of Chinese pottery all date from the T'ang period, and all reflect Western influence. (*Above left*) A Chorasmian dancer in glazed olive green, (*above right*) a youth in unglazed pottery who has distinctly Graeco-Roman features, and (*below*) a horsewoman playing polo, a game invented in Central Asia

nevertheless retained much of her influence and some of her powers in the south-eastern areas so that the trade continued to develop there and the attraction exercised by her artists made itself felt.

Numerous artistic currents flowed along the caravan routes leading to and from China. In addition to the Central Asian elements, the influence of Gupta India, which had already played so vital a part in forming the Buddhist art of central Afghanistan and which was now to leave a mark on Kashmir, China and Tibet, also penetrated to the Taklamakan, where it came in conflict with that of Sassanian Persia. Hellenism likewise reached the eastern cities both in the form into which it had been fashioned in Gandhara and also, according to Foucher, direct from the Western world. Its effect there was noted by Sir Aurel Stein who remarked that the paintings of Serindia 'reflect the Mediterranean delight in beauty, youth and life'. Grünwedel also refers to the presence of classical elements both at Kuça and in Khotan. Indo-Greek art was even produced in Kashgaria when it became a vigorous centre of Buddhist art and religion. Though Kashgaria fell under the influence of the Kizil school, yet both painting and sculpture developed there along the same broad lines as at Bamyan, with Hellenism remaining a potent force even when Chinese influence had become so pervasive that the final products were essentially Sino-Buddhist in character.

As Buddhism advanced towards the Taklamakan, Kashgaria with Yarkand and Khotan in the west, Tumsuk, Aksu and Kizil in the north, Sorçuk and Karasahr in the east, and Miran and Cerčen in the south became important centres of Buddhist art and thought. Kumtura contained within its cultural sphere the thriving monastic – and the term is in this context virtually synonymous with artistic – centres of Kizil and Kuça. These in their turn transmitted their artistic styles to religious strongholds such as those of Sorçuk, Karasahr, Koço and Turfan, all of which could keep in direct touch with Tun-huang by means of a subsidiary road. Tun-huang's artists encountered in addition styles which, though evolved in the Khotanese area, had undergone alterations in such places as Dandan-Uilik as they travelled north-eastward along the southern caravan route, passing as they did so through such artistic and religious centres as Keriya, Niya, Cerčen and, above all, Miran and Loulan in the Lopnor.

The sculptures and paintings from which we derive our knowledge of Serindian art were unknown until 1889 when Sir Aurel Stein discovered the first of the Taklamakan's buried cities. A Russian expedition set out to explore the area in 1897 and the German scholar A. von Le Coq soon followed their example. Like the religious art of Byzantium, the Buddhist art of Turkestan sets out to express abstract, mystical ideas by means of colour within a firmly defined iconographic form. But whereas Byzantium's Christian art was created for a nation revolving round a highly sophisticated court and clergy, that of Serindia set out to win the devotion of the relatively uneducated masses such as soldiers, traders and caravan leaders. Each faith evolved its own symbolism based on its own particular philosophy. Buddhism's concern with light and its relationship with Buddha was easily comprehensible to people familiar with the Zoroastrian and Mazdaian doctrines. As Bussagli has pointed out, Central Asia's artists must thus have devoted a great deal of thought to the inner meaning of light and colour. Their paintings, and more especially those of Buddhist eastern Turkestan, reflect their profound preoccupation with light and shade effects.

As in the Kushan empire so in the Taklamakan the majority of the Buddhist buildings which have come down to us are in the form of monasteries. The larger ones grew up in districts where the existence of numerous natural grottos and caves suitable for conversion into shrines and cells for the monks reduced the need for building to a minimum. Later many of the caves which had been used as shrines or temples were altered and enlarged, cylindrical vaults being chiselled into them and corbels cut to serve as bases for the domes which were hollowed out of the rock. Some grottoes were on the other hand given flat roofs with grooves cut in them to imitate the carved wooden beams usual in domestic architecture of the period. In all the shrines the main statues were free standing; they were placed in the centre of each grotto to enable the faithful to walk round them in the prescribed manner. The statues were usually made

169 Printed silk textile from Chien fo-Tung. Chinese textile makers often turned to Central Asia for their inspiration, and this piece shows horses, their flanks decorated with swastikas, which occur also on the Hasanlu bowl (*Ill. 55*)

of stucco and followed traditional lines, Indo-Greek conventions coming to the fore in Kashgaria, which ranked as an important Buddhist centre from the first to the tenth century A D, as well as in north-western India and Gandhara.

In the northern area, and more particularly in the Sorçuk district, the number of grottoes which were transformed into sanctuaries was so great that the word Mingoi, meaning 'A Thousand Caves', was used to describe the region. With the years it has come to be associated with the sculptures which adorned these shrines. These consist both of large, traditional figures of Buddhas and Bodhissattvas, as well as of numerous smaller, more individualistic works depicting with quite remarkable vivacity and precision people of every age and walk of life (*Ills. 171, 172, 173, 174*). They are as skilfully executed as the larger figures. In addition they reveal a remarkable understanding of portraiture and a keen sense of actuality, with a correspondingly sensitive grasp of pathos and humour.

170 Chinese figured silk from Loulan. The prototype for the lions which, amidst their setting of Chinese scrolls decorate this silk of the Han dynasty, is perhaps to be sought in the ▶ blue glazed tile lion frieze at Susa, rather than in China's own repertory of animal design

171, 172, 173, 174 (*left*) Carved stucco statuette of a warrior wearing armour almost identical to that worn by the knights in Soghdian and Chorasmian paintings. (*above right*) Stucco horse, recalling models from Persia of Assyrian and Achaemenid times. (*far right*) Camel, probably one of Bactrian breed, and (*below right*) head of a laughing boy, which can be paralleled in Kushan, Bactrian and Parthian art. All these carved stucco statuettes come from the Mingoi caves near Sorçuk, and although dating from the eighth to tenth century, they retain many points that link them to more westerly art of a far earlier date

Along the north-western route sculpture and painting developed along very much the same lines as at Bamyan, with Hellenism persisting, as at Yun-kang, into the fourth century, when it was superseded by the Indo-Iranian and Chinese elements forming the Sino-Buddhist style. Virtually nothing dating from the earlier period has been discovered at Kumtura where the Chinese lost their monopoly in silk (*Ills. 169, 170*) in the fifth century when cocoons reached Khotan. The earliest works to survive are assigned to the eighth century, in the third phase of Sino-Buddhist art; however, the first of these overlap with paintings of the second phase from Kizil. In the latter the people have the serene aloofness with which both the Sassanian and Chinese strove to invest their monumental figural works, but it is combined with the passionate gestures which must

have been learnt either from Gandharan intermediaries or, as Basil Gray suggests, from Indian silver work based on the type of carved Indian ivory panels which also inspired the Bigram ivories. In addition, the style reveals links with that practised at Varaksha. By the eighth century, however, Chinese influence, and more especially that of artists of the T'ang school, had become dominant. Indeed, with her preference for *Mahayana* Buddhism China might well have become the cultural leader of the north-western oases towns had not Western influences, and more particularly that of Sassanian stucco sculptures, penetrated to Sorçuk and Karasahr to equalize the situation. It is slightly ironical that it should have been the Manichaeans fleeing from Sassanian persecutions who were largely responsible for disseminating these Western, and more especially Sassanian elements throughout eastern Turkestan. However, Soghdian merchants also helped to transmit them together with certain details of their own costumes. The Sassanians also, helped to popularize their native arts, but, at Sorçuk, where the style is less narrative than at Kuça, and where T'ang realism breaks through, local conventions persist, even if tempered, as in the Mingoi caves, by Khotanese influence.

175 (*left*) Wall-painting of swimmers. The art of Kizil was strongly influenced by India and it is interesting to compare the treatment of the heads to *Ill. 140. c. 500*

176 (*right*) Amongst the ▶ loveliest of Kizil's many paintings is this goddess and celestial musician, who seem to express the beauty of heavenly harmonies by the delicate and graceful curves of their bodies. *c.* 600–800

177 Wall-painting of four female donors from Sorçuk who are vested with a personality and spirit of actuality which distinguishes them from the paintings of saintly personages. Eighth–ninth century

By annexing Kuça in 383 the Chinese made it possible for Buddhism to enter China, even though it was not till 658 that they chose the town as the headquarters of the Tarim region. Like Bamyan, Kuça quickly developed into a leading centre of *Hinayana* Buddhism and the earliest paintings to survive in the district, notably at Kizil, date from the first century whilst the latest are assigned to the eighth or very shortly after.

The earliest paintings in the Kuça region form a distinct group. To begin with they were strongly Indo-Persian in style, but the Persian elements quickly supplanted the Indian, to be in their turn overlaid in the sixth century by the Chinese. Kizil and Kumtura (*Ill. 178*), close to Kuça, created a school of a rich and varied character. One of the loveliest of its paintings is of a goddess with a celestial musician (*Ill. 176*). Artists of this school, like those of Byzantium, were fond of arranging their figures in rows rather than in tiers as was done in Gandhara. Bussagli notes that at the time when Indian influence was paramount artists took an obvious interest in such technical matters as volumes, contours and relief effects, but that, within another century, they had ceased to do so and their figural paintings became flatter and more stylized as a result. He ascribes this to the arrival in the East of Nestorian missionaries who

178 Wall-painting of a Bodhissatva from Kumtura which reflects the attention paid to volume and draperies absent at Kizil, where the style is more frontal and direct, and thus reminiscent of the Soghdian school. Eighth–ninth century

instinctively worked in the Byzantine manner which thus came to some extent to supplant the Indian (*Ill. 182*). Many of the earlier artists of the Kuça school also attempted to introduce architectural backgrounds into their works and endeavoured to master the laws of perspective; occasionally they signed their works. Fantastic backgrounds were also produced at this time, but geometric ones are more characteristic of the period. Some of the more decorative scenes include swimmers rendered in a style which recalls that of the famous painting of the bathers of Kizil (*Ill. 175*). Soghdian influence is, on the other hand, more clearly felt at Kumtura than at Kuça.

The Kizil paintings are the most important of this group, and this not so much because of any marked superiority in quality or individuality of style, but rather because more of them survive, with the result that it is they which furnish us with a complete time sequence for dating purposes. Thus Hackin assigned the earliest Kizil paintings to the period AD 450 to 650, with the second phase ending in about 750. As in Fundukistan so at Kizil the influence of Soghdia and Bactria is reflected in the cut of the clothes, more

180 (*left*) Four
ors from Kizil,
ng from the
nth century. It
teresting to note
similarity in
of the clothes
n in western
kestan (*Ill. 83*).
contrast Indian
ience is still
ngly apparent in
early wall-
ting, the Dance
Queen Candra-
ha (*right*), also
Kizil, which
s from AD 500,
n Indian influ-
prevailed in
area

particularly in those worn by donors (*Ill. 179*), whose tunics often
have the characteristically Soghdian single revere. Many of the ornaments, furnishing and armour which appear in the paintings, no less
than the proportions of the figures, also recall Central Asian prototypes yet, as in the rest of the Taklamakan area, the main influence
is still Hellenistic, and this is especially the case in the pictures of
Buddha. On the other hand, the women are closer in style to Indian
than to Iranian or Greek conceptions whilst the men are closer to
Sassanian models. Indeed, even during the last phase, though artists
were using highlights of the Chinese type, many of the men still
retained a markedly Persian appearance. At Kizil, as in the rest of the
medieval world, the more important personages are larger in size
than the others. Most of the paintings are of a narrative character.
Representations of hell were especially numerous in the seventh
century when the artists attempted to model limbs by means of
shading whilst outlining the contours of the bodies with a dark line.

181 Indian influence, combined with Graeco-Roman, is evident in this head of a young ascetic from the Cave of the Navigator at Kizil. *c.* 500

Paintings such as that of 'The Dance of Queen Candrapartha' (*Ill. 180*) are closely in sympathy with works of the Indian School, yet they adhere to the proportions followed at Piandjikent. However, the assymetric treatment of the scene, the sense of space and movement and the delicate colours, vividly recall the style which flourished not only in Bactria but also in Soghdia. Some of the Kizil artists were clearly striving to achieve decorative effects and in doing so they showed a marked preference for bright colours and lapis blue (*Ill. 182*). Later this was to some extent replaced by a striving for symmetry and it was then that Sassanian motifs such as ducks, pigeons and wild boars enclosed in pearl-studded roundels became popular. In contrast the sculptures at Kizil and Kuça have a touch of the Mingoi element which had made itself felt at Bamyan. The influence of both Taxila and Hadda can also be traced in them, though to a much lesser degree.

Turfan came under Chinese influence at an early date even though, in Han times, the nomads coveted it and many Turks settled there, mingling with its basically Indo-European speaking population. In

182 By the first half of the seventh century, when this head of the Ascetic Mahakasyapa was painted at Kizil, Western, and in this case, Byzantine, influence had reached the area, probably brought by Nestorian missionaries

the sixth century it fell to the Sui dynasty of China and in 640 it passed into the hands of the T'ang rulers, but even then it did not completely sever its links with Central Asia. These dated from early times and had been strengthened by the establishment of the northern caravan route round the Taklamakan. The T'ang rulers had been helped to power by the Uygurs who then proceeded to convert them to Manichaeanism and to introduce them to Persian art. The Chinese were grateful to the Uygurs for their military aid and expressed their appreciation by giving them Chinese princesses in marriage, but in 846 a passionate movement in favour of Confucianism swept across China. The Buddhists were overthrown and even the Uygurs were obliged, as Buddhists, to leave China. They moved to eastern Turkestan, to Tien-shan and Semirechie, eventually ruling over Turfan and the north-eastern section of the Tarim as far as Karasahr, near Sorçuk. Others fled to Khotan, Yarkand, Kashgar and Hami, but it was Turfan and Koço which developed into the

193

main Uygur centres. For a time Koço served the Uygurs as their capital even though the bulk of its inhabitants were Aryans speaking an Indo-European tongue. It was there that some Uygur intellectuals became converted to Christianity by the Nestorians, but the majority remained staunch Buddhists.

The Uygurs were hard-working and intelligent. They quickly learnt to grow vines and, by adopting Soghdian methods, they succeeded in transforming the Semirechie into a prosperous agricultural district and the centre of an efficiently run iron industry. They continued to delight in the Indo-Persian customs of their forebears, but the Nestorians taught them to respect dogma and ritual. Their monks were well educated; many knew Chinese and most were able to study the Buddhist texts written in that language though the majority used the Manichaean alphabet, whilst some preferred the Soghdian. The range of their learning is reflected in the astonishing diversity of books which Sir Aurel Stein discovered in the Monastery of the Thousand Buddhas, near Tun-huang, where the library had been walled up in the eleventh century. Its thousands of books were in excellent condition when Stein penetrated into the library and found there the world's oldest block-printed book (*Ill. 183*). It was published in China in the year A D 860, and its discovery has led to the belief that the art of block-printing may have been introduced into Europe from China by the invading Mongols. Many books in the library had been written on silk paper, others on the earliest rag paper known to us; some were in Chinese, some in Aramaic and some in the Syrian version of Soghdian used by the Manichaeans. The great majority were in the cursive Buddhist script of Central Asia, others in Syriac, some in Tibetan. According to Sir Aurel Stein all the canonical literary works had been written in areas where Chinese influence prevailed, as for example in Tun-huang. There were also some Uygur books in the library, several of which had been embellished with illuminations. These likewise consisted of Buddhist texts written for the most part in Soghdian in an alphabet derived from the Syriac, but some were in the runic Turkish used by the Orkhon Turks. In all these the paper had been folded and stitched in the Chinese manner. A unique find was the

183 Scroll from Tun-huang illustrating Buddha addressing Subhuti. This copy of the Diamond Sutra is the earliest example of block printing known to the world. 868

discovery of an original Turkish literary work dated to the eighth century. It is the oldest of its kind in existence, but already it is written in the form of a series of short stories of almost anecdotal character about people and. animals interspersed with moral comments and precepts in the manner adopted by the gifted group of north Persian poets of the twelfth century, such as Anwari of Tus and Suzani of Samarkand. They transmitted the tradition to the Turks where writers as different as the Sufi poet and theologian Celal ed'Din al-Rumi and the compiler of the 'Tales of the Nazereddin Hoca' adhered to it.

Uygur buildings have been found within recent times in the Ili and Chu valleys, across the Tien-shan. They are profusely decorated with paintings which are only slightly later in date than those which have been discovered in the Turfan area, but they are very like them, and more especially resemble those in the temple at Balasagun in Soviet territory. However, it is the Uygur paintings at Koço that most truly represents Uygur art (*Ills. 184, 185*). Koço was called

195

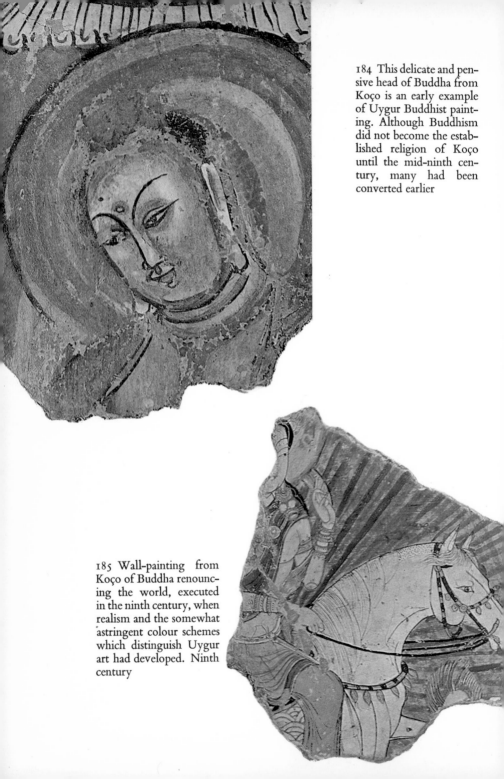

184 This delicate and pensive head of Buddha from Koço is an early example of Uygur Buddhist painting. Although Buddhism did not become the established religion of Koço until the mid-ninth century, many had been converted earlier

185 Wall-painting from Koço of Buddha renouncing the world, executed in the ninth century, when realism and the somewhat astringent colour schemes which distinguish Uygur art had developed. Ninth century

186 Wall-painting from Koço, thought to represent Mani with his followers. Before the advent of Buddhism, Koço had been a Manichaean stronghold, and it retained numerous adherents afterwards. Ninth century

Idigutschai, meaning city of Ilgut, by the Uygurs in honour of a Turkish hero of that name when they chose it as their capital. At first almost wholly Manichaean, having been founded by Mani (*Ill. 186*) in the third century, it soon attracted numerous Nestorians. Buddhism reached the town soon after the year 840 and took so firm a hold in this Manichaean stronghold that it survived the Uygur collapse in the tenth century to flourish there till the fourteenth. During the early phase of their art Persian and Indian influences receded in the face of the Chinese for the Uygurs were irresistibly attracted by the realism of T'ang art. However, under pressure from the Mazdaians and Nestorians, Persian elements regained their hold throughout the seventh and eighth centuries. It was then that a remarkable series of portraits painted on silk were produced (*Ill. 189*). In each case a single sitter was portrayed on a large silk panel in a hieratic pose, yet often shown holding a flower in one hand. The paintings combine physical exactitude with real psychological insight. After about the year 750 it became usual to inscribe the names of the sitters on the paintings; generally only

187, 188 Two wall-paintings from Bezeklik of a prince (*left*) and (*right*) two princesses.
interest which the Uygurs took in figural art led them to create a school which w
profoundly influence Persian and India miniature painting of Islamic times. Ninth cen

kings and soldiers of distinction appeared on these panels; sometimes,
however, monks dressed in robes cut on Indian lines were also
included. The military personages are generally painted in armour
of a somewhat heterogenous character for certain items of their
equipment recall Assyrian models and others Gandharan ones, but
.those made of solid pieces of engraved metal are obviously of local
origin. The helmets and shields, however, often resemble Persian
ones. The portraits are painted in a manner and style which fore-
shadows very similar pictures of a far smaller size produced by
Islamic painters in Persia. The Mongols also adopted the style,
adhering to it even more closely than the Persians, and so too
occasionally did the Chinese working in the Mongol period (*Ills. 190,
191*). Uygur work of the ninth century is less good than in earlier
times, but accomplished regional variations of the Koço school were

189 Silk portrait of an elderly prince from Koço. Ninth century

190, 191 (*above*) Persian miniature of a Turcoman prisoner, *c.* 1575, and (*left*) a portrait of Ghengis Khan, serve to show how the later schools of Persia were influenced by the artists of Bezeklik (*Ills. 187, 188*)

produced at Murduk and Bezeklik (*Ills. 187, 188*) during the closing phase.

At Bezeklik east of Kumtura, Gupta elements blended with the Chinese with the result that draperies came to be schematically rendered. At Sorçuk a temple contained paintings of knights wearing armour very similar to that shown in the frescoes not only of Kizil and Kumtura, but also of Soghdia. Another scene included some men wearing Arab dress and a saddle cloth bearing an Arabic inscription. They prove that the Uygurs had by then established relations with Islam. Murduk's art was more eclectic than that of Bezeklik. Here too knights wore the same type of armour as that current at Sorçuk and Kizil, but their helmets resemble those belonging to Sassanian Persia and, perhaps as a result of their contacts with the Western world, Buddha is represented there seated in the European manner.

Koço's Nestorian paintings (*Ills. 194, 195*) are particularly well

192 This wall-painting of a dragon leaping out of water from Bezeklik illustrates the sense of fantasy and colour which the Uygurs developed under Chinese influence during the ninth and tenth centuries

193 Wall-painting of musicians from Bezeklik shows that Turkish popular art, as it survives in the figures of the painted Karagoz parchment, had its roots in this animated painting of the eighth century

194 Palm Sunday. A wall-painting from the Nestorian temple at Koço where the Nestorians formed a small but influential community. Late ninth century

composed. They also reveal a keen feeling for space, and those which reflect Persian or Byzantine influences also display a clear under-standing of linear rhythm. Both the Nestorian and the Manichaean paintings in the area are enhanced by frequent touches of Chinese elegance. These appear in the backgrounds even of those paintings which adhere to Persian models. In some scenes the more customary architectural backgrounds are replaced by imaginary, romantic ones which stem from India. The demons which figure in so many of them are probably likewise of Indian origin, yet both the back-grounds themselves and the fierce creatures which inhabit them fore-shadow many aspects of Islamic painting. Links with Chorasmia are evident in the scenes in which the people, though shown full face, incline their heads, whilst the inclusion in later times of people of distinctly Mongoloid appearance testifies to the growing importance of that race of warriors.

Turfan, with the Sassanian elements in its sculpture and painting, together with Kuça, Kizil and Piandjikent surely influenced both the Buddhist art of Tibet and the Islamic art of the Ghaznavids, Samanids and Seljukid Turks. Mongol painters appear, on the other hand, to have been more deeply affected by the Uygurs for the figural art which the latter created did not die out when Koço and Tun-huang declined, but lived on among the Tunguz Khata who ruled over much of northern China and penetrated into Turkestan in the eleventh century. Furthermore, it was from the Uygurs that the western Mongols acquired their language and their alphabet.

Some of the Buddhist paintings which have been found in eastern Turkestan seem to be earlier in date than any that have so far been discovered in the vicinity of the Tumsuk–Turfan caravan route.

195 Woman worshipper, again from the Nestorian temple at Koço. This wall-painting recalls the donors in *Ill. 179*, although Uygur influence is probably responsible for the greater realism. Late ninth century

196 Painted wooden panel from Dandan-Uilik of two young horsemen, one riding a speckled horse, the other a camel. This probably depicts a religious ceremony, for the youths hold libation cups similar in shape to those which can be seen in the libation scenes of western Turkestan. *c.* seventh century

197 Wooden panel fr Dandan-Uilik which flects something of spirit of Kushan art. four-armed, three-fa deity sitting cross-leg in the yoga pose may represent the divi whom the Khota weavers chose as t patron. *c.* seventh cen

Khotan with neighbouring Yotkan must have played a very important part in developing the art of that south-eastern area, and to some extent also of China, for it became a major Buddhist centre in quite early times. Many monasteries are known to have existed there, but the greedy sands of the Taklamakan have swallowed them up and the ruins of only a few have been excavated. However, in c. AD 400 the Chinese pilgrim Fa-hsien saw them in all their glory, with their shrines replete with stucco statues, many of which were gilt. Here too Indo-Hellenism provided the basic ingredients of a style which also included Gandharan and Chinese elements combined with local forms. The frequency with which certain motifs, such as the Ganymede myth, the earth goddess, Nikes, wind deities, acrobats, sun-chariots, Buddha represented as an ascetic and ritual scenes recur must surely be ascribed to the influence of Indian Buddhists and thus ultimately of Greeks.

The shrines containing paintings and statues that have been discovered in south-eastern Turkestan date from the first ten centuries of the present era, and generally take the form of cave rather than free-standing buildings. In the paintings both Buddhas and Bodhisattvas are generally over life-size, their height being further accentuated by the small dimensions of the worshippers crouching at their feet. Their heads are generally surrounded by large haloes. When the small eighth-century temple of Dandan-Uilik near Khotan was excavated the external walls were found to have been adorned originally with paintings which included figural scenes. One showed a group of youths riding camels and horses, each of them holding a cup in one outstretched hand whilst a bird swooped down from heaven to accept the offering (*Ill. 196*). This theme was a popular one at the time. Some of the riders in the Dandan-Uilik version are Chinese looking, others Persian, and more particularly Sassanian. All have haloes to indicate that they are not only legendary but also holy personages. Dandan-Uilik was abandoned in 791, but in T'ang times Chinese influence had made itself particularly strongly felt there. It is easily observable in all the paintings of the Khotanese school with the exception of those of Dymoko in eastern Khotan, where the figures are two dimensional and presented frontally as in

198 Early examples of Tibetan art are extremely rare and seldom found outside Tibet. However, this sixteenth-century banner showing the Bodhisattva Namasangiti surrounded by divinities and emblems is a fine and charactertistic example of the work produced in western Tibet by a school of artists who delighted in profuse detail yet possessed the ability to create compositions of a monumental character

the Indianized panel-paintings from Dandan-Uilik (*Ill. 197*). However, even when Khotanese paintings conformed most closely to Chinese conventions, symbols of Indian origin continued to figure with the result that the Khotanese Buddhists soon came to regard their presence essential.

The Khotanese school of painting centred round the monasteries of Rawak, Dandan-Uilik, Niya and Endere was so much admired in contemporary China that certain Chinese artists were influenced by it. In late Sui times, that is to say in about A D 620, the works of the Khotanese artists Weich-in the elder and the younger were especially sought after in China's capital Ch'an-gan. The Khotanese school was also greatly esteemed in Tibet. Though the Tibetans had originally practised a form of devil worship resembling Shamanism, the marriage in 641 of one of their rulers to a Chinese princess marked the dawn of a new era in the country's history, for it coincided with the entry of Buddhism into Tibet. The creed reached Tibet from India, and not in any way as a result of the royal marriage. It came untouched by Hellenistic or Chinese art forms so that, from the start, Tibet's Buddhist practices followed those of India, adhering to the form of *Hinayana* Buddhism evolved many centuries earlier by its Indian founder, Prince Gautamo. He was born in about 620 B C, but his written works had been collected into an anthology by Kanishka, king of the Kushans, and a Tibetan translation of Kanishka's volume appeared in the first half of the seventh century A D. Gautamo's doctrine of non-attachment to material things appealed strongly to Tibet's small Buddhist community, for even in the eighth century the new faith was far from popular there and numbered only few adherents. However, Tibetan Buddhists had by then already adopted the elaborate ritual and galaxy of deities on which *Mahayana* Buddhism had come to depend; it had even widened its range to include the native form of Ponpo or animistic worship, and by then it was already too late for them to alter their ritual. Then an Indian preacher from the Buddhist University of Nalanda called Padonasambhava was invited to preach in Tibet. Whilst there he fused and transformed the Ponpo and *Mahayana* creeds into Tibetan Lamaism, and founded the sect of the Red Cap

199 This bronze figure of Maitreya succeeds admirably in combining elegance and the serene aloofness characteristic of Buddhist art with a feeling of vitality, which is shown in the treatment of the figure's shoulders and waist as well as from the linear rendering of the drapery. Tibet, fifteenth century

monks. They went about the country preaching his doctrine and it was quickly accepted by most Buddhists as well as by many Ponpo-ists. In 975 a new sect, that of the White Cap, was founded by the teacher Tilopu and the most widely loved of the White Sect saints, Mila-nepa. It too rapidly gained converts and the arrival in the tenth century of a new wave of monks seeking safety from Chinese persecutions greatly stimulated religious thought and the growth of monasticism. The monks were followed into Tibet by Khotanese artists bringing with them their own styles and iconographic tradi-tions which they imposed on the Tibetans. As a result the latter did

200 Wooden panel painted with three Bodhisattvas seated in the Oriental manner from Dandan-Uilik. The elegance and delicacy of line, together with the sense of movement, distinguishes the Khotanese schools from others. *c.* eighth century

not develop an artistic style of their own till well into the twelfth century.

Both Tibetan sects encouraged the inclusion of numerous deities in the decoration of their temples. Each Buddha in the Tibetan hierarchy was invested with a personal symbol and a colour appertaining to his rank, thus, for example, Vairocana was awarded dragon white, Ratnashumbava lion yellow, Akehobuya elephant blue and so on. Painted or embroidered banners (*Ill. 198*), many of them works of great beauty, came into use in the tenth century when painted replicas of these banners also started to appear on the walls of the poorer temples and shrines, besides paintings depicting religious ceremonies and divinities. Some of the banners were painted on canvas, some on paper and, occasionally, some on silk. The native style appears more clearly in them than on the wall-paintings, the subjects chosen to be shown on them being strongly mystical in content as well as including ritual dances. The work is generally delicate and evocative, gestures assuming an Indian expressiveness. All the paints used by Tibet's artists, with the exception of the blues and greens which were produced at Lhasa, had to be imported; yellows came from Kansu, red from both India and

201 Wooden panel showing the so-called Silk Princess from Dandan-Uilik. Silk played an all-important part in the economy of China and of the oasis towns along the caravan routes. *c.* seventh century

China, gold from Nepal. Reds, blues and greens predominate in Tibetan painting, perhaps partly for economic reasons. They are generally deep in tone and seldom strident as in certain Uygur works. Scenes are always presented against a background of clouds, hills or fruit and often include agitated figures. From the seventh century, when King Srong Tsan Gampo evolved the Tibetan alphabet from the Sanscrit and sent the Tibetan scholar Thonni Sambhota to Magadha to obtain a supply of religious books, calligraphy came to be regarded in Tibet as a fine art equalling painting in importance.

Sculpture was as widely practised in Tibet as painting (*Ill. 199*). Executed in anything malleable ranging from gold to butter it is believed to have been introduced into the country in the seventh century by two princesses, one a Chinese, the other a Nepalese, both wives of King Srong Tsan Gampo. It was they who were responsible for converting the king to Buddhism and persuading him to send to India for the holy images and texts necessary for the dissemination of the new faith. Both princesses must have been women of great strength of character for China and Nepal exercised an equal influence over Tibet's sculptors; as a result their statues of Buddha

are less stylized than the Chinese and are both smaller and also more delicate in style, conforming in their elegance to Indian standards of beauty. The inclusion of numerous nude female figures in Tibetan art is also in accordance with Indian tradition, but the treatment of the draperies seems to stem from the late phase of Gandharan sculpture.

But to revert to the oases cities on the south-eastern Taklamakan caravan route. In these a variety of styles, all of them of Khotanese inspiration, flourished simultaneously (*Ill. 200*). Yotkan was one of the more important of these towns. In Han times it established close links with China and also kept in regular touch with the Kushans at the time when Kanishka's influence was making itself felt among the artists of Khotan. As a result in early Buddhist times the art of Yotkan acquired a more marked Kushan flavour than did that of its neighbours. At Tarisluk the style is closer to that of Kizil and of Central Asia than of India. Many of the clothes shown on its paintings recall those of Balalyk Tepe. As at Dandan-Uilik, and more particularly in the enchanting painting of the Silk Princess (*Ill. 201*), the figures are elongated in accordance with Soghdian principles.

202, 203 Wall-paintings from Miran. They constitute the earliest of all Buddhist paintings to survive in Central Asia and owe their style to the artist Titus who signed one of the paintings. (*left*) Youths holding garlands show Western influence. (*right*) A religious scene. The convention of large eyes which is characteristic of the school may owe its origin to the influence of Coptic paintings. Late third century

At the same time the four-armed divinities were inspired by India (*Ill. 201*). The cup and short bladed knife which were used there as well as in other parts of Central Asia to symbolize Bodhisattvas frequently recur; their presence is in accordance with the *Mahayana* form of Buddhism favoured in Khotan.

Khotan also influenced the Buddhist communities which had grown up in the more distant staging points along the Tun-huang caravan route, and particularly in the important religious and artistic centre of Miran. During the third and fourth century AD numerous monasteries had come into being there which soon acquired a great many shrines and religious statues. Many of the shrines were set up in caves, the walls and ceilings of which were covered with paintings. Paintings also often appeared on stupas and in one case the scenes included one of children wearing Phrygian caps and carrying garlands (*Ill. 202*). Their appearance vividly recalls similar motifs produced in Hadda and Gandhara where they had been inspired by designs of cherubs made in Antioch. The Miran children are Oriental in appearance but their presentation recalls the Parthian style of Dura Europos.

Miran's art stemmed from India and Gandhara, but it was of a subtler character than either of these. Her artists treated perspective in the same way as did those of Gandhara and, in accordance with Buddhist practices, they attached great importance to figural art. It is indeed tempting to suggest that China may have acquired her interest in the human figure from Miran, where such renderings are particularly lovely, and that Tun-huang may have owed its delight in landscape and its preoccupation with real and imaginary animals to China, though the interest in fantastic beasts could equally well have been aroused by the Huns. Miran probably acquired the Graeco-Roman elements in its art by means of direct contacts with the West rather than indirectly.

Tun-huang adopted Miran's style and iconography as the basis for its own school of art. Indeed, Miran became the centre which influenced contemporary artists working at Niya, Cerčen and Loulan. Its importance, at any rate in so far as painting is concerned, is largely to be ascribed to the skill of an artist who signed some of his works with the name Titus. Sir Aurel Stein sums up his artistic style by describing Titus (*Serindia I*, 538) as 'a sort of Roman Eurasian by blood, brought up in the Hellenistic tradition . . . whom his calling had carried no doubt through the regions of eastern Iran, impregnated with Buddhism, to the confines of China'. Titus must undoubtedly also have been familiar with Byzantine painting for his draperies are modelled in the classic manner in which it appears in Byzantium. His use of chiaroscuro also reflects Byzantine influence; so too perhaps do the large eyes (*Ill. 203*) which are characteristic of the figural paintings of the Miran school and which could equally well have been inspired by Syria as by Coptic Egypt. Bussagli noticed that certain scenes recur in the Miran paintings without any very perceptible variations and considers this repetitiveness a sign of the existence there of a semi-industrialized art. If so, it must have grown up round Titus's studio.

It is now evident that, together with Koço and Miran, Tun-huang

204 Shrine at Tun-huang richly decorated with paintings and sculpture. The paintings cover the walls and ceilings in green, pink, pale blue, white and black often on a red ground. The sculpture, in this case Buddha and Bodhisattvas, are impressive, combining draperies treated in the flowing Hellenistic manner with a more linear and formal style. Eighth century

205 Silk hanging from Tun-
huang showing a Bodhisattva
standing on an open lotus,
holding a mottled green glass
bowl in his right hand.
Draped with flowing robes,
he is typical of the 'Chinese'
Bodhisattvas

206 Statue of a Lokapala in painted clay from Tun-huang. Eighth century

deserves to rank as a very important centre of Buddhist art. Buddhism reached it by way of both the northern and southern Taklamakan routes. The Monastery of a Thousand Buddhas is an outstanding example of this art. The monastery is situated in what has become the desert's edge and the insatiable sands have already covered much of its outlying territory. When Sir Aurel Stein visited the monastery several monks were still living there and the shrines remained revered places of pilgrimage. The monastery was founded in *c.* 333 on a site abounding with grottoes and caves. As the number of its inmates grew so did that of the caves which were brought into use as shrines. Eventually the whole area presented a vast complex of walls and shrines. Most of the buildings have now crumbled, but although no decorations dating from the fourth century survive many of the caves still contain the statues of Buddhas and Bodhisattvas which were set up in them many centuries ago (*Ill. 204*). They are for the most part made of stucco modelled with great skill. The delicate features of these deities are sometimes executed in the Graeco-Bactrian style, sometimes in that of Gandhara, and this also

217

207 Detail of a wall-painting from Tun-huang showing dancing ladies

208 Statues of the disciples Ananda and Kasyapa from Tunhuang. They are typical of the expressive, emotional style which appears at Tun-huang beside the reserved and formal one that is associated with Buddhist art. Early seventh century

applies to the many minor figures, such as satyrs, introduced into the decorations of the shrines. The paintings take the form both of murals and of figural compositions executed on either silk or gauze (*Ill. 205*). In the earlier works the iconography conforms to that established by Chinese artists of the first half of the fifth century but both the paintings and the sculptures range in date from T'ang and Sung to Yung times. The majority of the styles remain throughout predominantly Chinese, the Chinese element being most clearly apparent in scenes illustrating the lives of monks and in the floral motifs – its presence is easier to recognize if these works are compared to the more Indianized ones produced at Dandan-Uilik or even in Khotan. In contrast the draperies, poses and facial expressions continue to be rendered with the severity which characterizes the Graeco-Buddhist school, and this remains the case even when the linear treatment and grouping disclose a clear kinship with India. The colours which predominate are Malachite green, pink, pale blue, white and black set, as at Varaksha, against a red ground.

In the Tun-huang school figures are again often outlined with a dark, generally blue, line, but the highlights are applied in the Chinese manner as it is seen at Kizil. The scenes are based on scriptural texts and presented in sections, recalling the arrangement of the sculptures on Gandharan stupas. Nevertheless, the paintings must be regarded as offshoots of the Chinese school, more particularly of Shatung and Honan, rather than of Central Asia. On the other hand their colours are so brilliant that Stein was inclined to ascribe them to Tibetan influence. That Tibet should have left a mark on the region's art is scarcely surprising since, in the second half of the eighth century, Tun-huang lay in what Stein described as China's Western Marches, and was thus constantly in danger of being overrun by the Tibetans. Thus, when in 709, the Arabs conquered Bokhara, and a few years later occupied Tashkent and continued to advance into Ferghana, forcing the latter's prince to turn to China for protection and military aid, though the Chinese came to his help and reinstated him on his throne, at the same time forcing the emirs of Bokhara and Samarkand to recognize their authority, yet they were unable to exploit their success because of fear of the Tibetans. The latter had chosen that moment to march on China and the Chinese were obliged to abandon operations in Central Asia in order to hold the invader's advance. Even so, the Tibetans conquered Tun-huang in 759 and used it as a base first for the wars which they were engaged in waging against the eastern Turks and then, from about 790, as a springboard from which to attack the Chinese troops guarding the northern and southern borders of the Tien-shan. Indeed, in the eighth century Tibet was a major power in the east, holding much of Kansu as well as a tongue of territory stretching into central China. Nevertheless, China regained Tun-huang in 938 and, under the Sung emperors, her influence once again made itself felt in eastern Turkestan. However, in the course of the eighth century the growing influence of the Muslims in western Central Asia and of the Confucians in China resulted in the decline of Buddhism, and with it, of figural art. After 815 or so Chinese art went its own way in eastern Turkestan whilst in western Turkestan the rise of Muslim dynasties of Turkish origin, such as the Samanid, Ghaznavid and Seljukid introduced a new, early Islamic type of art to Central Asia, Persia and Anatolia, thus opening another chapter in the long history of the arts of these regions.

CHAPTER SIX

Armenia, Georgia and Caucasian Albania in Early Christian times

During the centuries when Buddhism was shaping life, religion and thought in eastern Turkestan and Islam was becoming the motive force in western Turkestan, Christianity was establishing firm roots in the Caucasian area and more especially in the countries which were known to their contemporaries as Armenia, Iberia (the heart of Caucasian Georgia) and Caucasian Albania. These three western states extended over Transcaucasia and what are known to us today as Azarbeidjan and southern Daghestan. At the start Armenia was perhaps the most important of the three since it is mentioned in Darius's Bisitun inscription. The Armenians were an Indo-European speaking peoples called Cai who probably originally came from the Erzincan area, in what is now eastern Turkey, but at the time of the retreat of Xenophon's Ten Thousand they already occupied much of the territory to the west of the Tigris and parts of the Euphrates region, though the river still separated them from Cilicia. They do not appear to have been in contact at the time with either Babylon, Phoenicia or India, but they had begun to trade with Anapa, near the Sea of Azov. By about 585 BC they were living in the region of Lake Van and the great imperial high-road described by Herodotus traversed their territory. The Persians called them Armena and their neighbours considered them good agriculturalists, horticulturalists and breeders of cattle and horses, for it was not until considerably later that trade became their primary occupation. Their towns were fortified by moats and walls from an early date but, according to Xenophon, in the Euphrates region they lived with their cattle and poultry in large subterranean houses. It was at about that time that they started to penetrate northward, to what had once been Urartu, in the process absorbing the surviving Urartians as well as Scythian stragglers and occasional emigrants from Central Asia. Before long they had taken possession of the high plateau bounded on the north and north-west by the Kura and Chorokh rivers, on the east by the Araxes and Lake Urmia and, on the south by Kurdistan and the Tigris valley. Surrounded as it was by hills this plateau formed a natural fortress, but to begin with the Armenians were relatively poor and weak, and unable to stand out against their powerful Persian neighbours. They thus became the vassals of the Achaemenids, adhering to the latter's religious beliefs to the extent of worshipping their gods Mithra and Anihita, adopting certain of their linguistic roots and allowing themselves to be influenced by their masters' distinctive artistic style.

With Alexander the Great the Armenians entered a new phase in their history, for they started to look to industry and commerce as a means of livelihood and established commercial relations with Mesopotamia, Egypt, Central Asia and India. Alexander recognized their growing sense of nationhood by installing Atropat as their petty king. He became the founder of their first royal dynasty. Seleucus I Nicephorus in his turn became so interested in Armenia that, according to Pliny, he had the Caspian area surveyed with the view of cutting a canal from the Caspian to the Black Sea – a project which never matured.

Under Tigranes II (95–56 BC) Armenia ranked as a great power, and deservedly so, for the country now stretched from the River Kura to the Caspian Sea and from Ecbatana to the Cilician Taurus. As a result she was coveted by both Parthia and Rome. Pompey was sent to conquer her and penetrated as far as Garni before retreating to the Euphrates in order to turn the river into a buffer against Parthia. In 54 BC Armenia was forced to recognize the Parthians as her masters. However, Rome's success in establishing its frontier on the Euphrates had the effect of encouraging the inhabitants of the Caucasian area to look south-west, to the Hellenistic cities of Syria and Mesopotamia, for alternative commercial outlets, and perhaps as a result, Tigranes II became an ardent Philhellene. He established his capital at Tigranokert, in the neighbourhood of Nisibin, somewhere it is thought in the Mayyafarikin area, and formed such close ties with the Greeks that the Armenians accepted many of their gods, fusing Zeus with his Armenian counterpart Aramazd, Athene with

Nanea and Apollo with Tin, to give but three examples. Nevertheless even when the Parthians were replaced in the East, first by the Sassanians, then by the Seljukid Turks and when the Holy Roman empire in the West was succeeded by Byzantium, Armenia continued to serve as a bone of contention between the great Eastern and Western powers. Weakened by the continuous quarrels, her rulers at last agreed in *c.* 1020 to cede an important section of their Transcaucasian territory to Byzantium in exchange for an area in the Taurus region, soon to be known as Little Armenia. Neither country benefited to any marked degree by this arrangement, for in 1071 Transcaucasian Armenia was overrun by the Seljukid Turks and some two centuries later the Mongols swept over the area. These invasions make clean breaks in the country's history.

Armenia was the first country to abandon paganism in order to become a Christian state. The nation dates its conversion to the year 301 and ascribes it to the missionary zeal of a native prince, St Gregory the Illuminator. The acceptance of Christianity strengthened Armenia's links with the Western world, more particularly since her Church was placed under the direction of that of Constantinople. It may, however, have been partly due to Persian influence that the Armenian Church developed along Monophysite lines. Inevitably this led to a breech with Constantinople and late in the sixth century the Armenian Church broke free from Byzantine control. Armenia's new, profoundly Christian art looked for guidance to Syria and Byzantium's eastern provinces rather than to the empire's young capital. The contacts she formed with the Western world aroused the anxiety of Sassanian Persia and, as a matter of course, the growing concern ended in a war with Byzantium. The treaty of 387 putting an end to hostilities can be compared to the partition of Poland many centuries later, for Armenia was, as a result, divided between Byzantium and Persia. Seven centuries of friction followed and would doubtless have persisted even longer had not the appearance of a third contestant, in the form of the Arabs, produced a lull which lasted until the Seljuks replaced the Persians in the struggle. The Arab occupation of Armenia falls into two periods. During the first hundred years (652–750) the country was ruled from Damascus by the enlightened Umayyads, but in the second period (750–887) their place was taken by the Abbasids who, by reigning from Baghdad, severed Armenia's links with Byzantine Trebizond, thus creating an economic crisis which brought much misery to the Transcaucasian Armenians. However, the situation soon improved, partly because many Arabs began to settle in Armenia, first using the towns as military bases, later developing them into trading centres. The need for the latter measure had resulted from the establishment in the eighth century on the lower reaches of the Volga of a flourishing Khazar kaganate. Its markets soon attracted Slav traders from what was shortly to become Kievian Russia as well as merchants from Varangian Scandinavia, Central Asia and the Arab world. The Khazar trading centres enabled the Slavs to by-pass Byzantium in their dealings with the south-eastern and eastern markets; Armenia benefited very considerably from this development, doing so not only at the cost of Constantinople, but also of Sinop and Trebizond.

In Armenia life had been easy during the Persian occupation and stagnant under the Arabs. The Armenians, with their strong sense of nationhood, had taken advantage of both situations to develop their national culture. The invention, by Mesrop Maschots in 396, of the Armenian alphabet did much to foster their patriotism for the new alphabet quickly replaced the Syriac in the Persian zone and the Greek in the Byzantine, thus unifying the country's intellectual life. In the fifth century books were being written in Armenian and many more translated into it, and by the seventh century many works were being embellished with illuminations carried out in very much the same style as the paintings with which the country's magnificent churches were then being adorned. Some of the finest of the earlier illuminations date from the sixth century and are bound up in the famous Etchmiadzin Gospels written for the Monastery of Sanadir in the tenth century. This magnificent volume is perhaps the finest of Armenia's many splendid medieval manuscripts (*Ills. 210, 211*). The earliest complete, and thus more truly representative, work is probably the Lazarev Gospel dating from 887. Both books are exceptionally sumptuous in appearance for the majority of the illuminated works were produced by monks who came from

209 Anberd castle which stands on a promontory at the confluence of the rivers Anberd and Arakshan. Armenia's independence was constantly endangered by invaders, and so her architects and engineers soon developed an impressive type of defensive building

relatively poor monasteries and who, therefore, used inexpensive materials and tended to prefer simply constructed designs. Backgrounds do not appear ever to have been included in the earlier illuminations but strong colour schemes were popular. In style the miniatures reflect the influence of the two countries which controlled their own. Thus the art, like that of Byzantium, is a basically figural one, but the style is often Eastern as in the empire's Syrian provinces, whilst the evident pleasure taken in geometric and floral motifs was doubtless encouraged by the Islamic world, Persia in particular probably fostering a fondness for animal designs.

225

210, 211 (*left*) The Annunciation and (*right*) The Baptism from the Etchmiadzin Gospels, now in t
Maternadaran Library at Erivan. Both miniatures were painted at the Monastery of Noravank, b

Gospel was transferred to Etchmiadzin cathedral, where it remained until quite recently. They are executed in the dark, linear style characteristic of the Armenian school. 989

During the opening phase of the Christian period the Armenians produced a distinctive type of tombstone (*Ill. 212*) which fell out of favour in the seventh century. In shape it resembled the Georgian stela in that it consisted of a vertically set-up stone slab the centre of which was adorned with a cross surrounded by elaborate sculptured ornamental design. But for the short-lived economic crisis Armenia was singularly prosperous in early Christian times. Much of her wealth stemmed from trade and, until Byzantium learnt to produce silk, more particularly from the silk trade. Caravans from China destined for Nisibin or Edessa travelled across Armenia, paying transit dues in order to do so. By the fifth century Dvin, the Dabil of medieval times, had become both an important trading centre and Armenia's capital. It had been founded in *c.* 330 by King Chosroe Kotan Arshakuni to replace Artashat as his capital. In 428 the Sassanians chose it as the headquarters of their governor and when, in the seventh century, the city fell to the Arabs the latter in their turn retained it as the capital of their emirate. Even after it had been almost destroyed by the wars and revolts which ravaged the country in the eighth century, the Arabs encouraged the Armenians to rebuild it. Thus when the Bagratids, who were to become the greatest of Armenia's royal dynasties, came to power, founding in 886 an independent kingdom in the northern part of Transcaucasia, they naturally tried to capture Dvin in order in their turn to use it as their capital. However, the Arabs resisted them so stoutly that, after a century of hesitation, the Bagratids decided to found a new capital at Ani. Ani quickly became the equal of Dvin both in beauty and importance for it developed into a thriving centre of trade and industry. Both towns became bitterly jealous of each other and never ceased to vie for primacy.

The decision to found Dvin and to use it as the country's capital in preference to an existing town is generally ascribed to the rising tide of Armenian nationalism. King Chosroe was strongly Philhellene and was in the habit of surrounding himself at court with Greeks rather than with his own subjects. He built his palaces, theatres, baths, even his churches – as, for example, Garni – on Greek lines, often adopting a Greek plan for them. The opposition he thereby

212 Stelae such as this one from Gaiana are typically Armenian. They provided the country's sculptors with an excellent opportunity of displaying their skill. In this example ancient designs, such as confronted birds and rosettes, are combined with Christian symbols. Ninth–tenth century

aroused is thought to have forced him to abandon Artashat, which was regarded as the centre of Hellenism in Armenia, and to found Dvin in order to make a fresh start there as, for example, Atatürk did in our own day, when he transferred Turkey's capital from Istanbul to Ankara.

Excavations have been carried out at Dvin since 1937. The city's foundations can now be dated to the fourth century. Beneath them are the remains of an as yet unidentified culture which flourished from the sixth to the third century BC and produced pottery vessels decorated with spirited hunting scenes. Dvin became Christian early in its history and a three-aisled pagan building of the third century was converted early in the fourth to serve as its first cathedral. The basilica form was used for all churches built in Armenia until the sixth century, when the Armenian dome came into being, bringing with it a new architectural skyline. Within a hundred years of its invention this turret-shaped dome (*Ill. 219*) was being set on four central pylons and side apses were being added to the straight body of the church to provide it with a cruciform plan.

229

Armenians excelled at building, generally using the fine quality stone which abounds in their country. In the fifth century the Catholicos of Dvin was provided with a handsome palace, even though it was only one storey high. It was square in plan, the smallish rooms facing onto a central hall of impressive appearance, for it measured 300 square metres. Four pairs of columns supported its roof, which included three wooden domes. In the sixth century this hall was used both as a place of assembly and as a treasury for valuable vessels, and also housed royal and clerical ceremonial robes. However, probably as a result of the transfer of the country's capital from Dvin to Ani, the Catholicos abandoned his palace in 893, establishing his See at Zwarthnotz, and the great hall was then converted into a mosque.

Dvin's citadel dates from two periods. The original structure was built of stone in the fifth century and comprised the royal palace. The latter was taken over by the Arabs when they conquered Armenia. It was built on a square plan, but its walls were destroyed by an earthquake in 893. They were rebuilt almost at once by the Bagratids, who used the original foundations but constructed the palace partly in brick, partly in stone. Use of brick may have been due to Persian influence just as the interior decorations in carved stucco were doubtless inspired by Islamic prototypes. The basement of the palace was given over to storerooms and workshops and it was in one of these that the excavators discovered some superb examples of both glazed and unglazed pottery, coloured glass and jewellery, much of it in gold.

The Dvin excavations have yielded very valuable results. The finds include tools, weapons and numerous objects made of iron. Copper appears to have been used only as a decoration. In its day Dvin was renowned for its metal work and textiles. Its carpets were world famous and its cushion covers and stoles made of a fabric with a raised pattern were in wide demand, as were its crimson goat-hair cloth, its furs, leather wares, brocades, gold embroideries and, above all, its silk garments. According to Ibn Haukal the latter were even finer than those obtainable in Constantinople. In the seventh century the Albanian historian Moses of Kalankatu described the

213 Detail of a textile reconstructed from four fragments found at Moschevaja Balka in the Kuban. It was most possibly made in Armenia and shows a sacrificial scene. Two men, probably priests, stand either side of a tree of life, holding their victims by the hair in the process of beheading them. *c.* 300 BC

banks of the Kura as being bordered with silk-worm farms; he added that the silk made at Partava (Berda) was exported to Persia. Typical of textiles being produced at this time is an Armenian figured silk discovered at Moschevaja Balka (*Ill. 213*). It is believed to represent a sacrificial scene and its design is made up of roundels. The only one to survive contains two confronted figures shown seated on stools with lion-headed terminals; they are dressed in soft bootees and cloaks, and their curled hair is adorned with half-moon shaped ornaments. They are separated by a tree, which may have had a ritual significance. Small figures with raised arms crouch at their feet. The bigger personages hold them by their hair whilst beating them with canes.

The Armenians have left us a great many objects which testify to their skill in the minor arts, yet it is in architecture that their creative gifts are seen at their best. The wealth derived from trade made it possible for much building to take place throughout the sixth and seventh century. Most of that which survives is in the form of

214 Carved wooden capital from Sevan cathedral elaborately decorated with confronted peacocks and ducks. Although some twelve hundred years separate them from the gold disc (*Ill. 11*), the ducks on the capital are descended from them. Ninth–tenth century

churches and tombs. The majority of the churches are constructed from neatly cut blocks of dressed stone, and both the style and quality of the masonry and the pointed, turret-like shape of the domes have led many scholars to conclude that the Seljuks of Anatolia acquired their technique and skill in building, even the basic features of their architectural style, from the Armenians. Many Armenian churches are, indeed, very much earlier in date than the Seljukid buildings which resemble them so strikingly, but it is hardly possible as yet to reach a definite conclusion regarding the origins of this style. Its roots may well lie concealed beneath the earth somewhere in northern Persia or western Turkestan, and the solution of the problem will have to wait till a great deal more field work has been carried out in those areas. The secret may even lie hidden in eastern Turkey, in areas still closed to research.

The Armenians were fond of decorating their churches with sculptures executed either in high relief, as at Zwarthnotz, or in low relief, as on the Sevan capitals (*Ill. 214*). They were as skilled at carving wood as the Islamic craftsmen and, like them, they often had recourse to carved stucco for ornamental purposes. In the tenth century a new wave of prosperity accompanied a new period of economic expansion and resulted in the rise of the towns of Ani and Kars. Then too, and doubtless for the same reasons, artists started to include the figures of donors in their paintings and sculptures. Most of the paintings that survive in Armenia's churches date from the tenth century onwards, but the finest were produced in the twelfth, thirteenth and fourteenth centuries (*Ill. 215*). In their broad lines and iconography they adhere to Byzantine traditions, but their style is

215 Wall-painting from the church of St Gregory Tigrane-Honentz, Ani showing St Gregory the Illuminator converting Armenia to Christianity. Below is shown the Dormition of the Virgin. Thirteenth century

216 (*above*) Defensive walls at Ani of the tenth century

217 Entrance to the palace at A

218 The cathedral at Ani. Blind arcading with its tall, slender lines and high narrow windows was used to give the impression of additional height. 989–1001

more Oriental. It is, moreover, so distinctive that it is clearly an essentially national product and one which is easily recognizable. When under Ashot III (953–77) Ani was being embellished in a manner befitting a capital, the best of Armenia's artists and builders were naturally employed there. Impressive walls were constructed round the city (*Ill. 216*). Within them a splendid palace (*Ill. 217*) was built as well as some large private houses, numerous churches and a magnificent cathedral (*Ill. 218*). The latter was designed by the architect Trdat, who was later asked to visit Constantinople to repair the capital's great cathedral of Hagia Sophia. King Gagik (989–1020) cannot, however, have been entirely satisfied with Ani for he built himself a town on the island of Aghtamar. It is thought that the throne-room in his palace was embellished with wall mosaics. The Armenians are known to have been fond of mosaic decorations and

to have been in the habit of decorating their most important buildings with these expensive adornments. They were such accom-
plished craftsmen that they probably excelled in this exacting art
and it is sad that no examples of their work in this field survive to
testify to their skill. The great palace of Aghtamar is now a ruin.
The most impressive monument to survive is the church of the
Holy Cross. On its walls is a sculpture of its founder, King Gagik
(*Ill. 220*), as well as an extensive sculptured decoration in low relief.
Even in their present lamentable condition the buildings at Ani and
Aghtamar remain works of outstanding quality, worthy of a high
place beside comparable works produced at a similar date in western
Christendom.

Iberia, the kernel of present-day Georgia, was already a kingdom
in Parthian times. From about AD 30 to 60 it was ruled from
Mskheta by King Farsman in the capacity of a vassal of Rome.

According to legend the country's inhabitants were descended from Japhet and came from Babylon. In the twelfth century B C they were definitely living in the Anti-Taurus mountains. From a very early date they were divided into the four social classes defined by early writers as royalty, the priesthood, the military and the rest. In classical times they were trading with Greece but worshipping the sun, moon and the planets as well as the mother goddess. Rome attached so much importance to this small and remote country that Hadrian invited Farsman to visit Rome on two separate occasions. Each time costly presents were exchanged and Romans gradually began to settle in Iberia. The artists amongst them first practised an essentially Roman form of art, but they soon started to combine Georgian elements with the Western ones. However, the Iberians remained throughout this period in regular touch with Sassanian Persia, often incorporating Eastern elements in their art and allowing themselves to be won over to the Eastern lunar cult and Sassanian Mazdaism.

220 Relief on the west façade of the church at Aghtamar, of King Gagik, 915–921, holding a model of the church in his hands. Armenian churches were often decorated with such figural, geometric and symbolic reliefs

221 Column capital in the form of a bull's head from the Sion at Bolinsk, Georgia, recalls this animal's importance in that area in prehistoric times. 478–493/4

222 (*opposite*) Capital from ▶ the south pilaster of the altar screen in the Sion at Bolinsk. Both the motifs recall those which were popular in the Caucasus in pre-Christian times, the treatment of the lion's mane is particularly reminiscent of early sculpture and metal work. Fifth century

Iberia became converted to Christianity during the first half of the fourth century. Some churches of that astonishingly early date survive there, if in a ruined state. They include the interesting churches of Nekressi and Cheremi. Like others of the same date they are very small and unadventurous in shape, leading one to conclude that their builders were feeling their way towards a new architectural style. Cheremi is square and was roofed originally with the same type of dome as that found on certain Mazdaian temples. However, in the fifth century basilicas started to be built and continued to be so in the tenth century. The form was new to Georgia, but some local features were incorporated into it. Thus the central aisle was wider than the others and contained no nave. Some of the churches of this type were truly superb buildings. The fine Sion at Bolinsk (*Ills. 221, 222*) still retains the inscription dating its construction to the years 462–77. It is a three-aisled structure built of dressed stone and already possessing a protruding altar apse. Five pairs of cruciform-shaped piers topped with capitals sculptured in the Sassanian style supported its roof. It had no narthex, but a large open gallery ran along the exterior face of its north wall whilst a double apsed baptistry was built along its south wall. Its roof was provided with a

centrally placed dome which was copied at Djvari (586–7) and at
Mskheta. Urbnissi is a basilica only slightly younger than the Sion at
Bolinsk for it dates from the fifth or sixth century. It is both a
narrower and a taller building than the Sion, but it too contains three
aisles, though the centre one is wider than the two others. This
development foreshadowed the invention of the typically Georgian
church-form evolved in the sixth century. Chubinashvili calls it a
triple church basilica because its shape is that of three adjoining,
intercommunicating churches spanned by a single roof, the central
church being taller and wider than the side ones. By the eighth
century the side churches had been transformed into porticos or
exo-nartheces. By the seventh century the dome was in general use
in Iberia but, as for example at Djvari (*Ill. 225*) and Mskheta (604),
it often assumed the pointed shape associated with Armenia (*Ill. 232*).
Churches such as these had a square central area to which corner
or side chapels were added to produce a cruciform plan. Djvari is
a tetraconch enclosed in a circle with arcaded apses opening into
it. The proportions of these churches are generally very impressive
and were rendered more so by the habit of dividing the outer
walls into three sections which helped to stress the building's

223 Relief of Stephanos I, Patriach of Kartli. The Georgians were perhaps not quite such accomplished sculptors as their neighbours the Armenians, yet in this rendering on the east front of Djvari church the artist has achieved a truly impressive result. Seventh century

224 (below) Relief from Opiza church showing its founder, the Kuropolate Ashot, presenting a model of the church to the Saviour. The style is a trifle primitive and archaic yet strangely appealing. 826

225 Exterior view of Djvari church seen from the south-east. This early building dates from the seventh century and made use of the Byzantine dome, rather than the Armenian conical, pointed roof

height. Often each section of the walls was adorned with sculptures. The motifs chosen for the purpose were drawn from a wide field and geometric, floral and animal forms appear to have been as popular as figural scenes. Djvari church was decorated with a sculptured portrait of its patriarch, Stephanos I (*Ill. 223*). Some of the sculptures produced for the churches were carried out in high relief, others in low (*Ill. 224*). Each wall was decorated with its own cycle of subjects. The majority of the themes chosen are Christian in content, and all form an integral part of the church's decoration.

The style of the sculpture is closely paralleled in the embossed and chased metal, usually silver, icons, gospel-covers or plaques which were produced in Georgia in considerable numbers from very early to very late medieval times. The Georgians were extremely accomplished metal workers and these plaques are particularly characteristic of their art (*Ill. 230*). They belong as much to the realm of sculpture as of metal work for in almost every case those who produced them

241

226 Silver disc of St Mamas riding a lion is only one of many hundreds of magnificent examples which testify to the skill of the Georgians in metal working. The treatment of the lion's head and mane recalls many earlier portrayals of the beast. Sixth-seventh century

possessed a real understanding of anatomy and feeling for modelling. Their makers remained anonymous till relatively late times, but in the twelfth and thirteenth century the goldsmiths Beka and Beshken Opizari signed their works (*Ill. 227*). Like many Byzantine artists of that period Beka elongated his figures; he also attached great importance to the ornamental settings which he devised for them. In comparison Beshken, if conclusions can be based on a single surviving work, was more archaic but also more monumental than the most illustrious of Georgia's medieval silversmiths. These metal icons are often very large in size. On all of them the designs were first hammered out from the reverse side of the sheet of metal and then finished off by hand. Only one example dating from the fifth century survives; it is a silver-gilt figure of St Gregory the Illuminator. A sixth to seventh century plaque of St Mamas (*Ill. 226*), patron saint of tax-payers, riding his lion is in a style which recalls that of Bactria's silver vessels, but the resemblance is probably due to the presence of certain east-Hellenistic elements in both.

242

227 Detail from the silver cover of the Bertsk Gospels showing St John, part of the Deesis group. It was made and signed by Beshken Opizari, probably a leading silversmith of his day. 1184–93

228 Silver plaque showing two saints. It is a work of considerable power for it succeeds in conveying the serene, yet severe, outlook of those who have withdrawn from the world. The draperies are strongly schematized. *c.* eighth century

The sculptured stone altar screens set up in the churches from the sixth century onwards are equally characteristic of Georgia. A fine example of early date survives in the sixth-century church at Tsebelda in Abkhasia (*Ill. 229*). Many screens were decorated in the Byzantine style, but some display strong Sassanian influences. Chubinashvili suggests that the one in the Sion at Bolinsk contains Soghdian rather than Sassanian elements. In the eleventh century the slabs were often decorated with figural designs and the tops of the columns into which they were set were elaborately carved from then onwards.

Some of Georgia's most splendid churches date from the eleventh and twelfth centuries, the period when the country was at the height of its political power and economic prosperity. The church at Ateni is a fine early example of this style, but it is buildings such as the cathedral at Kutais (1003) and Mskheta (1040) that are especially characteristic of it. In both, the domes are very high and very wide, the space beneath them assuming great importance. However, they are too late in date to be discussed in this volume.

229 Sculptured stone altar screen from Tsebelda church shows scenes from the Saviour's life. Notice that a disc with rosettes is included even at this late date. Sixth century

230 The church of Ateni is only one of many splendid churches built in Georgia during the eleventh and twelfth centuries, when the country was at the height of its political power and economic prosperity

231 (below) Column capital from the west porch which was added to the late tenth-century church of Bagrat III at Kutais during the first quarter of the twelfth century

232 East front of the chur of St Tzkhoveli at Mskhe It is interesting to compare with the almost contempo ary cathedral at Ani (*Ill. 21* and to note the more elabo ate treatment which t Georgians introduced in their architectural decoratio 1029

233 (*opposite*) Atzghuri cas which impressively mou guard over the plain a defends the entry to the p

234 (*below*) An old fortifi manor-house of a type whi has failed to survive to o day. It stood until the Fi World War in Swanetia at t foot of the Oashta mountai

The Georgians were as competent at building palaces, houses and castles as they were churches and monasteries. The earliest examples of domestic architecture to survive as ruins date from the tenth century. In Khakhetia the palaces were two-storeyed structures with the reception rooms situated on the top floor. They were lit by large, closely set windows and some scholars have suggested that when complete they must have resembled the Byzantine palace of the Blachernae in Constantinople. The ruined palace built at Gegat in 1156 by George III, the father of Georgia's great queen, Tamara, was square in plan and contained a large central hall. Both brick and dressed stones were used for its construction and glazed tiles, the pres-ence of which may perhaps be due to Islamic influence, for its roof.

235 The ruins of Tzromi church show that churches of considerable size, elaboration and merit were built in Georgia as early as the seventh century

Until the sixth century the Georgian Church was monophysite, and this, it is thought, may help to explain why the earliest churches do not appear ever to have been adorned with mural-paintings. The mosaic floors set up in the church at Pitsunda in the sixth century seem to have been inspired by Roman rather than Byzantine prototypes. Traces of another mosaic floor of much the same date are to be observed at Tzromi (*Ill. 235*), but so little of its design survives that it is impossible to form any conclusions about it (*Ill. 236*). When the Georgian Church came under the jurisdiction of the Byzantine the whole conception of a church's interior appearance altered and mural-paintings became customary (*Ills. 237, 238*). From the start they seem to have been regarded as embellishments rather than as visual means of religious instruction. The earliest paintings are at Djvari (545–86), but they are in too damaged a condition to be of stylistic value. Broadly speaking, Georgia's artists worked in the Byzantine style but they evolved their own method of presentation, often adorning the dome with a cross set in a medallion in

248

236 Tracing for a mosaic, with tesserae still visible, on the wall of Tzromi church. Originally it was lavishly decorated with wall and floor mosaics, none of which survive. Seventh century

237 (*below*) This mural from the apse of the cave church of Dodo at David-Garedzha is unusual, for it shows the Saviour as the personification of the sun and moon. Eighth–ninth century

preference to the Byzantine figure of the *Pantocrator*, displaying the *Deesis* in the apse in place of the Virgin and generally treating the apse as of more importance than the dome. All the finest paintings which survive, whether in the form of murals or as panels date from the eleventh century onwards and, as such, fall outside the limits set for this book.

Miniatures form an important part of Georgian art (*Ills. 239, 240*). The majority likewise date from the eleventh and twelfth century. Several examples may, however, be slightly earlier in date. Both in their iconography and style they adhere to Byzantine tradition. Indeed, many were painted by Georgian monks living in the Georgian monastery of Iviron on Mount Athos. Both they and their fellow illuminators in Georgia seem to have taken particular delight in evolving extremely ornate chapter-headings and in introducing architectural and animal designs into the scrolls and geometric motifs which they invented for the purpose. In rather later times Georgian artists produced secular miniatures which are closer in style to Persian than to Byzantine works. Persia, or rather the Islamic world, probably also provided the incentives which led the Georgians to

238 Detail from a wall-painting in the cave church of Do-do at David-Garedzha showing an archangel. Eighth–ninth century

239, 240 Two Georgian miniatures. (*left*) St Mark healing the Blind Man, and (*right*) St Mark holding his gospel. From the Dzhruchi Gospel dated 940

write and illustrate numerous books on astrology between the eleventh and seventeenth centuries.

Georgia took advantage of the enmity which led to a well-nigh permanent state of war between Byzantium and Sassanian Persia to grow strong and wealthy. However, when the Arabs invaded Asia and the Caucasus they put an end to her independence and prosperity. They established their headquarters at Tbilisi (Tiflis). During the economic crisis which followed the invasion many Georgians fled to the remote mountainous region of Khakhetia where the difficult nature of the country served to deter the enemy and made it possible for the native inhabitants to retain a fair measure of freedom. Others settled in Abkhazia, which had been under Byzantine tutelage since Justinian's day but had taken advantage of the Umayyads fall to proclaim its independence. It took the Arabs ten years to gain control over them but in *c.* 786 Leo II of Abkhazia managed to regain his freedom and to establish his capital at Kutais, for the old capital,

Mskheta, was still in Arab hands. Under his son Demeter II the Georgian Church broke free from Byzantine control and the Georgian prelate set up his See at Mskheta. From then onwards the country proceeded to gain in strength and by the end of the tenth century Georgia's southern frontier was on Lake Van.

Until the Mongol invasion of the thirteenth century, life in Georgia, even under the Arabs, remained sophisticated, lively and cultured. A traveller somewhat crossly remarked that the peasants aped the gentry, the gentry aped the princes and the princes aped their king. Literature flourished, living standards were high and craftsmanship so accomplished that sumptuous textiles, mosaics, fine jewellery and a variety of admirably made table utensils and richly ornamented weapons were produced in large numbers both for the home markets and for export. At Queen Tamara's court only vessels of gold were used, even silver ones being excluded. Georgia also became an important centre of production of delicate cloisonné enamels of the Byzantine type. Their numbers appear to have exceeded those made by the jewellers of Kievian Russia, though the latter are rather more delicate in style, conception and execution, and show a better understanding of colour than do the Georgian ones. The Georgian colours are a shade harsher and darker and disclose a marked preference for rather a deep shade of light green. Some contain errors in firing yet the honour of producing what is perhaps the loveliest of all cloisonné enamels of the Byzantine type falls to Georgia. It is a tenth-century enamel of the Virgin which, though so much damaged that only the face and hands survive, is nevertheless comparable in its beauty and expressiveness to the scarcely less damaged, famous twelfth-century Byzantine icon of the Virgin of Vladimir. This spiritual, delicate and, notwithstanding its minute size, truly monumental masterpiece serves as the centrepiece of a gold triptych known as the Khakuli icon (*Ill. 241*). The triptych is adorned with exquisite gold filigree work and granulations which provide settings for cabochon jewels and numerous cloisonné enamels (*Ill. 242*). Some of the enamels are of Byzantine workmanship, most, including that of the Virgin, are Georgian. The triptych was made for the Monastery of the Virgin which the kuropolate

David founded at Khakuli. When the Seljuks invaded Georgia it was moved for safety to the Monastery of Gelat in Imeretia, which had been founded by Bagrat III where it remained until recent years. It may have been in its honour that, between 1125 and 1130, the apse of the church there was adorned with a fine wall mosaic (*Ill. 244*). Though emotional in conception, and thus in accord with Georgian taste, the mosaic is elegant and severe without being ascetic. It corresponds in this respect with the style of the enamel. Both admirably reflect in their beauty, restraint and magnificence the Georgian way of life in pre-Mongol invasion times.

Caucasian Albania – the Aghovan of the Romans and the Aran both of the Parthians and of King Shapur's Sassanian rock inscription at Naksh-i-Rustem – was considerably poorer and politically less important than either Armenia or Georgia. Nevertheless, it ranked with them as one of the three foremost Caucasian kingdoms. Its territory extended in the north to the Derbend area, in the west to Khakhetia, in the south, in the third century, as far as the Kura river, and a century later as far as the Araxes, whilst in the east it stretched to the Caspian. The country was wild and mountainous. Access to it was so difficult that it probably accounts for the fact that Albania's art remained more individual and truly local than that of either Armenia or Georgia. Albania's history dates back to the fourth century BC when her soldiers were greatly respected for their valour and endurance. In 331 BC the Achaemenids were, nevertheless, able to gain control of the country; they then hastened to enrol Albanians into their army. However, the people's national consciousness was already so well developed by the time Pompey led his legions against them that he could make but little headway. The Albanians confronted and held the invaders wearing armour, that of the officers being made of metal, that of the men consisting of leather breastplates. Armour of this type continued to be worn in remote Caucasian hilltop villages, more particularly in Ossetia, in modern times (*Ill. 245*).

The Albanians were at first divided into numerous tribes and even in Strabo's time twenty-six of these were still in existence. However, in *c.* 215 BC they were already united under their first king.

241, 242 The Khakuli icon of gold repoussé and filigree work studded with precious stones and cloisonné enamels of Georgian and Byzantine origin. The central panel depicts the Virgin, of whom now only the face and hands remain. Tenth century. (*right*) Detail of part of the icon with inlaid Georgian enamels depicting Christ Pantocrater, the Archangel Gabriel, SS John and Mark and St Gregory the Theologian. Twelfth century

243 View of Gelat monastery founded by King Bagrat III at the turn of the tenth century. It presents a splendid complex of many turret-shaped domes and sloping roofs

244 Detail of a mosaic of the Virgin from the apse of the church at the monastery of Gelat. It was set up in the monastery at about the same time that the Khakuli icon was transferred there and may have been done in honour of this. 1125–30

245 Until the outbreak of the First World War, men in remote areas of the Caucasus still wore armour of leather covered with bone scales, very similar to those worn by the Tadjiks at the beginning of the Christian era

Writing in the seventh century A D the first of their historians, Moses of Kalankatu, noted that in 152 B C their ruler was a member of the Persian house of the Arsacids; his descendents retained the throne till well into the fourth century A D. Whilst under their rule the Albanians came into contact with eastern Hellenism, an encounter which left only a slight mark on their art. From the first century or so B C till late into the third century A D the Albanians, like their neighbours the Armenians and the Georgians, were obliged to defend themselves from the Romans, Parthians, Alans and Sassanians. In the fourth century King Shapur's conquests in the Caucasian area led to widespread revolts. The Albanian ruler, Vaie II, fared badly in one of these risings and was obliged to cede his powers to a Sassanian viceroy. In consequence the Persians became responsible for the safety of Albania's north-eastern frontier and, in order to protect them from nomadic raiding parties, Yazdagird I built a fort at what was then known as the Albanian Gates, but is called today the Derbend defile.

The country's capital was established first at Kabula, Pliny's Kabulaka, the Kabalah of the Arabs and the Shamakha of medieval times. Following upon Vaie's abdication the Sassanians moved it to what is now the Yevlakh district, to a point whence the Iberian and Armenian borders could be seen. They called the new capital Perosez (city of Peros) after Peros (Firus) the son of Yazdagird I because the prince had given the town's inhabitants permission to build defensive walls round the city. The name was soon altered to Perozbad, but it was pronounced Petrav by the Armenians. It came to be generally known by the latter name though the Arabs called it Barda'a. At the time the Albanians were so much under the influence of Persia that they ceased worshipping the forces of nature to become Zoroastrians. Then Gregory the Illuminator, having accomplished the conversion of Armenia, set out to establish Christianity in Albania. He was helped in this by Mesrop who proceeded to evolve an Albanian alphabet from his Armenian one. Nevertheless, the Albanians remained in closer touch with the Persians than with the Georgians, but though they maintained regular contacts with the Armenians they proceeded to use the Georgian and Pahlevi alphabets as readily as their own. In later times they made equal use of the Arabic.

The converted Albanians were fervent Christians. The Catholicos of their church combated paganism with the utmost intensity and, in the seventh century, only a couple of years before succumbing to the Arabs, he even sent missionaries to the Huns in an attempt to convert them. A northern bishopric was established at Kabula at an early date, but the Arab occupation brought many difficulties to the Albanians for they not only had to contend against the invaders, but they were also obliged to defend themselves against the Volga Khazars. Nevertheless, their craftsmen continued throughout the years to produce pottery, brocades and metal vessels which

257

246 Bronze cauldron with animals mounted on the handles. From mid-medieval times Daghestan was famed for its metal work and more especially its cauldrons, which, like those of the Scythians, were intended to stand in the fire and not to hang over it

won them wide renown. They were, in fact, as gifted artistically as their neighbours. Their crafts were at their best in the seventh century under King Jevansher, but they continued to produce till late medieval times bronze dishes, jugs, aquamanile, and more particularly cauldrons (*Ill. 247*) and incense burners which are now greatly sought after. Both the pottery and the cauldrons made in the Kubachi region of Daghestan are particularly lovely. The pottery (*Ill. 252*) often displays floral designs exquisitely delineated and produced in the most alluring deep pastel shades. The metal work, and the stone sculptures for which Daghestan is equally famous, often reflect Sassanian designs. They continued to be produced in Albania later than anywhere else, both because Albania was not easily accessible to outside influences and also because the diversion of the ancient trade route linking Persia to Dvin via Partav, southward of Ani, and thence to the Black Sea brought about the complete isolation of

247 Bronze cauldron from Daghestan. The upper half of the vessel is divided into 'ace of spade' sections of Central Asian origin containing a rider and horse. Thirteenth century

248 View from above of the same cauldron. The rim is adorned with lions, some of which are confronted, while others advance in single file. Thirteenth century

249 Sculptured relief from above a window of a mosque in Kubachi. It shows the intense love of horses and riding shared by the people of western Turkestan and the Caucasus. Eleventh century

Albania. As a result old traditions survived there for longer than elsewhere and in the twelfth century when Armenia annexed the southern part of Albania and western Georgia, the Albanians were still making open and rounded cauldrons with tripod bases similar in every respect other than size to the tiny gold ones which had been laid in the Maikop burials some four thousand years earlier. They continued to decorate the rims of many of the cauldrons with animal designs of Scythian character and to fashion their handles into animal shapes (*Ill. 246*). They also produced some spouted cauldrons equipped with lids which are as characteristic of the country as the pottery aquamanile in the form of goats or birds, often with strong Sassanian influence. The relief decorations which adorn a number of stone slabs of the same late date discovered by the late J. Orbeli in the Kubachi district (*Ills. 249, 250*), though they include Sassanian motifs, also recall certain designs in the felt appliqué worked objects found both at Pazyryk and Noin Ula. They appear in conjunction with others bearing a marked resemblance to

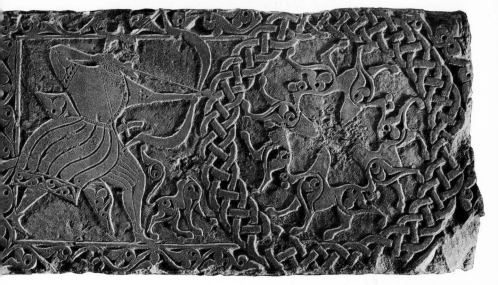

250 Stone relief from Daghestan. Hunting scenes were popular subjects in the arts of the Caucasian area from prehistoric times onwards. This late example still reflects influences from Achaemenid, Scythian, Sassanian, Parthian and Islamic styles. Twelfth century

251 Stone relief from Kubachi adorned with three scenes which are of particular interest. The first two seem to belong to the same cycle as the bronze plaques which Griaznov regards as illustrations from Central Asian epics. The last scene on the right shows a rider shooting backwards in the Parthian style. The slab serves to show that traditions lived on in the area longer than is generally supposed. Twelfth–thirteenth century

252 Kubachi potters excelled at producing pots and vessels of superb quality. They adorned them with floral motifs as gay and decorative as those which appear in the finest of Islamic miniatures. Sixteenth century

designs of a similar date evolved in such widely separated regions as Armenian Ani, Seljukid Anatolia and Russian Vladimir. It is thus to this remote corner of the Caucasus that we must turn to find elements which had been evolved many centuries earlier in Central Asia, still flourishing (*Ill. 251*) at a time when, elsewhere, they had already been fused into the framework in which the decorative arts of Europe developed in late medieval times.

Bibliography

Chapter One

ANDERSSON, J. G. *Hunting Magic in the Animal Style*, Östasiatiska Samlingarna, Bulletin 4, Stockholm, 1932

BOROVKA, G. I. *Scythian Art*, London, 1928

GIMBUTAS, M. *The Prehistory of Eastern Europe I*, American School of Prehistoric Research, Bulletin 20, Harvard, 1956

GRIAZNOV, M. P. and BOULGAKOV, A. *L'art ancien de l'Altai*, Moscow, 1958

GROUSSET, R. *L'empire des steppes. Attila, Genghis Khan, Tamerlan*, Paris, 1939

GROUSSET, R. *Chinese Art and Culture*, London, 1959

GROUSSET, R. *De La Grèce à la Chine*, Paris, 1948

KISELEV, S. V. *Ancient History of Southern Siberia*, Moscow, 1951. In Russian, French resumé by R. Ghirshman in *Artibus Asiae*, Vol. XIV, 1–2, pp. 169–89, Ascona, 1951

KUFTIN, B. A. *Archaeological Excavations at Trialeti*, Georgian Academy of Sciences, Tiflis, 1941. In Russian

MONGAIT, A. *Archaeology in the USSR*, Moscow, 1959

RICE, T. T. *The Scythians*, 3rd edition revised, London, 1961

ROSTOVTZEV, M. I. *The Animal Style in South Russia and China*, Princeton, 1929

RUDENKO, S. I. and M. N. *The Art of the Scythians of the Altai*, Moscow, 1949. In Russian

SALMONY, A. *Sino-Siberian art in the collection of C. T. Loo*, Paris, 1933

UMEHARA SUEJI. *Studies of Noin Ula finds in northern Mongolia*. The Togo Bunko Publications, Series A, No. 27, Tokyo, 1960

Chapter Two

DALTON, O. M. *The Treasure of the Oxus*, 3rd edition revised, London, 1964

DIAKONOV, I. M. *History of Media*, Moscow and Leningrad, 1956. In Russian

FRYE, R. N. *The Heritage of Persia*, London, 1963

GODARD, A. *Le Trésor de Ziwiyé (Kurdistan)*, Haarlem, 1950

GREKOV, B. D. and YAKUBOVSKI, A. G. *La Horde d'Or et la Russie*, Paris, 1939

NEGAHBAN, E. O. *Gold Treasure of Marlyk*, Illustrated London News, 28 April, 1962. *Further Finds*, 5 May, 1962

PIGULEVSKAYA, N. *Les villes de L'état Iranien aux époques Parthe et Sassanide*, Contribution à l'histoire sociale de la basse antiquité. The Hague, 1963

PIOTROVSKIJ, B. *History and Culture of Urartu*, Erivan, 1944. In Russian

POPE, A. U. editor. *A Survey of Persian Art*, London, 1937

TREVER, K. V. and ORBELI, J. *Sassanian goldwork, Objects in gold, silver and bronze*, Moscow and Leningrad, 1935. In Russian

TREVER, K. V. and ORBELI, J. *Excavations in Northern Mongolia, 1924–1925*, Leningrad, 1952

TREVER, K. V. and ORBELI, J. *Monuments of Graeco-Bactrian art*, Moscow and Leningrad, 1940. In Russian

Chapter Three

BERCHEM, M. VAN. *Die Inschriften der Grabtürme* in E. Diez, *Churasanische Baudenkmäler*, pp. 109–16. Berlin, 1918

FRYE, R. N. *Muhammad ibn Ja'far's History of Bukhara*, Mediaeval Academy of America Publication No. 61, 1954

GHIRSHMAN, R. *Iran, Parthians and Sassanians*, London, 1962
Persia from the Origins to Alexander the Great, London, 1964

GRAY, B. *Early Chinese Pottery and Porcelain*, London, 1953

MASSON, M. E. and PUGACHENKOVA, G. A. *The Parthian rhytons from Nissa*, Ashkabad, 1959. In Russian

PRIEST, A. R. *Chinese Sculpture in the Metropolitan Museum of Art*, New York, 1944

ROSTOVTZEV, M. I. *Dura-Europos and its art*, Oxford, 1938

Dura and the Problem of Parthian art, *Princeton Journal of Classical Studies, Yale Classical Studies*, Vol. V, pp. 157–304, Yale University Press, New Haven, 1935

SHYSHKIN, V. A. *Varaksha*, Moscow, 1963. In Russian

SMIRNOV, L. J. *Oriental Silverware*, St Petersburg, 1909. In Russian

YAKUBOVSKI, A. I. and others, *Paintings of Ancient Piandjikent*, Moscow, 1954. In Russian

TOLSTOV, S. P. *Ancient Chorasmia*, Moscow, 1948. In Russian

Chapter Four

DAGEN, E. LE BERRE, M. and SCHLUMBERGER, D. *Monuments preislamiques d'Afghanistan*, Paris, 1963

FA-HSIEN, *Travels of Fa-hsien, 399–414 AD, or Record of the Buddhistic Kingdoms*, edited by H. A. Giles, Cambridge, 1923

FOUCHER, A. *L'art gréco-bouddique du Gandara*, 2 vols. Paris, 1905–41

GHIRSHMAN, R. *Bégram. Récherches archéologique et historiques sur les Kouchans*, MDAFA, Vol. 12, Cairo, 1946

GODARD, A. and Y. and HACKIN, J. *Les Antiquities bouddhiques de Bamiyan*, MDAFA, Vol. 2, 1928; Vol. 3, 1933; Vol. 7, 1936

HACKIN, J. *Récherches archéologiques en Asie centrale*, 1931, Paris, 1936
Nouvelles récherches archéologiques a Bamiyan. MDAFA, Vol. 3, p. 90, Paris, 1933

ROWLAND, B. *The Art and Architecture of India*, London, 1953

TARN, W. W. *The Greeks in Bactria and India*, Cambridge, 1938

WALDSCHMIDT, E. *Gandara, Kutscha, Turfan*, Leipzig, 1925

Chapter Five

BARTHOLD, V. V. *Turkestan (Istoria Kulturnoj zhisni Turkestana)*. Lenin, 1927

BUSSAGLI, M. *Painting of Central Asia*, Geneva, 1963

GORDON, A. K. *Tibetan religious art*, New York, 1952
Iconography of Tibetan Lamaism, New York, 1939

GRAY, B. *Buddhist Paintings of Tun-huang*, London, 1959

GRÜNWEDEL, A. *Alt-Kutscha*, Berlin, 1920

HEISSIG, W. *Ein Volk sucht seine Geschichte*, Düsseldorf, 1964

LE COQ, A. VON *Buried Treasures of Chinese Turkestan*, London, 1928
Bildenatlas zur Kunst- und Kulturgeschichte Mittel-Asiens, Berlin, 1925
Chotscho, Berlin, 1913
and WALDSCHMIDT, E. *Die buddhistosche Spätantike in Mittel-Asiens*, 7 vols., Berlin, 1923–33

MARTIN, F. R. *Thüren aus Turkestan*, Stockholm, 1897

PELLIOT, P. L. *Les influences Iraniennes en Asie Centrale et en Extrême Orient*. Revue d'historie et de litterature religieuse, Fey, 1912
Les Grottes de Touen-houang, 6 vols. Paris, 1920–4

STEIN, SIR M. A. *Ruins of Desert Cathay*, 2 vols., London, 1912
Sand-buried Ruins of Khotan, London, 1903
Ancient Khotan, Oxford, 1907
Serindia, Oxford, 1921
Innermost Asia, Oxford, 1928
The Thousand Buddhas, Ancient Buddhist Paintings from the Cave Temples of Tunhuang, London, 1921, 22

TUCCI, G. *Tibetan Painted Scrolls*, Rome, 1950

Chapter Six

AMIRANACHVILI, C. *Les Emaux de Georgie*, Paris, 1962

DOURNOVO, L. A. *Armenian Miniatures*, London, 1961

DER NERSESSIAN, S. *Armenia and the Byzantine Empire*, Harvard, 1945

STRZYGOWSKI, J. *Die Baukunst der Armenier und Europa*, Vienna, 1918

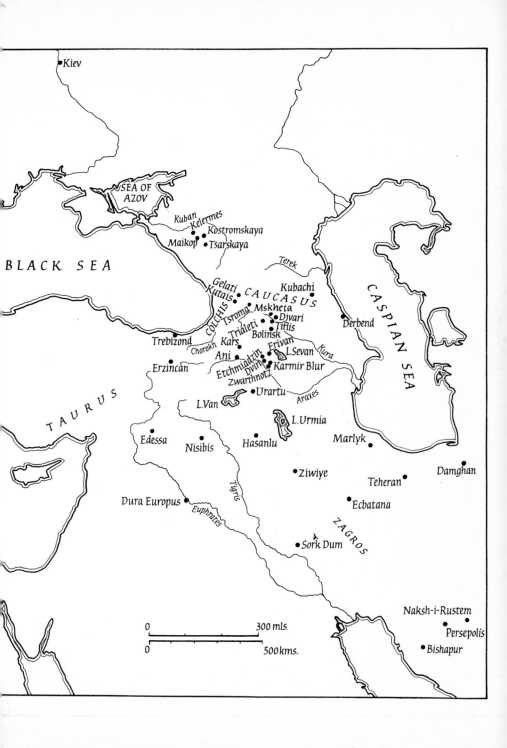

L. Baikal
Noin Ula
Amur
ei
Selenga
Ulan Bator
I
ORDOS
Great Wall of China
an
Tun-huang
Hwang-ho
CHINA
Lhasa

0   500 mls.

0   800 kms.

	ANCIENT ORIENT	GREATER CAUCASIAN AREA	RUSSIAN CENTRAL ASIA
3000		Princely burials of the KUBAN	Afanasievo culture in the Ob ar Irtysh areas
2000		Trialeti burials of Georgia	Andronovo culture in upper O and Yenissei areas
1000	Rise of Medes and Lurs MARLYK & HASANLU	Rise of Urartian kingdom	Metal working in Minussinsk basin
900	Luristan art		
800			
700	ZIWIYE	TOPRAK KALE	
	Fall of Assyrian Empire (612)	KARMIR BLUR	
600		End of Urartian kingdom (590)	Sakas, Turks, Huns amassing
500		Koban culture of Georgia until 1st century AD	ALTAIAN art at PAZYRYK
400	Death of Alexander (323) Fall of Achaemenids Rise of Seleucids (312–64)		Alexander the Great in area
300	Arsaces founder of Parthians c. 250		Rise of Zoroastrianism
200	PARTHIAN art		The Rise of SOGHDIA, FERGHANA, CHORASMIA
100		Armenia becomes great power under Tigranes	
BC AD	NISA monuments		
100	Rise of Sassanian Empire		First examples of Soghdian painting
200	Parthians conquered by Ardashir (226)		VARAKSHA paintings until 8th century
300		Founding of Constantinople (330) Christian states of Armenia, Georgia, Albania	PIANDJIKENT paintings until 7th century
400			TOPRAK KALA paintings, frescoes
500			
600	Death of Muhammad (632) Fall of Sassanian Empire	Arab conquest of area	PIANDJIKENT paintings, frescoes
700			VARAKSHA paintings, frescoes
800	Samanid dynasty		Arab conquest of area
900	Seljuk Turks begin to amass		
1000			

AFGHANISTAN	INDIA	EASTERN TURKESTAN	
			3000
			2000
		Chou dynasty c. 1027–221	
			1000
		Invention of silk-making in China	
			900
			800
			700
			600
	Birth of Buddhism		
			500
			400
			300
Rise of Bactrian kingdom until AD 155	King Asoka (264–227)	China trades silk to West ORDOS animal art	
			200
Yueh-Chi conquer Bactria c. 130	Demetrius conquers Gandhara c. 189 Buddhism reaches Gandhara	Han dynasty 206 BC–AD 25 Buddhism enters China c. 120	
			100
Rise of Kushans		NOIN-ULA burials Later ORDOS bronzes	
			BC
			AD
Rise of Graeco-Buddhist art HADDA & TAXILA	Expansion of Kushans Graeco-Buddhist art GANDHARA & MATHURA	Tadjik art (1st–4th centuries)	
			100
King Kanishka (144–185) Surkh Khotal temple	Kushans fall (241)		
			200
BEGRAM ivories			
			300
BAMYAN		MIRAN paintings	
			400
		Rise of Orkhon Turks Chinese enter Tarim KIZIL paintings	
			500
		TUN-HUANG art	
			600
	Buddhism in Tibet Height of Tibetan art	Kirghiz art T'ang dynasty (618–906) KIZIL paintings	
			700
		Uygurs	
			800
			900
Ghaznavid dynasty		TURFAN Nestorian and Manichean paintings	
			1000

List of Illustrations

The author and publishers are grateful to the many official bodies, institutions and individuals mentioned below for their assistance in supplying original illustration material

1 Gold bull: pierced for pole support to canopy. From Royal Tomb at Maikop, c. 2300 BC. Photo: State Hermitage Museum, Leningrad

2 Two gold diadems: decorated with gold rosettes, probably mounted on felt or cloth. Royal Tomb, Maikop, c. 2300 BC. Photo: State Hermitage Museum, Leningrad

3 Silver goblet: decorated with animals and a landscape. Royal Tomb, Maikop, c. 2300 BC. Photo: State Hermitage Museum, Leningrad

4 Projection of the decoration of a silver goblet: animals and a landscape. Royal Tomb, Maikop, c. 2300 BC

5 Cup: gold filigree work with mounted stones of agalmatolite and turquoise. Trialeti, 17th barrow, c. 1000–2000 BC. Photo: National State Museum of Georgia, Tiflis

6 Silver cup (two views): processions of men and animals. Kurukh Tash near Trialeti, 5th barrow, c. 1000–2000 BC. Photo: National State Museum of Georgia, Tiflis

7 Bronze belt with hunting scene. Trialeti, c. 1200 BC. Photo: National State Museum of Georgia, Tiflis

8 Belt buckle: stylized stag and dog. Iron. Fifth century BC. Photo: Georgian National Museum, Tiflis

9 Belt buckle: stylized horse. Bronze openwork, Scythian, Caucasus, c. fifth century BC. L. 5⅜″ (13·5). Photo: courtesy Trustees of the British Museum

10 Belt buckle: horse. Iron. Fifth century BC. Photo: Georgian National Museum, Tiflis

11 Horse's breast-plate (?): gold repoussé and filigree. Akhalgorisk horde, fifth century BC. Photo: Georgian National Museum, Tiflis

12 Gold head-dress terminals: Akhalgorisk horde, fifth century BC. H. 5⅛″ (13·0). Photo: Georgian National Museum, Tiflis

13 Silver bowl: so-called Kazbek dish from Stepantsminda, sixth century BC. Photo: National State Museum of Georgia, Tiflis

14 Silver dish (detail): Papak, pitiarch of Ardashir, 220–241. Photo: Georgian National Museum, Tiflis

15 Gold head of a stag from Tageloni, first century AD. Photo: Georgian Academy of Sciences, Republic of Georgia

16 Iron terminal of man standing on the horns of a bull. Stepantsminda, mid-first millennium BC. Photo: State Hermitage Museum, Leningrad

17 Dagger: inscribed with cuneiform, 'Marduk-nadin-abe, King of Babylon'. Bronze. L. 16¼″ (32·3). Kermanshah, twelfth century. Photo: Courtesy Trustees of the British Museum

18 Cheek-piece: human-headed, winged bull. Bronze. Luristan. Collection E. Graeffe, Brussels. Photo: ACC, Brussels

19 Gold stag: probably centre-piece to a shield. Kostromskaya, seventh–sixth century BC. L. c. 12″ (30·5). Photo: State Hermitage Museum, Leningrad

20 Gold leopard: chased and decorated with amber and enamel inlay. Probably centre-piece to a shield. Kelermes, seventh–sixth century BC. L. c. 12″ (30·5). Photo: State Hermitage Museum, Leningrad.

21 Felt saddle-cloth (detail): stag being attacked by an eagle. Pazyryk, Mound I, fifth century BC. c. 12″×7½″ (30·5×19)

22 Aigrette (?): lion-gryphon couchant. Gold, embossed and chased, head alone being completely in the round. Oxus Treasure. Scythian, fifth–fourth century BC. L. 2½″ (6·5). Photo: Courtesy Trustees of the British Museum

23 Wooden necklet: carved stags. Pazyryk, Mound 2, fifth century BC. Photo: State Hermitage Museum, Leningrad

24 Carved stag: wood with leather antlers. Pazyryk, Mound 2, fifth century BC. Photo: State Hermitage Museum, Leningrad

25 Wall-hanging (detail): human-headed composite creature. Felt appliqué. Pazyryk, Mound 5, fifth century BC. State Hermitage Museum, Leningrad. Photo: J. E. Dayton

26 Carpet (detail): border of elks and horsemen of Achemenian style. Wool 74½″×78¾″ (189×200). Persian, fourth–third century BC. Pazyryk, Mound 5. Photo: State Hermitage Museum, Leningrad

27 B-shaped belt buckle: The Hunt. Gold. Sarmatian, first century BC–first century AD. Photo: State Hermitage Museum Leningrad

28 B-shaped belt buckle: man asleep beneath a tree with horses and two people. One of a pair. Gold. Sarmatian, first century BC–first century AD. Photo: State Hermitage Museum, Leningrad

29 Belt buckle: wolf and serpent fighting. Gold, originally inlaid with stone and paste. Siberia, first–second century AD. Photo: State Hermitage Museum, Leningrad

30 Wall-hanging (detail): the so-called Great Goddess being approached by a rider. Reconstruction. Felt appliqué. Pazyryk, Mound 5, fifth century BC. c. 10′×6′ (3·05×1·83 m). Photo: State Hermitage Museum, Leningrad

31 Silver dish: warriors throwing down their arms. Kulagysh, seventh–eighth

century AD. Photo: State Hermitage Museum, Leningrad

32 Plaque: two men fighting, and their horses. Bronze openwork. Ordos region, c. third century BC. H. 2½″ (6·5), L. 5″ (12·8). Photo: Victoria and Albert Museum, crown copyright

33 Harness plaque: fighting horses. Gilt bronze openwork. Ordos region, c. first century BC. W. 4¾″ (12·0). Photo: Courtesy Trustees of the British Museum

34 Plaque: fragment of a gilt bronze creature. Ordos region (?), fourth–first century BC. H. 2″ (5·0). Photo: Courtesy Trustees of the British Museum

35 Horse trapping: stylized creature. Bronze. Ordos region. Han dynasty. Photo: Musée Cernuschi, Paris

36 Bronze ritual vessel (ting): Li Yü, Shansi. Chinese, sixth century BC. H. 6″ (15·2). Photo: Musée Guimet, Paris

37 Rug (detail): wild gryphon attacking an elk. Wool, embroidered. Noin Ula, Tomb 6, c. first century AD onwards. Photo: State Hermitage Museum, Leningrad.

38 Wall-hanging (detail): tigers. Wool, embroidered. Noin Ula, c. first century AD onwards. Photo: State Hermitage Museum, Leningrad.

39 Wall-hanging (detail): two horsemen. Embroidery. Noin Ula, 6th barrow, c. first century AD onwards. Photo: State Hermitage Museum, Leningrad

40 Wall-hanging (detail): head of a Hun. Embroidery. Noin Ula, 25th barrow, c. first century AD onwards. Photo: State Hermitage Museum, Leningrad

41 Death-mask: painted clay. Tadjik. Second century BC. Photo: John Webb

42 Sword sheath (detail): scenes from a royal hunt. Median workmanship. Oxus Treasure, seventh–sixth century BC. Gold. L. 10⅞″ (27·5). Photo: Courtesy Trustees of the British Museum

43 Bronze gates (detail): Assyrian army of Shalmaneser III defeating Urartians in 859 BC. Balawat, ninth century BC. Photo: Courtesy Trustees of the British Museum

44 Relief (detail): Assyrian melting down Urartian statues. Room XIII, Nineveh, seventh century BC. After a drawing by Flandin from E. Botta, *Monuments de Nineve*, Vol. II.

45 Bronze plaque: Urartian building. Toprak Kale, eighth–seventh century BC. H. 11⅞″ (30·0). Photo: Courtesy Trustees of the British Museum

46 Bronze model of a tower. Urartian, eighth–seventh century BC. Toprak Kale. H. 6⅝″ (16·8). Photo: Courtesy Trustees of the British Museum

47 Ornament: man standing on a bull. Probably part of a throne, now broken up. Bronze, engraved. Urartian, eighth–seventh century BC. Toprak Kale. H. 8½″ (21·5). Photo: Courtesy Trustees of the British Museum

48 Ornament: human-headed, winged bull. Probably part of a throne, now broken up. Bronze, originally with inlaid stone face. Urartian, eighth–seventh century BC. Toprak Kale. H. 8¾″ (22·2). Photo: Courtesy Trustees of the British Museum

49 Ornament: lion terminal from a throne, now broken up. Part of a throne now broken up. Urartian, eighth–seventh century BC. Toprak Kale. H. 8½″ (21·5), overall L. 11½″ (29·3). Photo: Courtesy Trustees of the British Museum

50 Bronze quiver: embossed with horsemen and chariots. Belonging to Sardur II. Urartian, c. seventh century BC. Karmir Blur. Photo: State Hermitage Museum, Leningrad.

51 Bronze helmet: embossed with horsemen and chariots. Belonging to Argysht I. Urartian, seventh century BC. Karmir Blur. Photo: State Hermitage Museum, Leningrad

52 Bronze helmet (detail): horsemen and chariots. Belonging to Argysht I. Urartian, seventh–sixth century BC.

Karmir Blur. Photo: State Hermitage Museum, Leningrad

53 Statuette: soldier. Bronze. H. 3¾″ (9·5). Urartian, eighth–seventh century BC. Photo: Musée du Louvre

54 Gold bowl: decorated with religious scenes. Hasanlu, Persia, ninth–eighth century BC. H. 8½″ (21·5), W. 11″ (28·0). Archaeological Museum, Teheran. Photo: Josephine Powell

55 Gold bowl (detail): goddess holding a mirror seated on a lion. Hasanlu, Persia, ninth–eighth century BC. H. 8½″ (21·5), W. 11″ (28·0). Archaeological Museum, Teheran. Photo: Josephine Powell

56 Spouted vessel: mythical figure with winged human body and two animal's heads, holding two sphinxes. Above, lion attacking a deer. Silver, inlaid with gold. Marlyk, late second–early first millennium. Diam. 7½″ (18·0). Archaeological Museum, Teheran. Photo: Dr E. O. Negahban

57 Gold vessel: winged bulls with heads in high relief, between, trees of life. Marlyk, c. ninth century BC. H. 7½″ (19·0). Archaeological Museum, Teheran. Photo Dr E. O. Negahban

58 Zoomorphic ritual vessel in the form of a bear. Pottery. H. 11″ (28·0). Marlyk, c. ninth century BC. Archaeological Museum, Teheran. Photo: Dr E. O. Negahban

59 Silver vessel: warrior struggling with leopards. Engraved. Marlyk, c. ninth century BC. H. 5½″ (14·0). Archaeological Museum, Teheran. Photo: Dr E. O. Negahban

60 Gold vase: double register of long-legged unicorns with scattered rosettes. Marlyk, c. ninth century BC. H. 7½″ (18·0). Archaeological Museum, Teheran. Photo: Dr E. O. Negahban

61 Cauldron handle: gryphon. Gold. L. 3⅛″ (8·0), W. 2⅛″ (5·3). Ziwiye, seventh century BC. Archaeological Museum, Teheran. Photo: Josephine Powell

62 Gold pectoral: two registers of processions of winged creatures, and, at each end, a Scythian feline and hare. Ziwiye, seventh century BC. L. 13″ (33·0), W. 5¼″ (13·4). Archaeological Museum, Teheran. Photo: Josephine Powell

63 Gold plaque: stags, ibexes and lions' masks. Comprises twenty-three fragments. Ziwiye, late seventh century BC. L. 11¾″ (30·0), W. 6¼″ (16·0). Archaeological Museum, Teheran. Photo: Josephine Powell

64 Dagger pommel in the form of a curled animal of Scythian type. Gold. H. ⅞″ (2·3), W. 1⅝″ (4·0). Ziwiye, c. 600 BC. Ernest Erickson Foundation, Inc. Photo: Metropolitan Museum of Art, New York

65 Horses head: green jade. Chinese, Han dynasty (206 BC–AD 220). H. 7⅝″ (19·3). Photo: Victoria and Albert Museum, crown copyright

66 Horse: grey unglazed pottery with traces of unfired paint. Chinese, Six Dynasties (220–589). H. 24″ (61·0). Photo: Victoria and Albert Museum, crown copyright

67 Tomb relief: battle on a bridge showing native Chinese ponies. Rubbing from a tomb in North China. Han dynasty. After E. Charrunes, *Mission archéologique dans le chine septentrionale*, Paris, 1909

68 Ivory rhyton: horned creature, with friezes of mythological characters. Old Nisa, Royal Treasury, second century. Photo: State Hermitage Museum, Leningrad

69 Ivory rhyton (detail): mythological characters. Old Nisa, Royal Treasury, second century. Photo: State Hermitage Museum, Leningrad

70 Statue: King Shapur I. Stone (*in situ*), 26′ (7·90 m). Bishapur (Mudan Cave), second half of the third century. Photo: Thames and Hudson Archives

71 Statue: Parthian prince. Bronze. Temple of Shami, Persia, 6′ 3″ (1·90 m). Parthian, second century. Archaeological Museum, Teheran. Photo: Thames and Hudson Archives

72 Bowl: Triumph of Dionysus with Ariadne and Heracles in relief. Silver. Diam. 9″ (22·6). Parthian, c. 200. Oxus Treasure. Photo: Courtesy Trustees of the British Museum

73 Relief: Parthian rider. Terracotta. H. 5⅞″ (14·8). Musée du Louvre. Photo: Archives Photographiques

74 Wall-painting (detail): horsemen hunting onagers. Parthian, second century. Dura Europos. Musée du Louvre, Paris. Photo: Thames and Hudson Archives

75 Bowl: Shapur II hunting. Chased silver with traces of gilding. Diam. 9″ (22·6). Sassanian, fourth century. Photo: State Hermitage Museum, Leningrad

76 Ossuary (fragment): figures beneath arches, showing Zoroastrian deities. Terracotta. Bia Naiman. Soghdian, fifth–seventh century. Photo: State Hermitage Museum, Leningrad

77 Ossuary (reconstruction): figures of Zoroastrian deities beneath arches. Terracotta. Bia Naiman. Soghdian, fifth–seventh century. Photo: State Hermitage Museum, Leningrad. After Borissov, 1940

78 Shield (fragment): horseman. Wood covered with leather. Mug Castle. Soghdian, eighth century. Photo: State Hermitage Museum, Leningrad

79 Stucco (fragment): carved decoration from a frieze. Soghdian, eighth century. Varaksha. Photo: State Hermitage Museum, Leningrad

80 Wall-painting (detail): drawing of a gryphon from Hall of Gryphons, Varaksha. Sogdhian, fifth–seventh century. State Hermitage Museum, Leningrad. After Shyshkin, *Varaksha*

81, 82 Wall-painting: men mounted on elephants fighting lions and leopards. From western wall of central hall of palace, Varaksha. Soghdian, fifth–seventh century. Photo: State Hermitage Museum, Leningrad

273

83 Wall-painting (detail): Tocharist painter. Second temple building, Kizil. Photo: Staatliche Museen, Berlin

84 Statue: 'Balbal' in stone, 6' (1·80 m). Photo: Historical Museum, Moscow

85 Wooden statuette of a woman. Piandjikent, seventh century. Photo: State Hermitage Museum, Leningrad

86 Wall-painting (reconstruction): the death of Syavush. Piandjikent, building XI, south wall, seventh–eight century. Photo: State Hermitage Museum, Leningrad

87 Wall-painting (reconstruction): ritual scene, probably depicting the Nu Ruz sacrifice, with traces of Soghdian inscription. Piandjikent, building X, north wall, seventh–eighth century. Photo: State Hermitage Museum, Leningrad

88 Wall-painting: men playing chess. Piandjikent, seventh century. Photo: State Hermitage Museum, Leningrad

89 Wall-painting: Rustram slaying the Dragon. Piandjikent, Room 41, seventh century. Photo: State Hermitage Museum, Leningrad

90 Wall-painting (reconstruction): horsemen. Piandjikent, seventh century. Photo: State Hermitage Museum, Leningrad

91 Wall-painting (reconstruction): Dehkans sitting at a feast. Piandjikent, seventh century. Photo: State Hermitage Museum, Leningrad

92 Wall-painting (reconstruction): woman harpist with a halo. Piandjikent, seventh century. Photo: State Hermitage Museum, Leningrad

93 Textile (reconstruction): ducks in roundels. Figured silk banner, blue and green on natural ground. Soghdian (Bokhara), early eighth century. Chien fo-Tung. Original in the British Museum. After Sir M. A. Stein, Serindia. Photo: Courtesy Secretary of State for Commonwealth Relations

94 Textile (reconstruction): elks in roundels. Figured silk banner, pink and green. Soghdian (Bokhara), early eighth century. Chien fo-Tung. Original in the British Museum. After Sir M. A. Stein, Serindia. Photo: Courtesy Secretary of State for Commonwealth Relations

95 Textile (reconstruction): figured silk. Soghdian, first century AD. Moshchevja Balka (Kuban). Photo: State Hermitage Museum, Leningrad

96 Wall-painting: woman holding gold cups. Soghdian, fifth–sixth century. Balalyk Tepe. Photo: John Webb

97 Textile: boar's head in roundel. Figured silk. Sassanian, sixth–seventh century. Astana. Photo: National Museum, New Delhi

98 Wall-painting (fragment): pigeon holding a necklace. Soghdian, fifth–seventh century. Gryphon Hall, Varaksha. After Shyshkin, Varaksha

99 Textile: bird-dog (senmerv). Said to have been found in the reliquary of the head of St Helena. Originally ornaments of a costume from a burial ground in Egypt. Figured silk. Sassanian, sixth–seventh century. Victoria and Albert Museum. Photo: John Webb

100 Ewer: decorated with ladies beneath arches. Gold. H. 6¼" (16·5). Photo: State Hermitage Museum, Leningrad

101 Dish: hunting scene. Silver. Soghdian, not earlier than seventh century. Photo: State Hermitage Museum, Leningrad

102, 103 Wall-paintings (fragments): human and tiger heads. Palace, Toprak Kala, third–fourth century. Photo: State Hermitage Museum, Leningrad

104 Sculpture: Alabaster head. Toprak Kala, third century. Photo: State Hermitage Museum, Leningrad

105 Statue: fragment of a woman. Unbaked, painted clay. Over life-size. Palace, Toprak Kala, third century. Photo: State Hermitage Museum, Leningrad

106 Frieze: rosettes and palmettes. Stucco. Teshik Kala. Photo: State Hermitage Museum, Leningrad

107 Statuette: river goddess (*yakshi*). Ivory, part of a piece of furniture. Begram, date uncertain, probably first–fourth century. Kabul Museum. Photo: Josephine Powell

108 Ivory: two water goddesses. Fragment of furniture. Begram, date uncertain, probably first–fourth century. Kabul Museum. Photo: Josephine Powell

109 Ivory: water goddesses. Fragment of furniture. Begram, date uncertain, probably first–fourth century. Kabul Museum. Photo: Josephine Powell

110 Glass bottle; probably imported from Syria. Begram, *c.* first–fourth century. Kabul Museum. Photo: Josephine Powell

111 Frieze: busts of youths and girls – musicians and garland-bearers. Stone. Possibly from a Buddhist temple, Airtam. First century. Photo: State Hermitage Museum Leningrad

112 Frieze (detail): bust of a musician. Stone. Possibly from a Buddhist temple, Airtam. First century. Photo: State Hermitage Museum, Leningrad

113 Coin: Eucratedes and (reverse) two horses. Silver tetradrachma, *c.* 180–150 BC. Photo: Courtesy Trustees of the British Museum

114 Coin: Demetrius helmetted. Silver tetradrachma of Demetrius. Photo: Courtesy Trustees of the British Museum

115 Coin: Euthydemus in old age. Silver tetradrachma wearing a laurel wreath, *c.* 230. Photo: Courtesy Trustees of the British Museum

116 Coin: Eucratedes. Gold stater. Bactrian, 170–165 BC. Photo: Bibliothèque Nationale, Paris

117 Silver gilt bowl: hunting scenes. North-west India, fifth–sixth century. L. 6½″ (16·0). Photo: Courtesy Trustees of the British Museum

118 Silver bowl: scenes from Tragedies of Euripides (Alcestis, Alope, Bacchae and Ion). Kustanai, first–second century. Photo: State Hermitage Museum, Leningrad

119 Silver bowl: two scenes from Syleus. Heracles, slave of Syleus, and Heracles slaying his master after a feast. Seventh century. Photo: State Hermitage Museum, Leningrad

120 Silver phalera: goddess with a bow. Photo: State Hermitage Museum, Leningrad

121 Silver disc: elephant and riders. Photo: State Hermitage Museum, Leningrad

122 Mirror; with graeco-bactrian designs. Bronze. Diam. 9⅛″ (32·3). Han dynasty (*c.* 200 BC–AD 220). Photo: Victoria and Albert Museum, crown copyright

123 Gold armlet; with gryphon terminals, and originally inlaid with coloured stones. One of a pair, the other is in the British Museum. Oxus Treasure. Persian, fifth century BC. H. 5″ (12·3), diam. 4½″ (11·5). Photo: Victoria and Albert Museum, crown copyright

124 Gold ring: embossed in the form of a lion (?). Originally set with coloured stones and turquoises. Oxus Treasure. Scythian, fifth–fourth century BC. Diam. 1½″ (3·6). Photo: Courtesy Trustees of the British Museum

125 Bronze lion-gryphon: cast and chased. Said to have been found near Helmund river. Bactrian, fourth century BC. H. 10″ (24·9). Photo: Courtesy Trustees of the British Museum

126 Pendant: figure of Hariti. Gold repoussé with pearls and garnets. Taxila area, third–fourth century. Photo: Victoria and Albert Museum, crown copyright

127 Pendant: gold-encrusted with jewels. Taxila. Kushan period, *c.* 100 BC–AD 100. Photo: National Museum, Karachi

128 Bowl: a *yaksha*, perhaps Kuvera, drinking. Silver embossed and chased. Kushan, third–fourth century. Buddhaghana, north-west India. Diam. 10″ (25·0). Photo: Courtesy Trustees of the British Museum

129 Reliquary: figures beneath arches. Gold, inlaid with rubies. Buddhist stupa at Bimaran. Kushan, first century. Photo: Courtesy Trustees of the British Museum

130 Statue: King Kanishka, inscribed 'The king, king of kings, His Majesty Kanishka'. Pink sandstone, originally enhanced with metal plaques. H. c. 5′ 7″ (1·70). Kushan, second century. Photo: Archaeological Museum, Mathura

131 Coin: Bull of Siva. Gandharan. Spalapati Dera, early tenth century. Photo: Courtesy Trustees of the British Museum

132 Coin: King Kanishka and (reverse) the goddess Ardoksha holding a cornucopia. Gold. Photo: Courtesy Trustees of the British Museum

133 Relief: Hariti and Pancika. Grey schist or limestone. Takht-i-Bahr. North-west India. Gandhara, third–fourth century. Photo: Courtesy Trustees of the British Museum

134 Head of a Bodhisattva. Pink sandstone. Kushan style, Mathura, second century. H. 4″ (10·2). Victoria and Albert Museum. Photo: John Webb

135 Relief: tree spirit (yakshi). Pink sandstone. H. 20¼″ (33·0). Jain stupa at Mathura. Kushan, second century. Photo: Victoria and Albert Museum, crown copyright

136 Head of Buddha. Red sandstone. Kushan, c. first century. Mathura. H. 1′ 10½″ (57·0). Photo: Archaeological Museum, Mathura

137 Head of Buddha. Lime composition with traces of red paint on the lips. Gandhara. Romano-Buddhist style, fourth–fifth century. Photo: Victoria and Albert Museum, crown copyright

138 Head of Buddha. Grey schist. Gandhara, second–third century. H. 1′ 4″ (40·5). Photo: Courtesy Trustees of the British Museum

139 Statue of a seated Buddha (Dharmacka mudra). Gandhara, second–third century.

c. 3′ (94·5). Photo: Courtesy Trustees of the British Museum

140 Statue of a Bodhisattva. Stone. H. 3′ 7″ (1·09 m). Gandhara, second century. Photo: Courtesy Museum of Fine Arts, Boston

141 Model stupa. Gandhara. Valley of Swat. Photo: Museum of Indian Art, Calcutta

142 Relief: Prince Siddartha (later Buddha) driving to school in a chariot drawn by two rams. Beside walk his companions holding inkpots and writing boards. Schist. Gandhara, Romano-Buddhist, second–fourth century. Photo: Victoria and Albert Museum, crown copyright

143 Relief: death of Buddha. Gandhara, Romano-Buddhist style, second–third century. Takht-i-Bahr, north-west India. Photo: Courtesy Trustees of the British Museum

144 Relief: Prince Siddartha in his harem. Stone. Gandhara, second–third century. Takht-i-Bahr, north-west India. Photo: Courtesy Trustees of the British Museum

145 Statue: goddess with flowers. Limestone. H. 1′ 7″ (48·0). Hadda, third–fourth century. Photo: Musée Guimet, Paris

146 Statue: head of monk. Lime composition. H. c. 4″ (10·0). Photo: Victoria and Albert Museum, crown copyright

147 Statue: head of a warrior. Lime composition. Romano-Buddhist style, fourth–fifth century. Hadda. H. c. 4″ (10·0). Photo: Victoria and Albert Museum, crown copyright

148 Statue: head of a demon (yaksha). Stone. Romano-Buddhist style. Hadda, fourth–fifth century. Kabul Museum. Photo: Josephine Powell

149 Colossal statue of Buddha. Rock-hewn, folds modelled on rope covered with plaster. West of Bamyan. H. 175′ (53·4 m). Fourth–fifth century. Photo: Thames and Hudson Archives

150 Wall-painting: Mandorla with Buddha preaching, surrounded by small Buddha

figures. From a dome, Bamyan, fifth–sixth century. Diam. *c*. 34″ (86·5). Kabul Museum. Photo: Josephine Powell

151 Wall-painting: the hunter king. From drum of a dome, Kakrak. Fifth–sixth century. L. 4′ 3½″ (1·3 m). Photo: Josephine Powell

152 Wall-painting: Bodhisattva surrounded by figures. Bamyan, group K, cave 3. Fifth–sixth century. Photo: Thames and Hudson Archives

153 Relief (detail): The hunt. Stone. Sassanian, fifth–sixth century. Taq-i-Bustan, Persia. Author's photo

154 Wall-painting: Buddha in meditation. Balawaste, mid-sixth century. H. *c*. 1′ 7½″ (49·5). National Museum, New Delhi. Photo: Josephine Powell

155 Wall-painting (detail): pigeons with necklaces. Bamyan. Photo: Josephine Powell

156 Wall-painting (detail): tusked boar. Bamyan. Photo: Josephine Powell

157 Sarcophagus cover: princely couple. Painted terracotta. Fundukistan, Niche E, sixth–seventh century. Kabul Museum. Photo: Thames and Hudson Archives

158 Wooden plaque: Blue Lotus Maitreya. Fundukistan, Niche E, seventh century. W. 9½″ (24·0). Kabul Museum. Photo: Josephine Powell

159 Ewer: horseman hunting with bow and arrow, the so-called 'Parthian shot'. Pottery, glazed with yellow and blue. H. 12½″ (31·8). Chinese, T'ang dynasty (618–906). Photo: Ashmolean Museum, Oxford

160 Ewer: bird-dog (*senmerv*). Silver. Sassanian, or post-Sassanian. After Y. I. Smirnov, *Oriental Silverware*

161 Amphora: handles are two stylized dragons. White pottery with brown glaze. Chinese, T'ang dynasty (618–906). H. 12¾″ (32·0). Collection Mr Samuel Lee, Tokyo. Photo: Thames and Hudson Archives

162 Seals: impressions from documents. Left, Chinese, right, Graeco-Romano

figure. Niya. Photo: Courtesy Trustees of the British Museum

163 Wooden chair: Niya, third century. H. 23″ (60·5), W. 26″ (61·5). Photo: Courtesy Trustees of the British Museum

164 Pilgrim flask: The Nativity. Red painted pottery. Eastern Mediterranean, *c*. fourth–sixth century. Photo: Courtesy Trustees of the British Museum

165 Pilgrim flask: flute player and dancer among foliage. Stoneware, glazed brown, over white slip. Chinese, T'ang dynasty (618–906). H. 8⅝″ (22·0), W. 7½″ (19·0). Photo: Victoria and Albert Museum, crown copyright

166 Statuette: figure of a dancer, probably a Chorasmian. Olive-green glaze. Chinese, T'ang dynasty (618–906). H. 8½″ (19·0). Photo: Royal Ontario Museum, Toronto

167 Statuette: figure of a youth with Graeco-Romano features. Unglazed grey pottery with traces of colour. Chinese, T'ang dynasty (618–906). H. 5⅛″ (13·0). Photo: Victoria and Albert Museum, crown copyright

168 Statuette: woman polo-player. Unglazed pottery with traces of colour. Chinese, T'ang dynasty (618–906). H. *c*. 11¾″ (30·0). Photo: Courtesy Trustees of the British Museum

169 Textile: ponies. Printed silk, blue and yellow. Chinese, ninth–tenth century, Chien fo-Tung. Photo: Courtesy Trustees of the British Museum

170 Textile: repeat pattern of animals and Chinese characters. Polychrome silk. Later Han dynasty. Photo: National Museum, New Delhi

171 Statuette: a warrior. Carved stucco, H. 12″ (30·5). Mingoi, near Sorçuk, eighth–tenth century. Photo: Courtesy Trustees of the British Museum

172 Statuette: fragment of a horse. Carved stucco. Mingoi, near Sorçuk, eighth–tenth century. Photo: Courtesy Trustees of the British Museum

173 Statuette: head of a camel. Carved stucco. L. *c.* 12″ (30·5). Mingoi, near Sorçuk, eighth–tenth century. Photo: Courtesy Trustees of the British Museum

174 Head of a laughing man. Carved stucco. Mingoi, near Sorçuk, eighth–tenth century. H. *c.* 2″ (5·0). Photo: Courtesy Trustees of the British Museum

175 Wall-painting: swimmers. Cave of the Navigator, Kizil, *c.* 500. W. 13½″ (30·9). Staatliche Museen, Berlin. Photo: Karl H. Paulmann

176 Wall-painting: goddess and celestial musician. Cave of the Painted Floor, Kizil, *c.* 600–650. W. 4′ 5″. Staatliche Museen, Berlin. Photo: Karl H. Paulmann

177 Wall-painting: female donors. Sorçuk, Cave VII, eighth–ninth century. H. 8¾″ (22·0). Photo: Staatliche Museen, Berlin

178 Wall-painting: worshipping Bodhisattva. Kumtura, eighth–ninth century. H. 23⅝″ (60·0). Photo: Staatliche Museen, Berlin

179 Wall-painting: donors. Cave of the Sixteen Sword-bearers, Kizil, *c.* 600–650. H. 5′ 3″ (1·6 m). Staatliche Museen, Berlin. Photo: Karl H. Paulmann

180 Wall-painting: dance of Queen Candraprabha. Treasure Cave, Kizil, *c.* 500. H. 5′ 3″ (1·6 m). Staatliche Museen, Berlin. Photo: Karl H. Paulmann

181 Wall-painting: head of a young ascetic. Cave of the Navigator, Kizil, *c.* 500. W. 13¾″ (30·9). Photo: Staatliche Museen, Berlin

182 Wall-painting: head of Ascetic Mahakasyapa. Large cave, Kizil, 600–650. H. 15¾″ (40·0). Staatliche Museen, Berlin. Photo: Karl H. Paulmann

183 Scroll: Buddha addressing Subhuti, from the Diamond Sutra. Chinese, 868. Tun-huang. Photo: Courtesy Trustees of the British Museum

184 Wall-painting: Buddha beneath a canopy. Koço, seventh–eighth century.

H. *c.* 8″ (20·5). Photo: Staatliche Museen, Berlin

185 Wall-painting: the future Buddha renouncing the world. Koço, ninth century. H. 10¾″ (27·4). Photo: Staatliche Museen, Berlin

186 Wall-painting: portrait of Mani (?). Manichean. Koço, Ruin K, early ninth century, 5′ 6″×2′ 10″ (1·65×0·96 m). Photo: Staatliche Museen, Berlin

187 Wall-painting: Uygur prince. Bezeklik, Temple 19, eighth–ninth century. W. 8¾″ (12·4). Photo: Staatliche Museen, Berlin

188 Wall-painting: Uygur princesses. Bezeklik, ninth century. H. 21¼″ (53·9). Photo: Staatliche Museen, Berlin

189 Silk: Uygur prince. Koço, ninth century (?). W. *c.* 14″ (31·0). Photo: Staatliche Museen, Berlin

190 Miniature: a Turcoman prisoner. Kazvin school, *c.* 1575 (MS. Ouseley Add. 173, fol. 1 r.). Photo: Bodleian Library, Oxford

191 Portrait of Ghengis Khan. National Central Museum, Tainan (Formosa). Photo: Thames and Hudson Archives

192 Wall-painting: dragon leaping out of the water. Bezeklik, Temple 19, ninth–tenth century. H. 25″ (32·0). Photo: Staatliche Museen, Berlin

193 Wall-painting: musicians. Bezeklik, eighth century. Private collection, Tokyo

194 Wall-painting: Palm Sunday (?). Nestorian. Koço, temple at Eastern Gate, late ninth century, 23½″×25″ (30·5 ×32·0). Photo: Staatliche Museen, Berlin

195 Wall-painting; worshipper, Nestorian. Koço, temple at Eastern Gate, late ninth century. 17⅛″×8¼″ (33·0×12·0). Photo: Staatliche Museen, Berlin

196 Wooden plaque: two youths riding. Dandan-Uilik, Sanctuary D. VII, *c.* seventh century. 13¼″×7″ (33·5×17·8).

Photo: Courtesy Trustees of the British Museum

197 Wooden plaque: four-armed, three-faced deity seated cross-legged on a cushion supported by two couchant bulls (recalling Brahmanic Siva Avolokitesvara). Painted on both sides. Dandan-Uilik, ruined dwelling, c. seventh century. c. 12¾"×8" (32·5× 25·4). Photo: Courtesy Trustees of the British Museum

198 Banner: the Bodhisattva Namasangiti. Western Tibet, sixteenth century. Photo Courtesy Trustees of the British Museum

199 Sculpture: Maitreya. Bronze. Tibet, fifteenth century. Photo: Courtesy Trustees of the British Museum

200 Wooden plaque: three seated Bodhisattvas. Painted on both sides. Dandan-Uilik, c. eighth century. Sanctuary, D.X.3. Photo: Courtesy Trustees of the British Museum

201 Wooden plaque: 'The Silk Princess'. Dandan-Uilik, Sanctuary D.X., c. seventh century. 7½"×4⅝" (19·0×11·5). Photo: Courtesy Trustees of the British Museum

202 Wall-painting: youths with garlands. Miran, Shrine V, late third century. Photo: National Museum, New Delhi

203 Wall-painting: religious scene. Miran, late third century. H. c. 29" (73·8). Photo: Nation Museum, New Delhi

204 Interior view of Cave CXCVI; Buddha, Lohans, Bodhisattvas and painted walls. Tun-huang, eighth century. Photo: Arthaud

205 Silk-hanging: Bodhisattva holding a transparent bowl. Tun-huang, 2′ 7½"× 10" (80·0×25·5). Photo: Courtesy Trustees of the British Museum

206 Statue: Lokapala. Painted clay. Cave CXCVI, Tun-huang, eighth century. Photo: Arthaud

207 Wall-painting (detail): dancing ladies. Cave CDXXVIII, early sixth century. Tun-huang. Photo: Arthaud

208 Statues: the disciples Ananda and Kasyapa. Tun-huang, early seventh century. Photo: Arthaud

209 Anberd castle on the promontory at the confluence of the Anberd and Arkhashan rivers. Photo: State Hermitage Museum, Leningrad

210 Miniature: The Annunciation. Etchmiadzin Gospel (Maternadaran 2374). Armenian, 989, executed in the Monastery of Novavank, Siunik. 11"×7⅞" (28·0×19·5). Photo: Thames and Hudson Archives

211 Miniature: The Baptism of Christ. Etchmiadzin Gospel (Maternadaran 2374). Armenian, 989, executed in the Monastery of Novavank, Siunik. 11" ×7⅞" (28·0×20·0). Photo: Thames and Hudson Archives

212 Stele of carved stone from a church at Gaiana, ninth–tenth century. Photo: Mme Thierry

213 Textile (reconstruction): two seated figures in a roundel. Moshchevaja Balka. Armenian, c. third century. Photo: State Hermitage Museum, Leningrad

214 Column capital: confronted peacocks. Carved wood. Sevan cathedral, Armenia, ninth–tenth century. Photo: State Hermitage Museum, Leningrad

215 Wall-painting: St Gregory the Illuminator converting Armenia to Christianity, and The Dormition of the Virgin. Church of St Gregory Tigrane-Honentz, Ani. Thirteenth century. Photo: Ara Güler

216 City walls, Ani, Armenia. Late tenth century. Photo: Ara Güler

217 View of the entrance of the Palace, Ani, Armenia. Author's photo

218 Cathedral, Ani, Armenia, 989–1001. Photo: Ara Güler

219 Church of St Gregory of Abughamrentz, Ani. Mid-ninth century. Photo: Ara Güler

220 Relief: King Gagik. West façade of the church of Aghtamar, Lake Van, 915–921. Photo: Josephine Powell

221 Column capital (detail): bull's head. The Sion, Bolinsk, 478/9–493/4. Photo: Georgian Academy of Sciences

222 Column capital (detail): lions and deer. South pilaster of altar screen. The Sion, Bolinsk, fifth century. Photo: Georgian Academy of Sciences

223 Stone relief: Stephanos I, Patriarch of Kavtli, east side of Djvari church, seventh century. Photo: Georgian Academy of Sciences

224 Stone relief: The Kuropolate Ashot. Opiza church, 826. Photo: Georgian Academy of Sciences

225 Exterior view of Djvari church from the south-east, seventh century. Author's photo

226 Silver disc: St Mamas on a lion. Georgian, sixth–seventh century. Photo: Georgian Academy of Sciences

227 Silver icon (detail): St John. Cover of the Bertsk Gospels. Silver. By Beshken Opizari, 1184–93. Photo: Georgian Academy of Sciences

228 Silver plaque: two saints. c. Eighth century. Photo: Georgian Academy of Sciences

229 Stone relief: altar screen from Tsebelda, sixth century. Photo: Georgian Academy of Sciences

230 Exterior view of Ateni church, tenth century. Photo: Georgian Academy of Sciences

231 Column capital: Kutais cathedral. Georgian, early twelfth century. Author's photo

232 East front of the church of St Tzkhoveli, Mskheta, 1029. Photo: Georgian Academy of Sciences

233 Atzghuri castle, Georgia. Photo: Georgian Academy of Sciences

234 An old house in Moshir at the foot of the Oashta in Swanetia. Author's photo

235 Exterior view of Tzromi church. Seventh century. Photo: Georgian Academy of Sciences

236 Sketch for a mosaic: Head of Christ. Tzromi church, seventh century. Photo: Georgian Academy of Sciences

237 Wall-painting: Christ between the symbols of the Sun and Moon. Cave church at Dodo, David Garedzha, eighth–ninth century. Photo: Georgian Academy of Sciences

238 Wall-painting (detail): Archangel. Cave church of Dodo, David Garedzha, eighth–ninth century. Photo: Georgian Academy of Sciences

239 Miniature: St Mark. Dzhruchi Gospel. Georgian, tenth century (H. 1660, fol. 92 v.). Photo: Georgian National Museum, Tiflis

240 Miniature: St Mark healing the Blind. Dzhruchi Gospel, tenth century (H. 1660, fol. 93). Photo: Georgian National Museum, Tiflis

241 Triptych: The Khakuli Icon. Gold repoussé and filigree, inlaid with Georgian and Byzantine enamels and precious stones. Central panel shows the Virgin. Twelfth and tenth century respectively, 6′ 6″ × 4′ 9″ (2 × 1·47 m). State Museum of Georgia, Tiflis. Photo: Cercle d'art, Paris

242 Khukuli Icon (detail): Christ *Pantocrater*; (*circle below*) Archangel Gabriel; (*below left*) SS John and Mark; (*below centre*) St Gregory the Theologian. Georgian enamels, twelfth century. State Museum of Georgia, Tiflis. Photo: Cercle d'art, Paris

243 Gelat monastery, founded by King Bagrat III, tenth century. Photo: Georgian Academy of Sciences

244 Mosaic (detail): The Virgin. Gelat monastery, 1125–30. Photo: Georgian Academy of Sciences

245 Photograph taken at the beginning of this century showing a man from Ossetia wearing armour consisiting of leather breast-plates, similar to that worn by the Tadjiks. Author's photo

246 Bronze cauldron, with animals mounted on the handles. Daghestan, thirteenth century. Photo: State Hermitage Museum, Leningrad

247 Bronze cauldron showing mounted rider, Daghestan. Photo: State Hermitage Museum, Leningrad

248 Bronze cauldron (viewed from above): confronted animals. Daghestan. H. 18¾″ (48·0). Photo: State Hermitage Museum, Leningrad

249 Stone relief: horseman. Upper portion of a window from a mosque at Kubachi, eleventh century. Photo: State Hermitage Museum, Leningrad

250 Stone relief: the hunt. Daghestan, twelfth century. Photo: State Hermitage Museum, Leningrad

251 Stone relief: horsemen fighting. Kubachi twelfth–thirteenth century. Photo: State Hermitage Museum, Leningrad

252 Bowl: floral decorations in underglaze colours. Kubachi ware, sixteenth century. H. 4½″ (11·4), diam. 12″ (30·5). Author's collection. Photo: John Webb

The maps were specially drawn by Mr John Woodcock

Index

Numbers in italics refer to illustrations

Abbasids, 224
Achaemenids, 25, 76, 77, 116, 222, 256; art, 20, 22, 69, 138, *123*
Afghanistan, 42, 75, 90, 106, 129, 148, 161, 177; under the Kushans, 143, 162; its Buddhist religion and culture, 162–8, 180; Sassanian influence in, 168–70
Afrasiab (Samarkand), 94–5, 96
Agathocles, coin of, 134
Aghovan (Caucasian Albania, q.v.), 253
Aghtamar, 235, 236, *220*
Airtam, 131, *111, 112*
Akhalgorisk hoard, Georgia, 22, *11, 12*
Aksu, 176, 180
Albanian Gates (Derbend defile), 257
Albaum, L. I., 100
Alexander the Great, 42, 80, 81, 87, 91, 92, 124, 222
Alexandria, 148, 161
Alexandria-Kapisu or Kapisha *see* Kapisu
Altai, the, 52, 168; art, 30, 32–4, 38, 39, 45; *21, 23, 24*
Amiranachvili, Professor, 25
Amphora, 175, *161*
Amu Darya, river, 76, 100, 123 *see also* Oxus
Anatolia, 14, 55, 67, 95, 122, 158, 165, 169, 220, 232, 262
Anberd Castle, *209*
ʿAni, 228, 232, 235, 236, *215, 216, 217, 218*
Anihita, 94, 124, 222
Ankara, 229
Anti-Taurus mountains, 237
Anwari of Tus, 195
Apollo, 151, 223
Arabs: invade Central Asia, 40, 51, 93, 122, 162, 169–70, 220, 251; destroy Toprak Kala, 118; occupy Armenia, 223–4, 228, 230; occupy Georgia, 251–2; occupy Albania, 258, 260
Aral, Sea of, 50, 93
Aral mountains, 42
Aramazd, 222
Aran (Caucasian Albania, q.v.), 253
Araxes, river, 222, 256
Ardashir I, king of Persia, 25, 86
Argysht I, king of the Urartu, 57, 64, *51, 52*
Argysht II, king of the Urartu, 58
Arin-Berd or Ereburi, 58, 60, 62
Armenia, 91, 221, 253, 256; Urartian kingdom, 54; people, 21–3; Eastern and Western powers contend for, 22–3; Christian, 223; Arab occupation of, 223–4;

develops national culture, 224; arts, 224–8, 230–1, 232–3, *210, 211, 213, 215, 220*; Dvin, 228–31; architecture, 229–30, 231–2, 235–6, *209, 214, 216–19*; annexes part of Albania and Georgia, 258
Armenian Church, 223
Armenians, 256; origins, 221
Armour, leather, 253, *245*
Arsaces, king of Parthia, 81, 83
Arsacids, 256
Artashat, 228, 229
Aryans, of Koço, 194
Ashkabad, 81
Asia Minor, 14, 26, 90, 124, 142, 168
Asoka, emperor of India, 148
Assyrian art, 57, 59, 65, *44*
Assyrians, 54–5, 57
Astyages, king of the Medes, 55
Ateni, 244, *230*
Athena, 83
Athene, 222
Athos, Mount, Georgian monastery of Iviron, 250
Atropat, king of Armenia, 222
Avars, 50
Avesta, the, 77
Azarbeidjan, 67, 221
Azes I, Scytho-Parthian king, 144

Babylon, 80, 221, 237
Bactria, 50, 76, 77, 80, 81, 99, 144, 145, 170, 190; conquered by the Achaemenids, 76, 123; absorbed in Kushan empire, 92–3, 143; extent, 123; standard of living, 123; religion, 124, 131; conquered by Alexander the Great, 124; its capital, 124, 127–8; under the Seleucids, 128–9; political maturity and intellectual sophistication, 129, 131; art, 131–4, 138, 154, 242, *111, 112, 117–22, 125*; coinage, 133, *113–16*; clearing house for India's trade with the West, 139; love of luxury, 140; Greeks in, ejected by Kushans, 140, 141
Badakshan, 93, 123
Baghdad, 224
Bagrat III, king of Georgia, 253
Bagratids, 228, 230
Bahram Gur, 106
Baikal, 44, 195
Balalyk Tepe, 100, 110, 121, 166; *96, 97*
Balbals or 'Stone Dames', 100
Balk, 124, 142, 162, 174
Balkash, Lake, 42

Bamyan, 142, 172, 184; Buddhist paintings at, 100, 122, 164, 180, 192; Buddhist monastery ruins at, 162; statue of Buddha at, *149*; painting from cave shrine at, 165, 166, *150*; wall-paintings from, 169, *155, 156*
Banners, embroidered, 210, *198*
Barda'a (Arabic name for Perosez), 257
Barger, Evart, 132
Barnett, Dr R. D., 72
Basilican churches: of Armenia, 229; of Georgia, 238, 239
Begram (Kapisu), 162, 165, 172; treasures from, 127–8, 161, 186, *107–10*
Belt buckles see Siberia
Bezeklik, 200, *187, 188, 192, 193*
Bia Naiman, 114, *100*
Bisitun, inscription, 76, 77, 123, 221
Bivar, A. D. H., 144
Black Sea, 90, 176, 222
Block-printed book, earliest, 194, *183*
Blue Lotus Maitreya, 172, *158*
Bodhisattvas, 154, 155, 182, 206, 213, 217, *140, 152, 204, 205*
Bogazköy, 62
Bokhara: Khan of, 50–1, oasis, 97; carpets, 111; Great Mosque, 115; conquered by Arabs, 220
Bolinsk, the Sion at, 238–9, 244, *221, 222*
Buddha, 150, 151, 156–8, 162, 181, 200, 206, 210, 211; statues, reliefs and paintings of, *136–9, 142–4, 149, 183–5, 204*
Buddhism: in Bactria, 131; westward movement of, 142; in Gandhara, 149–50; in Afghanistan, 162; in Bamyan, 162, 164; in the Tarim basin, 176; in China, 177, 188; among the Uygurs, 197; in Tibet, 208; in eastern Turkestan, 221
Buddhist art: eastern Turkestan, 100, 180ff., *83, 169–208*; at Bamyan (*see* Bamyan); in Bactria, 131, *111, 112*; in Kushan period, 146; in Gandhara, 148–54, *137–9, 141–8*; in Matura, 151, *136, 140*; influences and effects, 155–6; stupas and vishanas, 156–7, *141–3*; in Afghanistan, 162–8, 180, *149–56*; in eastern Turkestan, 180ff., *183–208*
Buddhist monasteries, 162
Bull cult, 14
Bussagli, M., 181, 188, 214
Byzantine influence: on Georgian art, 242, 244, 246, 248, 249; on Georgian Church, 252
Byzantium, 91, 94, 181, 188, 214, 223, 225, 228, 251

Cai (Armenians), 221
Carpets, 34, 111, 230
Caspian Sea, 81, 222, 253
Catal Hüyük, 26

Caucasian Albania, 221; early history, 253–6; its tribes attain unity, 256; under Persian control, 256–7; converted to Zoroastrianism, and then to Christianity, 257; under the Arabs, 257; arts and crafts, 258–62, *246–52*
Caucasian Georgia see Georgia
Caucasus, the, 67, 91, 116; conquered by Sassanians, 25; Scythians arrive in, 26; Urartian kingdom in, 54; Arab invasion of, 251; armour worn in, 256, *245*
Caucasus mountains, 14, 55
Cauldrons, 261–2, *247–9*
Cerčen, 176, 180, 181
Chandragupta, emperor of India, 148
Ch'an-gan, 208
Chensu bronzes, 43
Cheremi, church of, 238
China, 34, 77, 139, 141, 155, 168, 206, 211, 220; raided by the Huns, 43; nomadic style of art in, 43, *36*; and the Orkhon Turks, 51; raids Ferghana, 78–9; ponies, 79, *66, 67*; silk industry, 90, 140, 228; contact with Afrasiab, 94, 95; Han period bronze mirror, 133–4, *122*; transports gold, 140; relations with the Kushans, 141–2; trade with Tarim basin, 173; protection of caravan routes, 173–6; T'ang dynasty ware, 175, 178, *159–61, 164, 166–8*; Buddhism in, 177, 188; loses and regains Tun-huang, 220
Chinese Turkestan, 145 (*see also* Turkestan, eastern)
Chorasmia, 75, 76, 80, 85, 90, 123, 176, 202; under Achaemenids, 77, 116; under Parthians, 8; under Kushans, 93, 116; Bronze Age, 115–16; alterations of independence and subjection, 116; villages and castles, 116; religion, 117; capital, 117–18; 120; art, 120–2, *102–6*
Chorokh, river, 222
Chosroe I, Sassanian emperor, 93
Chosroe II, Sassanian emperor, 168
Chosroe Kotan Arshakuni, king of Armenia, 228
Chu valley, 195
Chubinashvili, 239, 244
Cimmerians, 19, 26, 27, 29
Cloisonné enamels, 252, *242*
Colchis, 18, 19, 91
Confucianism, 193
Constantinople, 51, 91, 223, 224; Hagia Sophia, 235; palace of the Blachernae, 246
Ctesiphon, 86
Cyreskatu or Kyropolis, 78
Cyrus I (the Great), king of Persia, 42, 55, 76, 77–8
Cyrus II, king of Persia, 55

Daghestan, 221; cauldrons made in, 258–60, 246–8; stone relief from, 260, 250
Damascus, 142, 223
Damghan region, 85
Dance of Queen Candraprabha, 192, 180
Dandan Uilik, 180, 206, 208, 212, 219, 196, 197, 200, 201
Dara, capital of the Parthians, 85
Darbucci, 111
Darius, king of Persia, 56, 76, 77, 80, 123, 148, 221
David, kuropolate, 252, 255
Demeter II, king of Abkhazia, 251
Demetrius I, king of Bactria, 127, 128, 144
Demetrius II, king of Bactria, 128
Derbend area, 256
Diakonov, I. M., 114
Diodotus, ruler of Bactria, 128, 129
Djambas Kala, 115
Djvari, 239, 241, 248, 223, 225
Duchtar-i-Nashirvan, 165–6
Dura Europos, 214
Dvin (Dabil), 228, 229, 230–1, 258
Dyson, R. H., 67, 68

Ecbatana, 55, 86, 90, 142, 155, 176, 222
Edessa, 228
Egypt, 14, 111, 138, 222
Egyptians, moved to Bactria, 80
Erdmann, K., 34
Erivan, 62
Erzincan, area, 221 ·
Etchmiadzin Gospels, 224, 210, 211
Ethiopia, 80, 91
Eucratides, king of Bactria, 128, 133, 140, 113
Euphrates, river, 221, 222
Euthydemus, governor of Kapisu, 128

Farmakovskij, 14
Farsman, king of Iberia, 236, 237
Felt huts (yurts), 28
Ferghana, 75, 76, 90, 123, 176, 220; Saka kingdom in, 42; horses, 77–8, 65; raided by the Chinese, 78–9; under Achaemenid suzerainty, 79–80
Firdausi, 40, 115; Shah-nama of, 106, 89
Foucher, A., 133, 180
Fundukistan, 128, 168, 190, 157

Gagik, king of Armenia, 235, 236, 220
Gandhara, 80, 129, 145, 148, 164, 182, 188, 206, 213, 214, 218; Greek influence in, 148–51, 154–5, 160, 162, 164, 180; coinage, 149, 131, 132; Buddhism in, 154–62; art, 144, 148–51, 154–62, 212, 220, 129, 133, 137–48
Ganges, river, 142, 149

Garni, 222, 228
Gautamo, Prince, 208
Gegat, palace at, 246
Gelat, Monastery of, 255, 243; wall mosaic, 255, 244
George III, king of Georgia, 246
Georgia, Caucasian, 256, 260; Bronze and Iron Age art, 14, 16, 20, 29; the name, 25; Sassanians, Romans and Sarmatians in, 25; the old kingdom of Iberia, 221, 236–8; art and architecture, 238–9, 241–2, 244, 246, 248, 250, 252, 221–225, 226, 228, 229–235, 237, 238, 239, 240
Georgian Church, 248, 252
Ghaznavid dynasty, 51, 122; art of the, 203, 220
Ghazni, 106
Ghirshman, R., 28, 72
Gobi desert, 50, 173, 174
Gold trade and its routes, 140
Gondolphus, Scytho-Parthian king, 143; ruler of Taxila, 145
Gray, Basil, 178, 186
Great Wall of China, 44, 173
Greece: and Cyrus, 42; trades with Iberia, 237
Greek influence(s): on Scythians, 26; on Turkestan, 81; on Parthian architecture, 86–7; and domination, in Bactria, 124, 127–9, 131 ff.; decline of, in Turkestan, 128; on Gandharan culture and art, 148–51, 154–5, 160, 162, 164, 180; in eastern Turkestan, 191; in Armenia, 228–9; on Georgian art, 244; on Albanian art, 256
Greeks; colonize eastern shores of Black Sea, 20; moved by Achaemenids to Kuzistan, 80; ejected from Bactria, 140, 141, 151; in Gandhara, converted to Buddhism, 150
Gregory the Illuminator, St, 223, 242, 257
Griaznov, M. P., 30, 39–41
Grousset, R., 79
Grünwedel, A., 180
Gupta India, 164–6, 180

Hackin, 146, 168, 169, 172
Hadda, sculptures, 161, 192, 213, 145–8
Hadrian, Emperor, 237
Han period, bronzes, 133–4, 122
Hasanlu, 65, 67–9, 54, 55
Haukal, Ibn, 230
Hekatompylos, capital of the Parthians, 86
Hephthalites, 101, 140, 166; overthrow the Kushans, 93
Herodotus, 77, 80, 221
Hinayana Buddhism, 164, 188, 208
Hindu Kush mountains, 93, 123, 142, 161
Hsing-p'ing, 173
Hunnu tribesmen, 48

284

Huns, 93, 173, 260; in Central Asian plain, 42–3; raid China, 43, 44; in Ordos region, 43; art, 43, *34*, *35*; in Mongolia, 43; graves in Mongolia and Baikal district, 44–8, *37–40*; avenge Turkish sacrilege, 50; of Mongolia, defeated by the Chinese, 174–5

Iberia, 221, 236–7, 238 *see also* Georgia
Idigutschai, 197
India, 42, 75, 90, 92, 93, 139, 141, 177, 208, 210, 212–14, 221, 222; Kushan empire in *see* Kushan empire
Indian art, 138, *128*
Indo-Celtic people, 141
Indo-Scyths *see* Kushans
Indus, river, 148
Ionia, 80, 142
Ionians, moved to Susa, 80
Iran, 90, 129, 170 *see also* Persia
Iranians, 52; and Parthians, 81
Irrigation, in Chorasmia, 116, 122
Irtysh district (Siberia), 37, 38
Isfahan, 116
Islam, 122; Uygur contacts with, 200; in western Turkestan, 221
Issyk Kul, lake, Turks of, 50
Ivory trade, 139

Jakubovskij, A. I., 106
Japhet, 237
Jevanshar, king of Albania, 260
Justin II, Byzantine emperor, 91
Justinian I, Byzantine emperor, 91, 251

Kabul, 14, 124, 142, 143
Kabul valley, 148, 176
Kabula (Kabulaka, Kabalah and Shamakha), capital of Albania, 257
Kakrak, 166, *152*
Kanishka, king of the Kushans, 144, 146, 149, 161, 208, 212, *130–2*
Kapisu (Alexandria-Kapisu or Kapisha), capital of Bactria, 127–9, 142; treasures from (*see* Begram)
Karakorum, 50; mountains, 81, 142
Karasahr, 176, 180, 186, 193
Karmir Blur, 55, 58, 62, 64, *50–2*
Karoshti script, 145, 162
Kashgar, 176, 193
Kashgaria, 52, 173; entered by Turks, 48; centre of Buddhism, 170, 182; art, 180
Kashmir, 150, 180
Katanda, 30, 38
Kazakstan, 40, 44, 100, 174, *84*
Keriya, 176, 181
Khaja-i-Khodja palace, 88
Khakhetia, 251, 253; palaces in, 246
Khakuli icon, 252, 255, *241*, *242*

Khotan, 145, 176, 180, 184, 193, 213; art of, 206, 208, 209, 212, 219, *196*, *197*, *200*
Khyber Pass, 142
Kievian Russia, 224, 252
Kirghiz people, 53
Kirghizia, headquarters of the Sakas, 42
Kizil, 176, 180, 200, 203, 212, 219; paintings, 169, 184, 188, 190–2, *175*, *176*, *179–82*
Koban culture, 19–20, *8–10*
Koço, 141, 180, 203, 214; as Uygur centre, 193; Uygur paintings at, 195, 197, 198, *184–6*, *189*; Nestorian paintings at, 200, 202, *194*, *195*
Kozlov, P. K., 46
Kubachi region, pottery from, 258, *252*; stone relief from, 262, *249*, *251–2*
Kuça, 168, 176, 180; art, 100, 186, 190, 192, 203; annexed by China, 188
Kuftin, B. A., 16
Kulagysh, silver dish from, 41, *31*
Kumtura, 176, 180, 184; art, 188, 190, *178*
Kunduz, river, 143, 148
Kura, river, 222, 231, 253
Kurdistan, 67, 222
Kushan empire, of north-west India, 92–3, 116, 142, 181, 182, 212; art, 143–6, *130*
Kushans: replace the Greeks in Bactria, 140, 141; their dress, 141, *126*, *127*
Kutais, 244, 251
Kwarasm *see* Chorasmia

Lamaism, Tibetan, 208
Lazarev Gospel, 224
Le Coq, A. von, 141, 181
Leo II, king of Abkhazia, 251
Lhasa, 210
Li-Ling, general, 174
Locatarra, or Lord of the World (Buddha), 162, *149*
Lopnor, 176, 181; annexed by China, 174
Loulan, 181, 214
Lurs, 26–7, 28–9, *17*, *18*

Mahayana Buddhism, 186, 208
Maikop, 12–16, 18, 260, *1–4*
Mamas, St, silver disc of, 242, *226*
Mani, 165, 197, *186*
Manichaeans, 186, 193, 194, 197; paintings, 202
Mannaeans, 27, 54, 68, 72; capital of, 67, 69
Marlyk, 65, 68–9, *56–9*
Marshall, Sir John, 145–6
Maschots, Mesrop, 224
Masson, M. E., 81, 86
Mathura, 129, 142, 144–6; carved figure of Kanishka, 146, *130*; Kushan sculpture of, *134*; Greek sculptors of, 150, 151, *136*; Indian sculptors of, 154, *136*

Mauryas, Scytho-Sakian king, 145, 150
Mayyafarikin area, 222
Mazar-i-Sharif, 143
Mazdaians, Mazdaism, 181, 197, 237
Medes, 54 ff., 58, 62, 67, 76, 80, 42
Media, 27, 91; conquered by Parthians, 81
Menander, king of northern India, 128
Mesopotamia, 14, 222
Mingoi caves, 100, 182, 184, 186, 171–5
Miniatures, Georgian, 250, 239, 240
Minussinsk area, 41, 52
Miran, 176, 180, 181; wall-paintings, 213–14, 202, 203
Mithra (Achaemenid deity), 222
Mithridates I, king of Pontus, 81, 128
Mithridates II, king of Pontus, 140
'Monastery of the Thousand Buddhas' see Tun-huang
Mongolia, 140; Huns in, 43–4, 44–8, 37–40; Orkhon Turks in, 50; outer Mongolia captured by China, 173; Upper, 50
Mongolian Hephthalites, 50
Mongols, 53, 122, 194, 203, 223, 252
Moses of Kalankatu (Albanian historian), 230–1, 256
Moshchevaja Balka, 111, 231, 95, 213
Mother Goddess, Chorasmian, 117
Mskheta, 236, 252; church of St Tzkhoveli at, 239, 244, 232
Mug Castle, 94–6; wooden shield from, 96, 100, 78
Muhammadanism, and Central Asia, 170 see also Islam
Mural-paintings, Georgian, 248, 237, 238

Naksh-i-Rustem, 166, 255–6
Nanea (Achaemenid goddess), 223
Nekressi, church of, 238
Nepal, 157, 211
Nestorians, 110, 188, 190, 194, 197; paintings at Koço, 200, 202, 194, 195
Nisa, 81, 83, 85; New, 81
Niya, 176, 177, 181, 208, 214, 163
Noin Ula, Hunnic grave near, 46, 260
Novosvobodnyj see Tsarkij

Ob district (Siberia), 37, 38
Opiza church, 241, 224
Opizari, Beka and Beshken, 242, 227
Orbeli, J., 106, 262
Ordos, bronzes from, 41, 32, 33; Huns in, 43, 44; evicted from, 48
Orkhon, Khan of the, 50–1
Orkhon Turks, 194; plunder Hunnic burials, 50; overthrow Avar rulers, 50; split into two groups, 50; wealth and strength, 50–1; their short-lived dynasties, 51–2; the Kirghiz their offshoots, 53

Orkhon valley, 44, 141
Ossetia, 256
Ossetians, 111
Ossuaries: Soghdian, 92; in Chorasmia, 117
Ottoman dynasty, 51
Oxus, river, 143, 155, 162 see also Amu Darya
Oxus Treasure, 32, 33, 39, 138; 42, 72, 123–5, 128
Oxyartes, 124

Pakistan, 75, 148
Palmyra, 158, 161
Pantaleon, ruler of Gandhara, 128
Papak, deputy of Ardashir, 25
Partava (Berda), 231
Parthia, 81, 83, 85, 86, 90, 91, 139, 222, 68, 69, 72, 73
Parthians, 42, 92, 110, 140, 141, 175, 223, 253, 256
Pazyryk, 30, 32–4, 38–9, 45–7, 53, 98, 111, 138, 168, 260; 21, 23–6, 30
Peros (Firus), 257
Perosez (Perozbad), 257
Persia, 34, 42, 50, 62, 67, 107, 116, 144, 176, 220, 225, 232; oldest woollen pile carpet, 34, 26; conquered by the Parthians, 81; silk, 140, 231; secures part of Armenia, 223 see also Sassanian Persia; Sassanians
Persian art, 88, 96, 198, 74, 138, 190, 191
Peshawar, stupa at, 157
Peter the Great, 37, 39
Phoenicia, 142, 221
Piandjikent, 95, 120, 121, 169, 203; art, 101, 103–7, 110, 114, 192, 85–92
Pilgrim flasks, 178, 164, 165
Piotrovsky, B. B., 60
Pitsunda, church at, 248
Pliny, 222, 257
Poiraiz, J. A. H., 26
Poland, 223
Pompey, 222, 253
Ponpo (animistic worship), 208, 209
Punjab, 170

Red Cap monks, sect of, 208–9
Rhytons: ivory, 83, 68, 69; clay, 116
Rindad (Tali Barzu), 94
Roman empire, 25, 86; and Georgia, 25, 236, 237; peace with Parthia, 90; Kushan contact with, 145; contact with N.W. India and Afghanistan, 161; and China, 173; and Armenia, 222; and Iberia, 237; and Albania, 255, 256
Roman influence, on Gangharan sculpture, 161–2, 145–8
Rostovtzev, M., 88
Roxana (wife of Alexander the Great), 124

Rudenko, S. I., 30, 34, 38, 46, 47
Russa I, king of Urartu, 62, 64, *50–2*
Russia: import of textiles, 111; Scythians in, 55

Sakas, 42, 93, 140
Samanid dynasty, 51, 122; art of the, 203, 220
Samarkand, 52, 78, 94, 101, 111, 123, 220
Sanadir, Monastery of, 224
Sardur I, king of the Urartu, 57
Sardur II, king of Urartu, 64, *50*
Saripul, 161
Sarmatians, 12, 25
Sassanian Persia, 223, 237, 251
Sassanians, 91, 141, 180, 223, 256; conquer the Caucasus, 25; seals, 81; art, 88, 165–6, 184, 186, *75, 99*; influence, 99, 100, 110, 111, 114, 128, 165–70, 175, 200, 238, 244, 258, 260, *95–8, 159–62*; and Albania, 256–7
Schlumberger, D., 128, 143, 144, 146
Schmidt, E., 28
Scythians, 19, 28, 42, 52, 221, 260; creative genius and technical skill, 12; gold work, 13, 30, 32, 33, 38, 43, 138, *19, 20, 22, 124*; influence Georgian art, 20; in the Caucasus, 26; conquer Media, 27; in Transcaucasia and the Zagros, 29; their burials, 46; sweep into N.W. Persia and eastern Turkey, 54–5; defeated by the Medes, 55, 58, 62; burn Karmir Blur, 62
Sehenga *see* Noin Ula
Seistan, 93, 129
Seleucids, the, 80–1, 124, 128, 148 *see also* Bactria
Seleucus I, 124, 222
Seljuks, 95, 116, 122, 158, 165, 169, 203, 220, 223, 232, 255, 262
Semirechie, the, 42, 193, 194
Serindia, paintings of, 180, 181
Sevan, Lake, 12
Sevan cathedral, 232, *214*
Shahlin Palace, 46
Shalmaneser III, king of Assyria, 54; palace at Balawat, 57, *43*
Shamanism, 122, 208
Shapur, Sassanian king, 168
Shapur I, Sassanian king, 161, 253, 256
Shapur II, Sassanian king, statue of, 85, *70*
Shibe, 30, 38
Shyshkin, V. A., 96
Siberia, 26, 43, 52, 87, 123; belt buckles from, 37–8, *27–29*; Scytho-Sakian and Scytho-Sarmatian periods, 39–40; tattooing in, 52–3
Sienpei, the, 44
Silk: industry, 90–1, 110–11, 140, 154–5, 228, *93, 94, 95, 97, 99, 169, 170*; banners, 197, *189*; Princess, 212, *201*

Sinan-ti, emperor of China, 174
Sinkiang, province of, 75
Siva, 149, 151, *131, 132*
Slab graves, of Mongolia, 43–4
Slavs, 224
Soghdia, 75, 90, 94, 95, 121, 123, 124, 168, 176, 190, 200; conquered by the Achaemenids, 76–8, 80; horses, 76–7; art, 91–101, 103–7, 111, 114–16, *76–92, 96, 97, 100, 101*; absorbed in Kushan empire, 92; textiles, 110–11, *93–5*
Soghdian script, 80
Sorçuk, 176, 180, 186, 200; wall-paintings, 169, 188, *177*; grottoes, 182 *see also* Mingoi caves
Soviet Armenia, 58
Soviet Turkestan *see* Turkestan, western
Srong Tsan Gampo, King, 211
Stein, Sir M. A., 67, 111, 141, 180, 181, 194, 214, 218, 220
Stepantsminda, 25, 27, *13, 16*
Stephanos I, Patriarch of Kartli, 241, *223*
'Stone Dames' *see* Balbals
Stupas, 156–8, 162, 163, 220, *141, 143*
Surk Khotal, 85, 143–4
Susa, 80
Suzami of Samarkand (Persian poet), 195
Syavush, 104–5, 124, *86*; Chorasmian companion of, 117
Syr Darya (Jaxartes), river, 50, 76, 77
Syria, 90, 178, 214, 222, 225, *165*

Tadjik burials, 52, 53, *41*
Tadjikistan, 75, 76, 81, 129
Tageloni, gold head of stag from, 25, *15*
Taklamakan, desert, 162, 173, 176, 180, 193, 206, 212, 217; buried cities of, 181; Hellenic influence in, 191
'Tales of the Nazereddin Hoca', 195
Tallgren, A., 26
Tamara, queen of Georgia, 246, 252
T'ang dynasty ware *see* China
T'ang school of art, 186, 197
Tarim basin: kingdom of the Yueh-Chi in, 140; Buddhist art of, 154, 162; the oases hamlets and trade with China, 173; conquered by China, 174, 175; wrested from China by the Turks, 176, 178; Uygur rule in, 193
Tarn, W. W., 127, 140–1, 145, 150
Tashkent, 76, 220
Tattooing, in Siberia, 52–3
Taurus mountains, 142
Taxila, 129, 142, 144–5, 162, 192; Gondolphus ruler of, 145; treasures excavated at, 145–6
Teishabani (Karmir Blur), 62
Tepe Maredjan, 164

Termez, 176; ruins at, 162
Teshik Kale, 122, *106*
Thomas, St, 145
Thonni Sambhota (Tibetan scholar), 211
Thracians: in Asia, 80; in Bactria, 124
Tibet, 42, 180; Buddhism in, 208; sects in, 208–10; art, 209–12, 220, *198–201*
Tien-shan, the, 42, 193, 220
Tiflis (Tbilisi), 12, 251
Tigranes II, king of Armenia, 222
Tigris valley, 221, 222
Tilopu, founder of White Cap sect, 209
Tiridates I, king of Parthia, 91
Tokharian empire *see* Kushan empire
Tokharians, 140, 141
Tolstov, S. P., 115, 118
Toprak Kala, 117–18, 120, *102–5*
Toprak Kale, 58, *45–9*
Transbaikal area, 41, 43
Transoxiana, 141, 168, 176
Trdat (architect), 235
Trevers, C. H., 134
Trialeti, 16–18, 64, 68, *5–7*
Tsarkij (Novosvobodnyj), 12
Tsebelda church, 244, *229*
Tumen district (Russia), 41
Tumsuk, 176, 180
Tunguz Khata people, 203
Tun-huang, 176, 180, 194, 213, 214, 217, 219, 220, *183, 207, 204–8*
Turfan, 141, 174, 176, 180, 192–4, 203
Turkestan: entered by Turks, 48; ancient divisions of, 75; adopts Greek customs, 81; end of Greek power in, 128; Indian influence in, 162
Turkestan, eastern, 42, 75, 116, 150, 154, 161, 162, 169; art, 100, 180ff., *159–208*; Soghdian silk textiles found in, *93, 94*; occupied by China, 173–4; struggle for oasis hamlets, 174–5; languages, 175–6; races, 176–7; infiltration of Chinese culture, 177–9; advance of Buddhism, 180, 221; Uygurs in, 193
Turkestan, western, 75, 87, 124, 138, 164, 232; Islam in, 221
Turkey, 56, 58, 221
Turkmenistan, 75
Turks, 42, 48, 169, 173, 176, 220; enter Turkestan, 48; dress, 48, 50, *172*; migrations, *50*; conquer Soghdia, *93*; conflict with Persians, 94; settle in Turfan, 192 *see also* Orkhon Turks
Turret-shaped domes, of Armenian churches, 229, *219*
Tzromi church: 248, *235, 236*

Ukhaidir, 88
Umayyads, 224, 251
Upper Zaravshan valley, 95
Urals, 12, 90, 116, 176
Urartians, 54, 56, 221
Urartu, kingdom of, 55, 68, 69, 221; destroyed by the Medes, 55, 58; defeated by the Assyrians, 57, *43*; art, 57–60, 62–5, 72, *45–9, 53*; sacks Hasanlu, 67, 68
Urmia, Lake, 57, 67, 72, 222
Uygurs: leave China, 193–4; their advanced culture, 194–5; art, 195, 197, 198, 200, 202–3, 211, *184–9, 192–5*
Uzbekistan, 52, 75, 76, 100, 129

Vaie II, king of Albania, 256
Van, Lake, 221, 252
Van, district of, 56, 58
Varangian Scandinavia, 224
Varaksha, 96–100, 121, 169, 186, 219, *79–82, 98*
Virgin of Vladimir, 252
Vishanas, 156, 157, 162
Vishaz, king of Bactria, 124
Volga Khazars, 257

Weich-in, elder and younger (Khotanese artists), 208
White Cap sect, 209
White Huns, invade Gandhara, 161
Wu-ti, emperor of China, 50, 90

Xenophon, 221

Yarkand, 174, 180, 183
Yazdagrid I, king of Albania, 256
Yevlakh district, 257
Yotkan, 206; art of, 212
Yueh-Chi tribe, 140
Yun-kang, 184
Yurts *see* Felt huts

Zagros, the, 27–9; occupied by the Medes, 54, 56
Zakin, Urartian metal belt from, 72
Zakis, Scythian disc from, 22, *11*
Zan Tepe, 168
Zaravshan, 101
Zaravshan, river, 76; valley, 101
Zendam, 111
Zidzha valley, Hunnic graves in, 45
Ziwiye, 65, 72, *61–4*
Zoroaster, 92, 124
Zoroastrians, Zoroastrianism, 94, 105, 110, 131, 257
Zwarthnotz, 230, 232